Spirits from the Edge of the World
Classical Shamanism in Ulchi Society

SPIRITS FROM THE EDGE OF THE WORLD

Classical Shamanism in Ulchi Society

J. Van Ysslestyne

PATHFINDER COMMUNICATIONS

Copyright 2018 by Pathfinder Communications

Find us at www.2pathfindercounseling.com

Cover Photo: Grandmother Nadia Duvan, Courtesy of Kiliii Yuan

Typesetting, Cover, and Illustrations: R. S. Teeples

ISBN-13: 978-0-692-10429-3

In memory of Grandmother Nadia Duvan, this book is dedicated to the Ulchi (Nani), people of the Earth.

Born on a cold shore
And tried by the harsh cold
Only now have I learned and am able
To warm people's hearts
With a singing voice

• *Leonid Laptsuy*

Table of Contents

All photos in this manuscript are provided by the author and Nadia Duvan except: pages 22 and 208, photos courtesy of Karen Lewis, pages 113, 241, and 276, photos courtesy of Nadia Han and the Olchi family. Cover photo and pages 198, 367, and 387 courtesy of Killiii Yuan.

Throughout this book are illustrative images of designs and patterns taken from some of the material arts of the Ulchi people, including: birch bark cut, paper cut, appliqué, embroidery, and the petroglyph and rock carvings of their ancient ancestors. There are two notable exceptions. First, the frontispiece is an illustrative rendering of *World Tree*, an original wood carving by Kolya U. Second, page 209 contains an illustrative rendering of *Lineage Tree*, a cut paper work owned by the author.

A typographical note concerning the electronic version of this book and accessibility tools such as screen or book readers. Glyph markers have been used in the commentary, narrative, and memories (Chapter 08) portions of this book to denote the follow changes: End of a commentary by commentator is indicated with a .(Unicode: 2024, Name: ONE DOT LEADER). Change from one commentator to the next is indicated with a ..(Unicode: 2025, Name :TWO DOT LEADER). The end of the commentary or narrative section is indicated with a ...(Unicode: 2026, Name: HORIZONTAL ELLIPSIS).

Preface

C lassical shamanism among the Ulchi (Manchu-Tungus speaking peoples of the Amur River Region) is an evolving animistic tradition. The Ulchi's call themselves the Nani or people of the earth. Their histories recount their earliest progenitor as the great Mammoth who instructed the first ancestral shaman in the secret arts. This apprenticeship, between Mammoth and man, became the seminal foundation for classical shamanism practiced amongst the people.

The fieldwork presented here is unique in many aspects. Grandmother Nadia Duvan was the last practicing shaman of the Ulchi until her death in April of 2016. Her father and mother were born in the late nineteenth and early twentieth centuries respectively. Having grown up in a traditional Ulchi household her memories and reflections, personally and through family members, reveal the never-ceasing role of the shaman within the cultural context of daily life. Her family members were the informants for the researcher Anna Smolyak and her aunt was married to the linguist O.P. Sunik.

We brought the shamans and other members of the tribe to the United States from the years 1994-2015. They traveled once or twice a year to the Pacific Northwest. Programs were arranged through the University of Washington, Burke Museum, and other venues open to the general public. Observing and participating with a foreign audience elicited a unique perspective about North American culture especially when it came to exposing them to the neo-shamanic teachings in the West. Their comments about these practices are found within the pages of this book.

Traditionally these peoples are very reluctant to share their cultural information with most outsiders. Grandmother Nadia and Grandfather Misha would always remark about the privacy and secrecy of all the Northern peoples. This is due partly to the fact that, in the past, information was usually filtered through the Russian language, in which all details of the subject matter either got lost or misunderstood, and partly to the cultural belief that discussion of the inner teachings is taboo and forbidden by the spirits. Speaking of spiritual matters may displease the spirits, so if a discussion is necessary, the information given is measured and succinct. In 1994 Vera Duvan, a local teacher of the Ulchi-English language, took me under her tutelage. She not only instructed me in the Ulchi language but guided me more deeply into the implicit conceptual meanings of her native tongue. Serving as the Ulchi translator during their visits to North America this training allowed me to express a more layered and nuanced explanation to English speaking audiences.

The Ulchis never sit down and lecture about their philosophies or their beliefs about the reality of existence. They make it a point to wait for the petitioner to ask questions. Moreover, in asking a question, one should not presume that one will receive an answer. Answers to questions are dependent upon the emotional affect states of the particular spirits or shamans on any given day. If the spirits don't want you to talk, then you obey their dictates.

The commentaries that I provide in each section of the book denote those few and glorious times that my "Why?" questions were not met with the response: "Quit asking why, because your questions are tiring, and bothersome" or "The spirits are becoming angry and don't want me to keep talking"—or with silence, often accompanied by a cold, rather solemn stare in my direction. Many times, my questions didn't even elicit a stare but were completely ignored.

Choosing the narrative voice for this manuscript was easy. The material was compiled from over twenty- five years of audio and video recordings from both their native villages and their travels to the United

States. I have chosen to convey this book's voice in the form that was provided to me: factual, pragmatic, detail oriented, and verbatim. The only variance comes when I have been a participant in an event.

Grandmother Nadia always reminded me that for the first ten years of her own shamanic exploration, she never received any information from the elders. After twenty years, they began to provide her with bits and pieces concerning the deeper aspects of the practices. When her work with the shamans verged on a thirty-year partnership, they began to speak of the inner details. It was only before the impending death of one of her teachers that all of the secrets were passed down to her to carry on the tradition. Within these narratives are found many details of Manchu-Tungus shamanism that have never been revealed, yet I am keenly aware that this information is just the tip of the iceberg.

J. Van Ysslestyne

SPIRITS FROM THE EDGE OF THE WORLD
Classical Shamanism in Ulchi Society

CHAPTER I

Ways of Nature

The Ulchi (*Nani*) conception of the world is based on a foundation of animism; everything in their environment is perceived as a living being endowed with reason and spirit. Like their ancient ancestors, the Ulchis believe in the existence of spirits whose actions affect people, animals, plants, objects, and occurrences in the natural world. According to this worldview, everything—from mountains, rivers, lakes, and forests to people—is governed by invisible powers and spirit masters.

The structure or model of the world is divided into three distinct sections: the Upper, or Heavenly World; the Middle World of earthly, mortal humans; and the Lower World of the dead. These regions are adjacent and parallel to each other, and are similar in geography, relief, and inhabitants; there are mountains, forests, rivers, oceans, villages, animals, people, and shamans. The three regions overlap and combine to form a harmonious, unified macrocosm, symbolized by the World Tree, whose top branches reach into the heavenly sphere, while the trunk stands in the earthly realm and the roots grow deep into the world of the dead. Although living humans reside in the Middle

World, they can attain temporary access to both the Upper and Lower Worlds during dreams or waking states in which, it is believed, spirits impinge upon the conscious mind.

LAWS OF LIFE

Doro are a set of orally transmitted natural laws reflecting the Ulchi sense of environmental ethics. They are biocentric in nature; all forms of life are considered equally valuable, and humanity is not perceived as the center of existence. These laws take into consideration many variables and are ambiguous in the best sense of the word—they allow for many interpretations, and there is room for uncertainties. Historically, there were no canons, edicts, or institutional laws governing the clans as a whole. Instead, there were guidelines for living a moral and ethical life within the parameters of the Ulchi worldview.

ULCHI HOUSEHOLD, MID 19TH CENTURY

These "Laws of Life" have been passed down orally to children by their parents, grandparents, and other elders of the family group. First and foremost among them are the laws specifying how to be a "proper human being" on the earth. These involve a set of virtues and principles to be cultivated by each member of society. They stress modesty, kindness, gentleness, humbleness, generosity, an economy of nature (not wasting anything), and avoidance of premature death. To expose or render oneself vulnerable to nature's destructive forces is a great taboo. Long life is valued, as it comes with a ripening of wisdom that will be transmitted to the younger generations.

In the vast Siberian landscape, the home has been the only environment to afford the Ulchis a modicum of physical and spiritual protection. Stepping outside the front door conveys them into a different home—that of the Middle World spirits. There, as in the homes of humans, the social obligations of hospitality and reciprocity inherent in the host-guest relationship inform and guide the behavior of each individual. They consider it vital to maintain a balance with Nature and the world of spirits, whether as hosts in their abodes or guests in the Middle World.

When traveling through a forest, mountainous region, or body of water, it is taboo to speak loudly or make unnecessary noise because this may disturb the homes and lives of the animals. When hunting, fishing, or gathering from Nature, one should procure only what one needs to survive. Before these activities, a ritual of gratitude is performed, and offerings of food and tobacco are given to the spirits of nature. They never ask for abundant amounts of fish or large game. As Grandmother Nadia would say, "You don't place an order or make demands!" Most requests of Nature ask her to send the little animals or whatever she can spare. Proper behavior requires that one never speak unfavorably, jest, or make offensive comments about the spirits, as they may seek to punish a person for those actions. Living a comfortable life is a gift from the spirits of the three worlds.

COMMENTARIES

GRANDFATHER MISHA:

Our ancestors have passed down their knowledge from generation to generation. Our ancestors, our children, and our selves will always make gestures of thanks to the trees, the grasses, the sky, and waters of the earth because all life grew out of the earth. Men and women prospered on the land, and they had their children. Animals prospered upon the earth, and the people hunted and made their living from them. The spirit of the Earth and the spirit of the Sky are forever arguing among themselves, and that is why we make our living on the land as we do. No matter where one travels to, whether it is in the mountains or the taiga, or to the water, one must tread lightly and always offer thanks and give offerings to the spirit that one finds there at journey's end. We make our offerings to the spirits of the mountains, trees, and land so that we may stay in balance with and among them. We do this and ask for happiness for our children and our children's children.

.

Do not cut down trees for firewood. Take only the fallen trees and branches for burning. Never harm a tree. If you needed to cut down a young, healthy tree for the backbone of a house, fishing equipment, arrows, bows, or for boats and paddles, you would cut it down, but first you would perform a special ritual, "explaining" to the tree what you had decided to cut it down for, telling the tree it would become a spirit sacred to the people.

..

Grandmother Nadia:

When stepping out your front door, you enter another's home. When entering this "home," you must display proper etiquette. Remember that you are a guest, and a good guest displays courtesy, politeness, and respect. The animals, rocks, grasses, and every spirit understand all human languages. They watch and remember a person's actions and listen to everything a person says while outside.

.

4

GOGA DUVAN, CA. 1940

My parents were very old when I was born. This transference of knowledge happened day by day unnoticeably. It was possible when I was a child that I didn't understand everything, but as I grew older, I have come to understand the way of my ancestors. My parents would say, "Never think that you are greater, stronger, or more powerful than Nature. Once you begin to understand, you will find that it becomes easier to live and grow upon the earth, but one will never understand everything.

•

It is important to address one's environment with great humility. We have many stories about people who ignore the laws of Nature. Nature can harm and punish you at any time and at any age. This is the counsel given by the elders of my village. This counsel is a huge gift to us all. People forget that we have a limited time here on this earth. If we forget our harmony with Nature, then we will contribute to evil. Evil comes from greediness and jealousy. Always walk the middle way. Always forgive people and help those poorer than yourself.

•

The elders would always echo these phrases: "Treat Nature with love and respect. She is your mother and teacher. Follow the Doro, remember the traditions, respect all of the spirits and your life with be happy, and you will live long."

•

My parents always told me to never send harmful tidings to anyone and to always live in peace. They would tell me never to forget to give offerings to the spirits and ask for forgiveness. They would say, "Give offerings to the Sky, Sun, Water, and to the Taiga. Give offerings with vodka, water, special rice, and berries. White or red fish is permissible but never give meat.

•

Everything around us is a living spirit. Everything is its own person. This understanding of the world comes from the fact that we depend on the living earth for our food and life energy. Each part of nature is a living being, and these spirits can be offended. All spirits need to be worshipped and shown respect. We ask for forgiveness if we make a mistake. Everything around us has given us life and the continuity of our clans. This is why each object and part of the world that surrounds us is treated with great respect and care.

•

Every area has its Master spirit, mountains, trees, and rivers. Every area has a Master spirit who sees everything going on in that place. The Master spirit of a place can help you, accept you, or harm you.

•

Today, all people on the Earth are in need of ecology of the soul. People have forgotten the order of their ancestors: to live in harmony with Nature and themselves, to care for everything that lives around them. We, humans, are temporary guests upon earth; Nature is eternal.

•

The Doro educates each person how to live in harmony with Nature, other people, and finally with oneself.

CHAPTER 2

• • •

Creation Myths

The creation tales of the Ulchi explain how humans and specific clans came into existence and grew out of the Earth. Ulchis speak of a time long ago, when a beautiful maiden married a great Siberian tiger. Grandmother Nadia said, "A long, long, time ago, there were five brothers and six sisters. The five brothers married each of the sisters, but one beautiful young girl remained alone. She traveled to the forest, and there she met a tiger. The tiger and the beautiful girl were married and produced offspring. These children were the first Ulchi people."

It was from this primordial union that the Ulchi grew into this world. The first people were half tiger and half human, and as they journeyed forth and they continued to marry and form alliances with other beings in nature, forming clan groups. Some clans relate how they came into existence through the mating of an early ancestor with a specific tree or animal spirit. Others claim that their origins are connected with a particular land spirit; these include the Duvan clan, whose name refers to the top of a spirit mountain.

In other creation myths, the human race issues forth from the land above the starry heaven as divine frogs which make their way to earth as the progenitors of all mammalian, aquatic, reptilian, and bird life. Another tale speaks of humans arriving from the volcanic core of the earth. No matter the legend, what is emphasized here is the notion that, rather than humans being "made" by a supernatural being, the human race grew organically out of nature.

CREATION STORIES

GRANDFATHER MISHA:

Long, long, long ago, the great Guardian of the Heavens and the Guardian spirit of the Earth argued among themselves. "Who better to give birth to new people?" they asked. The Sun spirit high in the heavens said, "There is another land high above us, a transparent land (space between the stars) above the heavens. There is a clear place higher above the heavens, and from this place, the rains fall."

From that higher place fell a rain of frogs, and as those frogs fell to the earth, each one went on their way. Each one grew; each one found mates and became their own people. Some became dog people, some became animal people, and some became human people. The frogs began to argue among themselves about who would become whom and which people would be which. Who would become a dog and who would become a human. And in the arguing, the people would become dogs, and the dogs would become people.

The Great Spirit in Heaven said, "Fine, I'll watch how these people make out and how they make their decisions and then I will decide who will become who and which people will become which peoples."

Under the guidance of the Great Spirit of Heaven, the new people of the earth grew and prospered. The humans grew and prospered, the dogs grew and prospered, and the birds grew and prospered. Then the numbers grew bigger, and the peoples of the earth began to argue among themselves.

The Great Spirit looked down and gave them things to do. The Great Spirit had given them peace because they had things to do. The Great Spirit gave them crops to raise, animals to take care of and look after, animals to hunt, and fish to catch.

The peoples of the earth were arguing with themselves, so they sent their leaders to the Great Spirit and asked, "What can we do to live well? We are always arguing with each other, and this is causing great strife."

The Great Spirit said, "Divide up the land equally and fairly and then you can live peacefully. You must divide up the cows, horses, the dogs, everything must be divided equally among yourselves, and you will prosper and live well in peace."

The spirit of the Earth said to the Great Spirit, "We understand that everything depends on you and that all prosperity comes from above. We will look to you when we petition for our health and prosperity." The Earth spirit then said, "So tell us how we should be with the fish. The fish have grown so great and prosperous in number that they threaten to spoil the water so that it will be good for neither fish nor fowl."

The Great Spirit replied, "Yes, I understand. I will make the fish travel up and down the rivers, and I want you to catch them and eat them." In this wise way, the lives of the people continued and were prosperous. They were able to feed themselves, clothe themselves, and make tools from the different parts of the fish.

Then the people looked to the Great Spirit *Enduri*, the Sky spirit, and said, "We need to grow gardens and grow food to feed ourselves." The Great Dragon spirit said, "Look among yourselves and see who is the wisest and richest of the people. You will see that the Manchu people are living well. They have much skill and know how to raise gardens. Go and ask them for their wisdom and they will teach you how to make a garden, how to grow vegetables and fruit because they are truly a wise people who have prospered. Now this happens all the time with the people of the earth. They always turn to the Great Dragon spirit of the Sky and ask for assistance, wisdom, help, and advice when they are in need of anything.

The Great Spirit is known by many names and is seen as a heavenly dragon named *Enduri* or *Ba*.

In the early days, when the Earth was still hot, and the rocks were boiling, five men and four women appeared on earth. The earth boiled for nine years and then gave birth to people. These people appeared out of the boiling earth, and from these nine people, all of the people of the earth came into existence. Some gave birth to boys, and others gave birth to girls, and still, yet others gave birth to twins. They spread themselves across the earth and developed their own languages, cultures, and traditions. Ba/Enduri gave them each the color of their skin and gave them directions about how to live and grow in this world.

• • •

GRANDMOTHER TIKA VALDU ANGA
WITH HER DOG, BULAVA VILLAGE

GRANDMOTHER NADIA:

Variation of Grandfather Misha's story

A long, long time ago, people were born. The Sun master and the Sky master said, "Above us is the territory of *Ba*. It is a clear and transparent land, and we travel in this place." A frog fell from the heavens to the earth, and people were born and continued to be born. Later, some of the people became dog people. The Sky master said, "Good. Now I see everything and how the people are living on the earth." The people began to fight all the time between one another, so the Sky master gave goodness to them, and they stopped fighting and became friends. The people lived well, grew strong, became hunters, and everything went well in life.

The Star in the sky, the Moon, has one dog and a very, very old grandmother who all day and night carries water. The Earth master asked how the future will be if everyone is always fighting each other. The Sky master said, "We will divide everything on the earth. We will send some people to this part of the earth to live and send others to a different place to live." So the earth was divided, and everyone was sent to different places and never again was there a war between the peoples.

They took the cows, horses, and dogs and divided them equally among the different groups of people, and later these people lived and lived and never again fought amongst each other. The Moon Grandmother didn't know what had happened. She was too busy carrying water all day and night.

A black cloud can be the same as people. When it fights, it shakes and thunders in the sky. Now, why do we Ulchi people say this? It is because you can divide people, but you cannot divide the clouds in the sky. The Red Star must always be given offerings. It will make a person live well upon this earth, and the people will be given happiness.

The Earth master said, "This is fine and well. You are the Dragon spirit who lives high in the heavens, and it is you who organizes the people of the earth. Whatever you decide is fine. You will decide how the people will live and grow in the future and you will create all things."

Then the Earth master asked the Sky master, "How shall the fish live?" The Sky master replied, "There is the master spirit of the sea called Temu. Let's ask him!" The Earth master replied, "How can we do this? The water is so great, and there are so many fish!"

"Who knows?" said the Sky master. "Maybe the water will run down and seep deep within you. You must create rivers so that the water runs through so that the people can find and eat the different fish and animals. Let the water move over the top of you!"

The Sky master said, "And it will be this way!" And one more thing said the Sky master to the Earth master: "Tell these people the history of the Manchu people and how they made gardens and how to grow things. The people will live and live as they learn to hunt and fish and travel in the forest. The Dragon Sky Master said, "The Manchu people will be the richest people around, and all the other people will have made good contact with those Manchu folks. Have the people construct a special altar house and give offerings all of the time, and they too will become very rich and happy people."

The Earth master said, "This is a very excellent plan." The Sky master said, "I see this is wonderful and a very good way to organize these people on the earth."

When the earth was born, the Earth mother became the Water woman who gave fish to the people. She sent her daughter to the heavens to become the Master of the sky. She sent her husband and her two sons to become the animal people of the forest.

·

Our elders say that the earth is made of water or perhaps it is made of bird feces. There were three people who lived along the Amur. Their names were Shankai, Shancloe, and Shanka. They sent three swans to dive deep into the waters to recover stones and sand for the earth. The swans dived for seven days, bringing back with them the material that was deep upon the ocean floor. The people looked and saw that the land was growing, and the Amur River began to flow, and this is how the earth was formed.

. . .

Grandmother Nadia remarked to me "There are so many creation tales in the Ulchi culture that one would have to sit all day to hear them all."

Anga Clan Legend as told by Grandmother Tika

A very long time ago, there lived a young woman on the banks of the Amur River. She was an only child when tragedy struck her life. Her parents died suddenly, leaving her alone to fend for herself. She was my grandmother.

One day, a great rainstorm came up from the river. She looked out to the Amur and saw a great, large fish head rising up from under the waves. He was a *laha* (catfish) with very large whiskers. First, she saw a head and then a tail.

The storm grew stronger and stronger as she watched that fish moving towards the shore. The fish came out of the water and began to roll uphill toward her home.

My grandmother thought to herself, "This must be the master of the river!" The great fish rolled up to the threshold of the home and spoke to her in a human voice. "Cook me quickly, eat me, and go to sleep!" She was too frightened to disobey the River master, so did what was instructed of her. She cooked and ate this fish and fell fast asleep.

Later, she woke up in the middle of the night. The house was almost completely dark. A small fire was burning in the hearth. My grandmother had thought she'd had an unusual dream. As she looked around her home, there, standing in the corner, was a great large fish. She watched the fish transform into a handsome young man.

He entered her bed, and they became as man and wife. They lived together and gave birth to three sons.

The family was happy, but their children were sometimes lonely. Within a few years, the whole family decided to move across the river to be closer to other people. They all moved across to the right bank of the river. The children began to play with the other youngsters who lived across the river, and they grew into strong and handsome men.

My grandmother was a Jurchen. Our family comes from the fish.

CHAPTER 3

· · ·

Upper World

The Upper World is the domain of the great dragon spirits who preside over the lives of humans, spirits, animals, rocks, rivers, trees—basically everything in Heaven and on Earth. They are the originators and organizers of creation; the animating life force itself. This life force is imagined as a dragon or a pair of dragons called by many names: *Ba, Ba Adja* (Master), *Enduri, Ama* (father) *Enduri,* and *Unya* (mother) *Enduri.*

This region is composed of three distinct and overlapping layers. The lower level of Heaven is called the iron level, the middle is the silver, and the top is golden. Although the three layers are a commonly held belief among the people, an individual shaman may purport a different cosmology based on their direct experience in this region of space. Grandmother Tika, for example, spoke of layers upon layers in multiple levels of the heavenly realm. These variations and nuanced descriptions are explained by shamans who penetrate beyond the vault of Heaven to realms beyond the known universe.

Each cosmological body in these regions has its own legend. The heavens contain the same elements as are found on earth: villages, homes, people, animals, mountains, and bodies of water such as lakes and oceans. Deceased ancestors such as clan leaders, shamans, and hero/ines would reside in the Upper World if they exhibited special talents during their lifetimes. These ancestors became protective spirits and judges to their clansmen on earth.

The spirits of the Sun, Moon, stars, celestial birds, and all other types of flying things are the powers, rulers, and organic intelligence who reside in this territory. This region is also the home of the cloud and thunder spirits. The inhabitants of the Upper World observe and remember everything that goes on in the Middle and Lower realms. The elders say that "those beings who rule these upper regions can have a direct effect on the lives of those who exist in the other realms."

Ba as the Unifying Principle of the Universe

The term *Ba* is probably the most complex Ulchi concept and encompasses various levels of meaning and forms. First, *Ba* is known as the source and principle of all things and is congruent with the Chinese conceptions of the Tao or undifferentiated Nature. *Ba* includes the universal life force, the organic patterns of the universe, and the

GRANDMOTHER NADIA DUVAN ROWING ON THE AMUR
RIVER, BULAVA VILLAGE (BACKGROUND)

natural rhythms and cycles within all of life that unify the opposites and diversity of everything in the corporeal/incorporeal world. *Ba* can also refer to a geographical location, an element, a spirit, or forces and processes within the natural world. When speaking of *Ba*, the specific translation is determinate upon the context of the sentence or idea that is being expressed.

Ba encompasses all three worlds and the entirety of Nature, but can also be ascribed to a specific location, namely, the Upper World. In this realm, one finds the celestial inhabitants called the *Bakini*, the people who originate and reside in this starry territory.

When traveling to a location or territory, one will ask for directions to that specific *Ba*. When speaking about the weather, one may ask about the condition of *Ba*. In conclusion, *Ba* is the microcosm and macrocosm of the known cosmos and all of the parallel universes that make up form and space in-between form.

COMMENTARY

GRANDMOTHER NADIA:

I remember my father would say to me, "Never, never forget, and remember this well! Never ask Ba, 'Why is it this way and why is this that way?'"

"It gets very tiresome to ask why, why, why. Now listen well. Ba makes everything go round for people, makes the thunder, and causes the waters to flow and all of life to exist. Ba could slap you down or grind you into the ground. You are a little person, and the great Ba can always do this at any time. Never gossip about different things but only speak the truth."

. . .

MAJOR SPIRITS OF THE UPPER WORLD

DRAGON SPIRIT

As the Sky spirit, *Ba* can take the form of a single dragon, a pair of male and female dragons, or an elderly human being. *Ba*, as the Great Spirit, may be called *Ba Enduri*; this term distinguishes *Ba Enduri* as appearing as a dragon rather than as its human counterpart. In this animistic reality, *Ba* is the supreme governor over all other tutelary spirits. *Ba*, as Sky spirit, is not an autocratic ruler or architect of the universe, as in the Judeo/Christian concept of God, but rather a spirit that unifies all of the other beings and presides over them as a type of spiritual regulator.

Many descriptions tell of how *Ba Enduri*, as a dragon, flies over the earth each day, listening, watching, and taking note of the deeds and activities of humans. All prayers and rituals are addressed foremost to *Ba*, followed by the specific spirit to which a particular offering is made by the petitioner. Shamans can have direct interaction with *Ba* in a shamanic song or dream and

GRANDMOTHER NADIA WEARING HER KUYSALI CLAN ROBE

may carry this information to the common people during one of their ecstatic flights to the heavens. Ordinary people, as well, can have intimate contact via their dream states, and such dreams are deemed as highly important and significant to their lives. This spirit is also responsible for the "fate" of each living person on their day of birth. This fate is written in a sacred book hidden in a mystical cave located in the invisible worlds.

Commentaries

Grandmother Tika:

There is a mark on a special stone book that tells how long each person will live in their lifetime. This is called a saycha mark. There is a cave in a magic mountain where there is a stone table. Around this table stand three stone chairs. On this table lies the stone book of fate.

••

Grandmother Nadia:

Ba knows and sees all. If your life is good, then Ba has given this goodness to you, and if your life is unfortunate, then Ba has given this to you also. Ba is Nature, so if you walk the middle way, then your life will be in balance, and if not, then your life will reflect this also.

• • •

Sun Spirit

The spirit of the Sun (*seu*) is portrayed as either female or male, depending on individual interpretation. S/he is but one of the retinue of cosmic spirits that inhabit the sky. The ritual to the Sun is the prime component of the New Year's Festival, as its rising marks the beginning of a new cycle of growth and change for each and every family member. The hours of the day are traditionally divided up in a manner somewhat dependent on her position in relation to the natural terrain. The trees, mountains, and other elements in the environment stand as a type of sundial, indicating the hours upon the earth. The time periods of day or night increase or decrease depending upon the season of the year. During the spring and summer, the Sun spirit makes her appearance in the land of *Ba* for extended periods, but when autumn and winter grow closer, she journeys with greater velocity through this region of space. The Ulchi territories lie along the same latitude lines as the major cities in Canada. Thus, complete seasons of darkness or light are unknown to the Ulchi, unlike their neighbors to the far north.

Throughout the year, daytime—or, to be exact, the hours before noon—are a period in which various rituals are conducted in the outdoors. The following day after a house ritual is performed; the remaining food offerings are taken outdoors and offered to the family's sacred tree (*tudja*) before the Sun travels to her noon position. Shamans also follow this criterion when placing the used wooden streamers (*gemsacha*) and other contaminated ritual paraphernalia outside after an evening healing. Ritual taboos demand that the next morning, they bring these polluted objects to a protected outdoor setting. Spirits are always active outdoors but especially during the hours of the night. The daytime is a more secure and protected period for humans to perform rituals and offerings in the outdoor world.

Sky shamans could travel to the Sun with the aid of the iron eagle spirit called *Koori*. This spirit could assist the shaman in a journey into the Upper World regions. Only the most powerful shamans could travel to the Sun, and Grandmother Nadia remarked that a bronze mirror (*toli*) was necessary to protect a shaman from dire consequences when coming into direct contact with this potent solar spirit.

Moon Spirit

The Ulchi lunar calendar marks the phases and delineations of each month. Patterns of growth, renewal, and decay are calculated in accordance with the Moon's phases. The Moon (*bay*), with her monthly and seasonal cycles, serves as a barometer indicating upcoming weather patterns, bringing portents of danger and distress, and heralding auspicious periods for conducting various types of rituals.

There are many stories about the Moon in which she appears as an old grandmother. For the Ulchi, the Moon in this guise is responsible for the atmospheric conditions that issue forth rain. There are also legends that say the Moon is a young man chasing his female love (the Sun) across the sky. During the time of the new Moon, when this celestial body can no longer be seen in the heavens, it is said that the young man has caught up with his beloved.

Commentaries

Grandfather Misha:

Grandmother Moon collects the water that falls down from the transparent heaven. She carries it back and forth each day, and she has a white dog that runs alongside her. When she grows weary of carrying all of that water, the buckets spill out, and that is how rains fall upon the earth.

·

If the new Moon is born on its side, then expect a bad month. There will be many sicknesses, deaths, and tragedies among the people. But if the Moon grows evenly, expect a month that is good and fortunate in every way. When a light-colored circle appears around the Moon, it means that the Moon has built herself a house and to expect cold weather. Only a good house can save itself from a big frost. Where can a hunter take cover from a cold and fierce storm? He must also hurry to a home. What kind of hunt can there be in such weather? Just sit and wait. Not every living person on earth can see the Moon people. Even a person with very good sight may not see them.

. . .

The "growing Moon," when the celestial orb is in its waxing period, is considered the Moon of the living, but the waning phases are relegated to the land of the dead and/or the ancestors. The monthly family ritual is normally performed on the night of the full Moon. There have been differing opinions by shamans about conducting healing ceremonies during certain lunar phases.

COMMENTARIES

GRANDFATHER MISHA:

When the Moon is growing, it is the time to conduct healing rituals for the living. When the Moon is dying, then this Moon belongs to the deceased. Never perform rituals for the living during this time.

..

When asked about this lunar taboo, Grandmother Tika had a different viewpoint.

GRANDMOTHER TIKA:

Don't conduct rituals for the living at the dying Moon? Are you crazy! You must be kidding me! What if a patient is very ill and needs your help right away? What are you going to do? Are you going to wait a couple of weeks before you treat them? They could be dead by then! You do your conjuring when people need you.

You never wait for a specific Moon phase to conduct the work.
You make your ritual when your spirits tell you to do so. It has
nothing to do with the placement of the Moon in the sky!

• • •

SAVING THE MOON LEGEND – LUNAR ECLIPSE

A very long time ago, when our people lived along the Amur River, a great misfortune came into their lives. You know that our people lived well, but when the Sun fell behind the mountains and evening arrived, we hid in our homes.

The night was the time that belonged to wicked spirits who controlled the Earth and the skies. Those spirits traveled everywhere, twisted and turned, and knocked beside our windows and doors searching for a careless person to abduct to their underground or celestial lairs.

Then the Moon was born and came down from the heavens to help our people. She was first born in the shape of a thin sickle mouth. Those wicked spirits became frightened and confused at her appearance and flew away. Each night, the Moon grew and grew and grew, until she transformed herself into a full and round celestial beauty. This was the time that the Moon was at her greatest force and power. It was at this time that those wicked spirits flew away and hid in their musty lairs.

These full moon nights are the time that we can walk joyfully and freely upon the excellent earth. This is the time that we sing our songs honoring the Moon.

A time came when, with each night, the Moon began to decrease and decrease until her death. Now we know that the Moon dies to be reborn and grow once again. This will be for all time to come. She taught us how to divide the hours of the day and night, the months, and when to recognize the arrival of summer, autumn, winter, and spring. She taught us that this celestial cycle travels round each and every year. We lived well and were friends with the Moon.

Once, when the Moon died and was not reborn, the wicked spirits gathered together and planned to destroy her forever. When she grew and grew into her greatest beauty (full Moon), those wicked spirits turned into evil celestial dogs and attacked her on all sides. They ripped at her and tore her into pieces and greedily ate her! She began to decrease and became half her size, and her beautiful face grew red from blood.

We were so frightened that we ran back into our homes and hid, but we loved her so greatly that we knew we must overpower our own fear and try to save her. The men traveled out with their bows, arrows, and spears and climbed to the top of the highest hill. The women came and brought their drums and saucepans, and even the children found their courage and with sticks and stones began to battle the evil celestial dogs.

Together we drove off the wicked spirits from the Moon and saved our celestial beauty from being eaten. So, from time to time, those evil spirits still try to destroy her, but we understand that when they try, we must leave our homes and rescue the Moon. Otherwise, there will be nothing. There will be no Moon or people.

. . .

Star People

Khadai is the spirit of the constellation Orion and is known as the "organizer of the world." S/he is the heavenly first ancestor/shaman of the Ulchi. In the ritual of "Praying to the Sky", hunters would bring special gifts to *Khadai*. They hoped that the offerings would please the celestial Master and, in turn, this Master would send the "furry animals" to them. Small special totems, usually of larch wood, were carved of this Sky master. Grandmother Nadia told me once that every person has their special star and that the spirit of the star is in some way connected to that person's life. She did not elaborate on this comment to me.

For the Ulchi, there was no differentiation between stars and planets, so all lights in the heavens are called stars. Stars are not only spirits but specific cosmological territories as well. They contain a mirror reflection of everything on earth, with villages, people, mountains, and lakes.

Ulchi shamans, when setting out to see the Upper World spirits, rest on the Pole Star, called the Great Blue Star or *Galbu Khosta*. The Spirit master of this star has been called Ancient Grandfather. Some shamans say that the Pole Star is a powerful ancient grand- mother who protects the souls of children and provides help and direction to the shamans while they are traversing this region of space. Each shaman will describe the image of this spirit in their own way.

ILKA DUVAN AND HIS WIFE ACHINDA, CA. 1950

Shamans have different stars or earthly locations where the souls of adults can be kept for safekeeping and protection, but children's souls are usually placed in the Pole Star. Sky shamans also use these locations as a place to rest during conjuring. The other two major stars used by shamans during their otherworld journeys are the Red Star (*Burikta*, or Venus), and the Yellow Star (Vega). The path of the Milky Way, which travels north-south across the circumpolar region of space, is the celestial highway that Sky shamans traverse to various secret stellar lands. This starry path shifts throughout the seasons from west to east, passing through at least thirty different constellations. Whether taking this north-south access across the cosmos or flying directly west toward the land of the dead, each Sky shaman navigates their journeys along this ancient road known as the Path of the Musk Deer (*Udey Poktoni*).

There are hidden apertures in the starry sky that lead to other levels of the heavens. These openings convey the shaman to higher spiritual realms where specific Master spirits live and make their homes. Only the most potent Sky shamans know where these doorways exist. Trying to gain access to these higher levels is always fraught with obstacles and impediments, as protective spirits, whose duty it is to keep guard at these entrances, seek to block or harm anyone who tries to enter.

They relied more upon the circumpolar stars (the constellations of Ursa Major and Minor, Cassiopeia, Cepheus, Camelopardalis, and Draco) than the equatorial or ecliptic regions of space. Basically, they were oriented to what was directly above their heads. Other constellations would rise and fall in their own seasonal cycles, but the never-setting stars in the circumpolar regions were not only the time keepers of the night but the portals to the land of the Upper World spirits. It was this region of space that they turned their attention toward for all matters, earthly and spiritual.

Legend of the Big Dipper

A heavenly mother-in-law asked her son to set up three racks for drying fish nets. He was young and inexperienced in these matters and accidentally set them up in a quadrangle. The mother-in-law was very upset that her son had constructed them improperly. She started chasing her son, and the father-in-law started chasing his wife, crying, "Wait, wait, wait! This is causing domestic chaos!"

The Big Dipper (*Kombo*) is also a celestial rest stop for shamans during their travels in the Upper World. Sometimes referred to as the Seven Transparent Stars, the region of Ursa Major is a type of way station for journeys through and around the circumpolar regions of the night sky. Grandmother Nadia spoke of traveling to the Pole Star and peeking in through the opening. She said she felt cold like never before, but through this portal, she saw a wondrous land. During his conjurings, Grandfather Misha would travel to the Red Star, Yellow Star, and Blue Star to rest briefly while gathering his strength during both dreams and in conjurings.

Commentaries

Grandmother Tika:

When I travel to the underworld, I journey westward between the constellations of Ursa Major and Minor (Big and Little Dipper). This is the way you travel to the land of the dead.

•

There is a small opening in the sky. When traveling there, you must fly past the Big Dipper. It is guarded by seven star women holding hammers. They sit there playing with their beautiful earrings and are sometimes distracted from their duty. When you fly there, you must travel past them, but you must not yawn and lose your attention; otherwise, they'll bash you with their hammers. This hole leads to a transparent silver land in the cosmos, and there you will find a golden Manchu Enduri nine stories tall. Sometimes this Enduri will appear as a golden dragon or old man. When I travel there, I wash my hands in the golden water. When I journey there, I wash my hands and face, and this is where I keep the souls of children. There are seven layers to the Upper and Lower World. I travel there in my conjurings and my dreams.

••

Grandmother Nadia:

The Ulchi did not have names for all of the stars or constellations. We tuned our attention to special stars that we would appeal to for rituals or guides during our hunting. The Milky Way is the path that a hunter would take through the sky as it marks the trail of his skis. The Pole Star appears first in the heavens, and we call it the Blue Star.

•

The stars are spirits that hold these glowing rocks (stars) in their hands.

•

When traveling in the sky, I found my way to the opening near the Big Dipper. I looked inside and saw one large eye staring back at me. It was Ba. I slowly entered this land, but it was so very dark and so very cold that I didn't want to proceed any further. I backed off, but I will always remember that great singular eye looking back at me.

• • •

Clouds, Thunder, Rainbows, and Lightning Spirits

The clouds are both animate beings and places of repose for traveling Sky shamans during a conjuring. They are also the home of the great Thunder spirit *Agdi*, who was greatly respected and feared by all peoples. Grandfather Misha's grandfather (whom he called father) was a Thunder shaman who controlled the weather and other meteorological conditions. Sitting close to a window while inside the home is taboo during a lightning and thunder episode outdoors.

Grandmother Nadia spoke about the fact that it was not uncommon for lightning to find its way into a home via a window or crack in the wall. In this way, many people experienced tragic deaths inside their dwellings, and such an event was seen as the wrath of *Agdi*. When *Agdi* was active, it was best to sit inside and remain quiet. When a rainbow (*Agdipanyani*) appeared in the skies, the peoples experienced this meteorological condition as the manifestation of *Agdi's* soul.

GRANDFATHER MISHA DUVAN, BAINBRIDGE
ISLAND, WASHINGTON STATE, USA, 1995

Commentary

Grandfather Misha:

The clouds also have their own lives and own spirits. They travel back and forth across the sky and also argue among themselves. When you see them turn dark and black, then they are beginning to fight and argue with each other. That is where lightning and thunder comes from, the arguments of the clouds. The thunder master is called Agdi. He lives among the clouds.

• • •

BIRD PEOPLE

All types of birds are beings that belong to the realm of the heavenly worlds and are venerated as the original creators of the earth. Before a human incarnates into the Middle World, their soul takes the form of a small nestling and waits upon the Tree of Life to enter the womb of a human female. All birds are great assistants to the shaman—an eagle, crow, swallows, swans, ducks, geese, owls, cuckoos, etc. Each specific shaman is served by a sole spirit or a cortege of these beings during their healing ceremonies. A powerful shaman can consciously transform themselves into a bird and, through this act of transmogrification, visit family members or clients, or just keep general surveillance upon the activities of a certain location or clan territory.

COMMENTARY

GRANDMOTHER TIKA:

My father, after he died, would always come back to me as a bluebird. I would go outside, and he would fly to visit me. Each time I saw that bluebird; I knew it was my father looking out for me and seeing how my life was progressing. We would talk to each other for a while.

. . .

SKY VAMPIRES

The harmful spirits of this upper region can be specific flying birds, star people, cloud people, etc. The most well-known are the Ebaha, also called Busawu. Both the common people and the shamans know well of these predatory spirits that can have direct physical or dream-like encounters with them from time to time. The Ebaha are vampiric beings that fly about searching for humans. They are seen as beautiful females, and their voices are heard as either melodic or discordant. Here are some of these firsthand encounters and dreams.

COMMENTARIES

GRANDFATHER MISHA:

When the Earth was destroyed by fire, the Ebaha/Busawu stole the shaman's clothes from my clan. The nine women (Ebaha) had clothing that was the color of bright light. They took my soul. I was turning around and around as if I had wings in flight. Their clothes were sparkling and transparent, and their voices were so beautiful. They wanted to suck my blood, so I quickly went away from them. That's all.

•

Ebaha would fly high above the taiga, and the hunters and fishermen would see them often. In the 1930s, when more and more airplanes appeared in the sky, they were rarely seen. Those who were in boats on the water would be safe, but those who camped in the land would disappear. Their bodies would be found only seasons later in the spring, when the snow melted, or in the fall. Their bodies would have been sucked dry and desiccated of all moisture. That's all.

•

Once I went with my brother to fish. We had prepared our nets, eaten dinner, and lay down to sleep in our boat. The sky and land were so very beautiful at sunset. There wasn't a cloud in the sky and a Full Moon was rising in the heavens. My brother went to sleep, and I was getting ready to lie down to sleep also in the bow of the boat. I was prepared to shoot any Ebaha if they planned to attack us that night.

From the side of Bear Mountain—and we call it Bear Mountain because there are a lot of bears that live there—there rose three Ebaha with the most beautiful voices. In truth, they flew toward us and attacked us! They circled and circled in flight around us. They kept circling around us and then quickly flew away.

I cried out to my brother, "Quickly, quickly, wake up!" I couldn't catch my breath, but I was slowly able to breathe again. I called out again, "Wake up, wake up!" I pushed on him to arouse him from his sleep.

He asked, "Where did they go?" I pointed in the direction and said, "They flew over there."

The following morning, we collected our net from the river and returned home. At the same time, my father was on the other side of the river.

My father had caught a great deal of fish. When we told our father the story, our father told us a story of a family from the Detu clan. He said, "A husband and wife had gone fishing, and they never returned. People from all over had searched and searched and searched for them, but they were never found. They disappeared, and no one ever knew what happened to them."

"Where did they go?" my father said. "I heard the voice of the Water master saying that when you are close to water, you cannot be captured by the harmful Ebaha/Busawu women."

"They cannot steal you because the Busawu lose all their strength when they are near water. The Water spirit knows and sees all," Father said.

Because we were nearby the water, the Busawu could not harm us, but people who do not sleep on the bank of the river can be attacked by the Ebaha/Busawu. They will drink all of your blood, and afterward, they will cast your body parts throughout the land. That's all.

•

Achi Dechuli was a very beautiful woman in her youth. She went fishing with two other people. She had not returned for three days. We thought she would return, but we never saw her or her two companions. We then set out to search for them, taking one of our hunting dogs along with us. We couldn't find any trace of them. Finally, we discovered that those people had returned home by themselves, but Achi was not with them.

The old man (father of Achi) said, "You have found your way back, and that is why you are alive; otherwise the Busawu would have surely taken you. Those Busawu will drink and suck the blood of the people they find, and they will steal the souls and dismember the body, scattering the body parts here, there, and everywhere. Those Busawu women are harmful and crazy." Later, Achi found her way home. That's all.

•

The Ebaha were born deep within the earth. They were cooked there inside the earth, which later gave birth to nine young Ebaha women. That's all.

•

There were eight or nine Ebaha flying. They travel throughout the world. They can live in the clouds and create misfortune for people. The elders say, "Whether you are traveling, hunting, fishing, being a guest in another's home, or even just walking in the forest, always remember to protect yourself. Always remember to give offerings to Ba. That's all.

••

37

Grandmother Nadia:

My cousins had a very large farm in Bulava. They had much livestock. One day, three Ebaha came to the farm. Viktor Duvan saw them flying down from the sky.

Viktor's mother grabbed him and held him close to her. Viktor is the brother of my cousin , and he was Vera's younger brother. I was about four years younger than Viktor. Viktor wanted to shoot the Ebaha, but his mother protested saying, "It is forbidden to harm them!" Viktor said okay to appease his mother, but he really wanted to kill those Ebaha.

Perhaps five or six months later, Viktor took his own life. I was a child when this happened, but I remember the event well. This is why we teach respect for all things, even the Ebaha or other harmful spirits. That's all.

· · ·

From what we can ascertain from these encounters, vampiric beings have been around since the beginning of time. All Ulchi children grew up being warned about their existence. When traveling through the woods for hunting, fishing, or gathering purposes, they would not only be aware of the predatory animals of the taiga but would take precautions regarding these harmful spirits of the Upper World. If a person stayed in the taiga after sunset, camping near the river would be necessary to avoid any nocturnal attacks. These spirits were rendered powerless to assault a person who was near a body of water. When the *Ebahas* arrived in someone's dreams, this unfortunate event would probably require a shamanic conjuring to return the person's soul from their grasp. *Ebaha* were also natural scavengers with the ability to sense a person's demise before the actual event. After death, they could come and feast upon the body.

I listened long and hard to these tales of the *Ebaha*. I asked Grandmother Nadia about the unfortunate event befalling her cousin Viktor who, although he didn't harm them, was driven by them to take his own life. Nadia replied, "Viktor didn't shoot them because of the pleas of his mother, but in his heart, he wanted to kill them, and the Ebaha knew this and came back to punish him. You must remember to show respect to all of the spirits, especially the harmful ones!"

COMMENTARY

GRANDMOTHER NADIA:

Now, human people could be Busawu. You know everyone is a Busawu from time to time. Every person can naturally be a little vampiric. When you are tired and have no strength, you may want to go to a river, mountain, a special place in nature or go dancing or be out among other people. You will draw good feelings into yourself by being around nature or happy and energetic events. This is natural for all human beings. It reinvigorates oneself. Now, there are living people who are full-time Busawu. There are those people with a negative state of mind or who perhaps are predatory by nature that are constantly draining the life energy from those whom they are around. These are people who make you feel weak and spent after spending any time with them. These types of people should be avoided at all costs because they will suck all of your strength and you will become ill in your mind and body.

• • •

TOP • GRANDFATHER MISHA DUVAN CONDUCTING THE SUN RITUAL,
BAINBRIDGE ISLAND, WASHINGTON STATE, USA, 1995
BOTTOM • VILLAGE MARRIAGE CEREMONY, NADIA DUVAN (THIRD FROM LEFT)

Upper World Rituals

The Sun Ritual and New Year's Celebration

The Ulchi New Year is observed according to the Eastern lunar calendar. This ritual occurs on various dates in late January and/or early February. It is a holiday that the whole family observes together and is considered the most auspicious time of the year for each clan. All members of the family remain awake all night and guard a lit candle that will burn from late evening until the early morning. After sundown, the clan prepares special foods and pastries that are traditional to this holiday. There are various types of fish dishes but never red meat. Offerings to the spirits include the usual wild berries, tobacco, and assorted grains. A person begins by taking branches of *sankura* (Ledum Palustre) and burning it as a type of incense to purify and cleanse the home including the family members.

Many families owned a special Spirit house that is brought out one day before the event. This Spirit house was usually rectangular in shape around eight inches wide, twelve inches long, and six inches deep. A piece of red wool or cotton is attached at the top and hangs down to the bottom of the structure, serving as a curtain or doorway. Also, there are small porcelain cups that are used for this ceremony. They are placed on either side. Offerings of vodka or other clear colored alcoholic beverages are poured into each cup. There is one cup per family member as well as sacred cups assigned to the different spirit helpers associated with the New Year. This Spirit house is kept safe in the rafters of the roof during the rest of the year. The upper sections of the roof are seen as spiritually and ritually pure. When the Spirit house is brought into the central part of the home, it is placed beside the New Year's candle, which is next to the home's altar (*mali*).

When the Sun rose the next morning, the men and boys of the clan carry the candle and the Spirit house outside. If there are no males in a family, then a woman would go outside to perform the ritual. When the ritual was complete, the candle is blown out. Those outside return and collectively make an offering to the House spirit. Each family member, in turn, expresses their personal wishes for the upcoming year.

COMMENTARIES

GRANDMOTHER NADIA:

We would begin the ritual in the early morning around six o'clock. I would want to sleep, but I had to wake up to participate. I remember that there was always snow on the ground because it was usually February. The Sun had not risen over the mountains at that time. It was so very dark, so we would use our kerosene lanterns. We had no electricity at that time. Only lanterns and the fire in the hearth illuminated our homes.

We would bring down the idols from the rafters in the ceiling. We cleaned them and fed them and made a special offering to them. We even had long conversations with each one. These idols were between two and three meters tall, and our home had so many of them, like the Masi, Dusey, Kuljamu, and Buchu. We would dress them in new clothes made of either fur or material.

Then the light would slowly appear from the east as the Sun rose. We would carry the small plates and Chinese porcelain cups and then make offerings. Those Chinese cups were so small. I remember that when I was a child, I really liked to play with them. There were so many plates, about nine of them. We would pour the araki (a clear alcoholic beverage) from the bottle. That bottle looked just like a Japanese sake bottle.

..

GRANDFATHER MISHA:

When making the New Year's ritual, you first speak to Orion and then to the Sun. Speak your own words, then make an offering.

*Then petition for your needs and the needs of the family and then
bow three times. After you have finished the outside ritual, bring
the Spirit house back inside and extinguish the candle. The New
Year has begun, and every clan has its own spirits and therefore
their own ways and rules of living dependent on the nature of
the clan spirits.*

. . .

Ritual to Orion

Known as "Praying to the Sky", it was also performed separately by
hunters during the winter chase. If this ritual took place on New Year's
Day, the Orion constellation would be addressed prior to the ritual to
the Sun. If the prayers were separate, then hunters would commence
the rite on arrival at their first encampment. Offerings were given
via the spirit portal of the campfire, and prayers and requests for a
successful hunt were made by each person individually.

Commentary

Grandmother Nadia:

*We don't have as many legends about the stars, but we use them,
as they are important guideposts for hunters and fishermen. I
remember bringing offerings to the three stars in the belt of Orion
each February or at the time of the New Year's Festival. When
Orion rose, we would take a small wooden table with tiny cups
outside. In this candled procession, the males of the household
would follow my father outside, then would fall to their knees
and petition those stars. My father would speak his wishes and
hopes to those stars. The women and girls would remain inside
the house and prepare food.*

.

*By the stars, we can determine what the weather will be in the
next few days. In the morning, the stars travel to the other side*

of the sky. Sparkling in the transparent ceiling of the cosmos, they make their home. There is a certain type of rain called "frog rain." From the stars, you'll know if this rain is coming. This type of rain comes quickly and then disappears.

. . .

Rituals to the Pole Star and the Big Dipper

Separate rituals to the Pole Star and the Big Dipper were conducted by Sky shamans due to their importance in conjurings, and these rituals would take on an individual flavor rather than following a prescribed cultural tradition. They were usually performed at the beginning of a shaman's song, asking for help and permission to fly to these celestial territories from the Master spirit of each specific star, especially by those shamans who protected the souls of children.

Ritual for Lunar or Solar Eclipses

Lunar and solar eclipses were thought of as events that portended danger and destruction. Everyone had the responsibility to go out of his or her homes to carry out the ancient ceremony of Saving the Moon or Sun. The ritual was conducted by the women, men, and children of the village, using drums, metal spirit belts, pots and pans,

and everything else that could make a loud and cacophonous noise. People were obligated to go out into the streets and begin to yell and drive off the offending spirits.

This began at the onset of the eclipse and continued until it had passed. It was believed that harmful spirits, in the form of celestial dogs, were eating the Moon or Sun. The dragon spirit, *Enduri*, had sent his dogs to bite that celestial body, and it was the duty of the people to drive these wicked spirits from the sky. When those cunning dogs were dispatched, the spirit of the Moon or Sun would quickly fly to the heavenly meadows to ingest healing grasses as an antidote, for self-healing, and then return to the night or day sky and again begin to shine in the heavens.

Although lunar eclipses were more common, the same ritual elements were enacted in those rare astronomical periods that produced a solar eclipse in their geographical region.

CHAPTER 4

Middle World

The name given to the Middle World is *Duentey*, which means "taiga" or "forest." This is the realm of terrestrial animals, rocks, rivers, mountains, and so forth. Animals are referred to as *Duenteyni*, which means "people of the forest." This is also the territory where human beings reside. It includes everything around us, the entire mortal world.

The Middle World is divided into two distinct regions: the territories of land and water. The land is co-ruled by the spirits of the tiger and bear. The realm of water, considered the most powerful and dangerous region of the Middle World, is ruled by *Temu*, the Master spirit of water.

Other major Middle World spirits include the Master spirits of Fire and Earth, and the *Kuljamu*, an ancient race of humanoid beings who act as the protectors of children.

Major Spirits of the Middle World

Siberian Tiger

As the tiger is the progenitor of the Ulchi people, it holds the distinction of being the primary land Master of the Middle World. In traditional Ulchi society, people wish to inherit the tiger's soul and its powers of dexterity and strength. As the Chief spirit, it must not be addressed as "tiger" (*dusey*) but instead is given the honorary name Amba, or "powerful one." Calling this spirit "tiger" would be considered denigrating and disrespectful.

The tiger was never hunted, as to kill or injure one would bring spiritual and physical harm to the hunter and their family members. Surviving an attack by a tiger could imbue the survivor with special powers that would lead that person down the road of the shaman. Grandfather Misha's brother survived a tiger attack and later became a tiger shaman. Grandmother Tika became a wife to a tiger spirit and gave birth to flying tiger offspring, who served her as spirit protectors and guides in the other worlds. Flying tigers were spirits associated with the celestial worlds, as these heavenly tigers were easily identifiable by their birdlike wings.

COMMENTARY

GRANDMOTHER NADIA:

The most sacred animal for the Ulchi is the tiger. One must never hinder the tiger if you meet her in the forest. You must bow to the tiger and walk around so as not to disturb the tiger on her path. It is a great taboo to speak loudly about the tiger.

•

We would appeal to the tiger spirit when leaving for the hunt or when treating various illnesses such as boils or tuberculosis.

•

Remember that not all Amba (tigers and spirits) are harmful.

• • •

Tiger Tale told by Grandmother Nadia

This is a story about a hunter who traveled into the forest and saw a tiger. He saw the tiger crying. The tiger was in great distress. The tiger was weeping because she had a piece of wood that was lodged in her paw.

The tiger pleaded with the hunter to help her remove the offending splinter. The hunter was afraid of the tiger. He was fearful to offend and refuse a request from this Great Spirit, went over and removed it from her body.

The tiger then spoke to the hunter, saying, "Do not be afraid of me, and now I am asking you to return to your own home." The hunter had caught nothing that day, and the tiger then again spoke, saying, "Go home and eat and sleep, and come back here tomorrow."

When the hunter returned to that same place in the forest the next day, he found many minks, sables, and other fur-bearing animals left for him by the tiger. He was so very happy. He took them into his hunter's cabin in the forest. He had a meal and then went to sleep.

Later that night, he had a dream that the tiger visited him in the form of a beautiful woman. In the dream, she said to him, "Do not worry and do not be afraid. I want you to travel to this place and that place in the forest. You will find my gifts of sables, minks, and other animals, as I will always help you as you have helped me. In the future and forever, you will always be known among your people as a great hero, a great hunter."

In the morning, the hunter woke up and remembered the places in the forest that the tiger told him to go to find her gifts. He found beautiful pelts of sables, mink, and other fur animals waiting there for him. He took this back to his village, and the people were amazed.

Each time the hunter went into the forest, he would return with the most bounty of beautiful pelts and food. Before he traveled on his future expeditions, he would make a great ritual offering to the spirit of the tiger and the spirits of the forest."

· · ·

Bear

The bear (*Buyu*) holds the secondary position of Master in the Middle World. Known as *Mapa*, or "ancient one," this spirit connects all living beings to the world of their ancestors, and its image usually represents the main House spirit for the clan. The bear is also considered the emissary between humans and the Master spirit of the animal people, who resides in the other worlds. The bear is the only spirit in the Ulchi pantheon that is responsible for creating semi-divine people among the living.

Traditionally, women who gave birth to twins were transformed into demigods amongst the clans because of the Bear spirit's involvement in such occurrences. The offspring of these women also held this sacred distinction. The Bear spirit would arrive in the dream state, in either the form of a bear or that of a young man, and would mate with a human woman. Afterwards, a set of twins would be born, altering the life and status of the woman and her children forever among the people.

The union of Bear spirits with human women were venerable events. Such alliances occurred as far back as anyone could remember, and they would reinforce and strengthen the cooperative partnership between humans, animals, and the spirits of nature. An Ulchi legend dating from the distant past relates the story of two sisters who became allied with bears in a specific mystical landscape.

THE TWO SISTERS

Long ago, there lived two sisters. Living together, they gave birth. The older sister gave birth and the younger sister also. The older sister had a daughter, and the younger sister had a son.

Later, one beast came down. You know a bear. The bear came down and entered the house and lay down next to the older sister on a plank bed. This is the way they lived. The younger sister was afraid of the bear.

Then, not long after, another bear traveled down to the house. That bear went to the younger sister. The older bear was with, the older sister. The younger sister wrapped herself up with clothing when the second bear entered the house, and she lay next to her child. She touched the bear with her foot and then kicked him. Not long after, the younger bear went away, but the older bear continued to live there.

Later, the older big bear went back to his home. Not long after, the younger sister went outside and followed the older bear to his home. She found the tracks of the bear and traveled and traveled and walked and walked till she found his home. Half of the house was made of wooden shavings, and the other half was made from fir branches. She parted the branches with her hands and looked inside through the small hole and saw the bears inside a cave.

The older bear said to the younger bear, "You found a son, so did you make a bow and arrows for him? I found a daughter so that I will make her a dress from lynx skin." Then another bear in the cave said, "Where is my child? I have no child to make something for." "That woman is very squeamish about me," said the younger bear.

Later, after listening to the bears, the younger sister returned home and asked her sister, "Did my baby cry?" "No," said the older sister. After this, they passed the night together.

The next day, the older big bear went to the older sister, but the younger sister was nowhere to be found.

Later, the younger bear traveled back to the house. He came inside and washed his hands. He brought a fish and lay down on the bed, and later he went outside to lie down. He gathered lots of wood and brought it into the house, where he made a great fire in the hearth. He took an offering bowl full of many types of food and made a ritual to the Fire Spirit. The younger bear said to the younger sister, "You will find a good man and he will be tall." Then the younger bear jumped into the fire.

Not long after, the younger woman came back and went into the house. She found a beautiful fur coat. She had been collecting berries, which she brought into the house and placed on the bed. Later, she collected some firewood and kindling and made a fire in the hearth. She wrapped up her child and took the ritual container with food and made an offering to the Fire Spirit. While holding her child, she jumped into the fire.

She and her child traveled through the fire. They journeyed for a very long time. The clothing of the child became loose and open, so she rewrapped it to make it secure. She tied the child to her back and continued to travel. They traveled for a long time until they reached a house made of grass and straw. Inside this home lived a very old grandmother.

"Oh," said the young woman, "it is so very cold outside." "Why are you carrying such a small child with you?" said the old woman. "Okay, please come inside and get warm."

"Okay," said the young woman, "I'll come inside the house." They all spent the night together. The old woman said, "Your husband said not to worry and asked you to come to him. Don't wander here and there, just return to your home." The young woman said, "What shall I do? I will just continue on my way and travel up to his mother country."

The next day, the young woman continued on her journey. The old woman instructed her to keep on traveling until she and the child arrived at a thicket. The old woman said, "Past the thicket is a lake. When you arrive at the lake, wash your child, and then wash yourself. Do it this way. Then hold the child close to your breast. Where you begin to ascend, you will find berries all around. Make a ritual offering with the berries from this mountain using the sacred food container. Then keep traveling and traveling along this path until you arrive at the top of the mountain. Follow the trail through the berries and keep going and going until you see an old woman. Pour berry juice, like water, and keep making ritual offerings to the spirits along your way."

The young woman followed her instructions and arrived at the top of the mountain, where she met the next old woman. That old woman said, "I thought you went back home." The young woman replied, "I will not go home. I will continue to travel toward my husband's mother country. I want to travel on the road of my husband's clan, the blood clan of the bear. I will search and find it."

Later, the old woman said, "Come into my home to rest and sleep for a time. You are tired and want to sleep, and then tomorrow you can wake up and go along your way. In the future, you will find your own way. Do as I instruct. In the future, I will not teach you anymore because from this day on, you must find your own road."

The young woman and her child spent the night. The next morning, she awoke and set off down the road. She traveled and traveled until she arrived at a house made of grass and straw. She gathered firewood, and as she entered the house, she saw another old woman.

"Ho ho ho," said the old woman. "You have found our mother country." The young woman brought her child inside the home where they all lived together, but there was no husband. They threw the wooden streamers into the taiga.

Later, the old woman said, "Oh, it is so dangerous outside in the evening that I will take you and your child to my own home." They all traveled to a different house, and when they arrived, they went inside to rest and sleep.

Later that evening, harmful Ebaha and twins flew down with powerful voices. The husband had just arrived at the home. He saw the twins outside the house, playing rhythms on a musical beam using sticks. The sound was very loud as the twins beat and beat out those rhythms. Under the house was a little baby bear with strong legs. This little bear was learning to walk. He was just learning to balance himself as he swayed back and forth.

All those spirit people appeared, and the old woman came out of the house and hit them. The Ebaha said, "We are heavenly spirits, and we fly down to capture the earth spirits."

All the people ran away except this one man and his mother. The old woman, her son, the young woman, and her daughter were finally able to rest that night, having driven off the harmful spirits.

They slept the whole night, and in the morning, the husband went out on his skies. The young woman followed her husband and saw him disappear into an opening. She looked through the hole and saw a small house. She said nothing but remained quiet as she watched.

When the husband and the young woman returned from the taiga, the old woman said, "Now it is finished! All is fine. You'll never have to be worried again about harmful spirits. They have all flown away!"

The young woman and her child remained in the home with the old woman, and every evening the husband would come home. They all lived together for a time. The young woman was afraid that he might make some trouble. That was what she was fearful of, and that is what she worried about each day.

Many days later, he returned home on his skies and went into the house. His wife was inside. His child was fine. The young woman had made an outfit for her child including gloves. She quickly took the child and soothed him. They all slept the night together.

The next day, around evening time, the man said to his mother, "I want to sleep with my child." The old woman replied, "But the child will cry in the night without a breast to feed on." The man said, "If he cries in the night, I will give him back to his mother." Now they all rested, and there was no crying, so they slept through the entire night.

Early in the morning of the next day, they quickly awoke. The wife was in a good mood. The old woman said, "It is not allowed. You cannot live here. One who was born in the other world cannot live here in the Fire World. You should return to your mother country and live there. Go away!"

The young woman left with her husband and child. They made a sled and went away. They pulled that sled and traveled and traveled until they needed to rest. They wrapped themselves up in warm clothing. They traveled and traveled and later saw their own house and went inside. They had arrived at their true place. There they found the older sister and her husband, the old bear. They all lived together, hunted and fished together, and lived their lives. Enough!

• • •

WATER SPIRIT

Temu is the Master spirit of all bodies of water, including rivers, lakes, and oceans. This spirit makes its appearance known to people in various ways. Sometimes *Temu* is seen as an old man or old woman, an old man and an old woman together, a seal, or another aquatic creature.

Temu lives in a beautiful underwater kingdom containing villages and people, and inhabited by the creatures of the sea. Although there is no "lord of the underworld" in the Ulchi tradition, the souls of those kinsmen who have drowned remain in *Temu's* domain.

Temu, like the Dragon spirit, sees and hears all that is said and observes the actions of humans. This is why one must be very cautious when addressing the Water spirit. One must never defile or spoil the sacred places associated with this spirit, and one may not laugh or speak loudly when around any water source. Speaking harshly of a Water spirit is a great taboo.

The Return of the Salmon ritual, which involves prayers and offerings to *Temu*, is performed twice a year, at spring and fall. This is one of the central seasonal rituals of the people.

SASQUATCH

The *Kuljamu* are an ancient race of people who inhabit the mountains in the Russian Far East. In the oral traditions, this race has always existed upon the earth. They are an ape-like humanoid creature that other cultures refer to as a Yeti, Sasquatch, or Bigfoot.

These beings stand over eight feet tall and are said to speak the language of humans, wear clothing, and use rudimentary tools such as axes and knifes. They are also referred to by the name *Googda Ni*, or "the tall people." Their idols are carved from the larch tree and are recognizable by their conical heads.

They live in stone houses/caves. Their homes duplicate human houses inasmuch as stone beds, tables, chairs, shelves, pantries, and hearths are found within. They are among the most important beings in the Ulchi pantheon, as their species is seen as semi-divine. They are the protectors of children, travelers, and the general household clan.

Special rituals are dedicated to the *Kuljamu* by hunters visiting areas deep in the taiga or traveling through mountain passes. As Master spirits of the mountains, they can assist in a successful hunt and a safe journey to and from a hunter's home. As a helpful spirit, it is the female of this race that is venerated. The female of this species is said to telepathically soothe the cries of a child in the night.

Two stories of the *Kuljamu* people, recounted below, have survived in the Ulchi oral history.

The Harmful Tall People

There was an old man who had a very beautiful daughter. The old man wanted his daughter to get married. This was very long ago, and this old man lived and lived for a long time. He had only one child, and this child was a girl. The girl wanted to get married to another man, but this man was very poor. The old man wanted his daughter to have a rich husband. He quarreled with his daughter because he wanted a rich son-in-law. Every day, the two of them would argue and quarrel.

The old man said to his daughter, "Search my head!" The daughter searched and found a large tick in his scalp. What did he make later with the skin of this tick? He made a shaman's drum.

Later, the old man, having made this drum from the skin of a tick, called all the people of the village together. He wanted the villagers to guess what type of skin the drum was made of, and whoever guessed correctly would become

KULJAMU SAVENS, BULAVA VILLAGE MUSEUM

the husband of his beautiful daughter. This was very long ago.

The servant women of the household were busy carrying all the water to the home. They were preparing for the arrival of the villagers who were called to try to answer the question of the drum skin. At that time, the windows of the home were constructed of fish skin instead of glass. There were two Kuljamu hiding outside the window, and they listened and listened to everything that was said by this old man.

When the servant women went down to the river to gather water, the Kuljamu followed them. The Kuljamu approached the women and said, "So tell us, what kind of skin did the old man use to make that drum?" The servant women were very afraid and did not answer. The Kuljamu then said, "If you don't tell us, we will throw you into an ice hole!" Out of fear for their lives, the servant women said, "He made it from the skin of a tick that his daughter found in his head, and from that tick skin, he made the shaman's drum." The Kuljamu walked back toward the house as the servant women continued their journey to gather water at the river for the village guests.

The Kuljamu, standing behind the window, said to the old man, "We know what type of skin you used to make the drum." "Now give us your daughter!" demanded the Kuljamu. The daughter, who wanted to get married, cried and cried. That poor woman just cried and cried because she wanted to marry the poor man of the village. She approached the Kuljamu and said, "Of course, my father will honor his promise, but what can I do to change your minds?" The Kuljamu were not about to change their minds.

That woman cried and cried and prepared for the journey. She took a comb and silver ingot and placed it in her bosom. She gathered some white paper and hid this in her clothing, at her abdomen. Then she took some scissors and cut out an image of a horse on another piece of paper. She sat down and went off with the Kuljamu.

"The rock house is our home," said the Kuljamu. They traveled and traveled and traveled and still didn't arrive at the destination of the rock house. It was very far away. The young woman thought, "I will deceive them because I do not want to marry them, whatever they do."

They finally arrived at the home of the Kuljamu. There were two rock houses near one another. The Kuljamu said, "You can stay at this rock house." She said, "I will clean and organize your home. I will wash everything, and once I am finished, the two of you can come inside the house." So the Kuljamu waited on the road between the two rock houses.

She went inside the house and saw stone shelves. On these shelves were raisins, peaches, berries, and different kinds of fruits. They were the Kuljamu's food. She thought, "Now I will deceive them." She cleaned and organized the home and took out the paper-cut image of the horse. She blew on the horse, and it came alive. You know in fairy tales such things are possible.

She mounted the horse and escaped. They flew and flew and flew through the sky. When both she and the horse grew tired, they rested back on the earth along the roadway. She was so tired that she just fell off the horse, and of course, the horse was tired and needed to rest also.

The Kuljamu searched for her. "Where has she gone?" they asked. They searched and searched and decided to track her down. Little by little, the Kuljamu came closer to where she was resting. She got back on her horse and flew into the heavens, away from the tall people with bad spirits. She traveled and traveled, and she and the horse grew very weary.

Later, the horse said, "Let's rest! I am so tired, but do not worry or be afraid. Let us take a little rest." The woman said, "I understand, but when we are on the land, the Kuljamu came closer and closer to us. They are catching up to where we are."

The woman then took the silver ingot from her bosom and threw it up into the sky. It turned into a large mountain to block the pursuit of the Kuljamu. The Kuljamu were still trying to catch her and grumbled and complained to one another.

She flew through the heavens with the horse, until the horse became so tired that they landed back on the earth. That horse was so exhausted that it could no longer go on, so she took out another piece of paper and cut an image of a new horse. On this new horse, she continued her escape.

The journey was so hard that she took out her awl and needle and threw it into the sky. It turned into a large iron net. "Hopefully, this iron net will slow them down," she thought, but the Kuljamu were gaining on her quickly.

She picked up a small tree branch and threw it perfectly into the sky. It turned into a large wooden pillar that extended from the top of the heavens to the bottom of the earth. It blocked the progress of the Kuljamu. She flew to the top of the pillar, but the pillar was unstable, and slowly it began to tip over.

The woman was angry and said, "I need some more paper." She reached into her clothing and found one small piece remaining, so she made her last horse, and they went on their way. She ran and ran and ran until she had completely left those Kuljamu far behind her. "What is happening?" cried the Kuljamu. "Where has she gone?"

Later, the horse became so tired that it just fell over. The horse said to the woman, "I am dying. Please don't cry or be sad. When I am dead, take my blood and use it to draw an image of a house and it will turn into a real home. Take my skin and sleep upon it." The woman cried and cried and said, "Of course, I will draw an image of a house with your blood."

Later, she drew the house and took the skin of the horse, wrapped it around herself, and fell asleep. She awoke to find herself inside a wonderful home. A large fire was burning in the hearth. There were many cups and bowls and even a large cast iron pot with hot water inside. She looked around the house and saw a bow and set of arrows, a gun, and other types of provisions. Outside the house were a barn and other small storage buildings.

She was alone, so she had to hunt for herself. She traveled into the taiga. She traveled and traveled for an entire day. "Oh, I am tired," she thought to herself. "I will take a little rest, and perhaps someone will come to my place and help me."

The next day, she saw a little boat approaching from the other side of the river. In the boat was sitting the poor man from her village, and she recognized him from very long ago. She also saw in the boat one of the Kuljamu she had escaped from, and he was accompanied by his father. She thought, "This makes me frightened, and now surely I will be killed!" She kept thinking and thinking of her fate, so she ran quickly into her house and grabbed the bow and arrow.

Later, the man, whom she had loved a long time ago, was the first to arrive at her door. The woman said, "Why have you come?" The man replied, "I have no wife, and I am looking for anyone who might have me for a husband. I have searched and searched and searched."

She remembered that, in the past, this young man had come to her father's house and wondered if he would find a wife. She also remembered those Kuljamu arrived on that same day. As she stood at the door, she thought, "What will I do when the Kuljamu arrive?" She was so worried.

The young man had come to her house alone, and she asked him, "Why did you bring those other people with you?" The young man said, "I was on my journey when I ran into them. The old man Kuljamu wanted me to take him and his son along with me." The young man was deceived into taking them along so that they could discover where the woman, whom they recognized, was hiding.

"How can I kill them?" she thought. "I am so tired, and I have thought of everything I can do." She walked down from her house, along the shore toward the boat. She came closer and closer and shot at the old Kuljamu man and his son. The boat quickly left the shore and headed down the river, away from the house.

She married the young man, and later they gave birth to one child, a son. The child grew up strong and healthy and learned to be a good hunter from his father.

• • •

Kuljamu in Auri Village

Long ago, when the earth was warm, Kuljamu lived at this time. Kuljamu was a very tall person. He was close to the size of a tall tree but was taller than a small tree. Kuljamu spoke the human language, but his head was pointed.

There was a great larch tree in Auri village. Its branches were large and spreading. Kuljamu would take our children and hang them from the branches and rock them like they were in a cradle.

When the water rose during inundation, Kuljamu walked through the water and said, "Not deep, not deep." When the water was little, Kuljamu kept saying, "Deep, deep." This kind of person was Kuljamu.

AURI MOUNTAIN IN THE ULCHI TERRITORIES

There was a small house at the end of a nomadic camp. A husband and wife and son lived there. The son was very young, about six years old.

A Kuljamu got into the habit of visiting this house. Kuljamu came to the house every evening when it was getting dark. Kuljamu would say, "Give me your child, give me." The husband and wife were very afraid.

An old man lived in that nomad camp. People always came to him to ask his advice. The people said, "Go and ask the old man what to do." So the husband and wife set off to ask his advice on the matter. The old man sat silently and listened to what they had said.

"What shall we do?" asked the husband and wife. "When it is getting dark, the Kuljamu comes and says, 'Give me your child, give me.'"

Then the old man spoke up and said, "Tomorrow, when Kuljamu comes, ask him to wrestle. He will say yes, and then open the door and quickly send your son outside. Let the boy run and, using his flint, tell him to cut off Kuljamu's tobacco pouch and then run back into the house. Kuljamu is tall and clumsy, and as he bends over, the boy will run away." The parents listened to the old man.

A day or so later, Kuljamu arrived in the evening and said, "Give me the child, give me." The father answered, "Kuljamu, let's wrestle!" "Yes, let's wrestle," said the Kuljamu.

The father opened the door, and at that moment the boy ran out, cut off the tobacco pouch with his flint, and ran back into the house. They closed the door, and Kuljamu went away, back to the mountain through the taiga.

The next day, the parents went to the old man and said, "Grandfather, what we shall do when Kuljamu returns for his tobacco pouch?"

The old man said, "Take an iron ax head and put it into a fire until it gets hot. When Kuljamu asks for his tobacco pouch, you should throw this out the window." The old man ordered them to do this.

Later, that evening, the Kuljamu came back to the house. He was standing near the window when he said, "Give me my tobacco pouch, give me!"

Then the husband and wife took the white-hot ax out of the fire and threw it through the window, saying, "Take your tobacco pouch!"

Kuljamu caught that white-hot ax and cried out, "This is hot, this is hot!" Kuljamu ran away into the taiga, and since that time he has never returned to that place.

That's all.

. . .

I asked Grandmother Nadia about this race of beings extensively, since they hold the distinction of being a primary Middle World spirit. Grandmother Nadia said that it had been a very long time since the *Kuljamu* had direct contact with the Ulchi people. In the past, they would occasionally visit clan territories and converse with the people in the area. I asked her about Grandfather Misha's youth when he was taken to a *Kuljamu* home by his relatives. I inquired whether, before Grandfather Misha's death, he had ever taken her to this place in nature. She said no, so I asked her if he had ever given her a map of the location or spoken of how to reach this area. She said, "He probably would not divulge that secret to me because I am not from his clan. This is a secret that only his clan would know."

EARTH SPIRIT

The Earth spirit (*Na Adja*) appears in the form of a grandmother, dragon, or bear. Each shaman would see this spirit in its multiple variations dependent on which image she would choose to take during any type of dream or conjuring .

Commentary

Grandfather Misha:

The spirit of the Earth is always moving and knows and sees how people are treating each other. The Earth trembles and shakes because of people's anger. The Earth is a dragon named Na Enduri (earth dragon). Na Enduri can determine the fate of a person upon the earth. This Earth dragon differentiates people from animals or other living beings.

•

When the people indiscriminately cut down trees, then the earth becomes lighter and shakes and rolls like thunder.

• • •

Fire Spirit

The Spirit of the fire is called *Pujen*, which translated means "ancestral heroine". Like many other Ulchi spirits, *Pujen* appears in various forms. This spirit is female and can be viewed as an old woman wearing a red robe or in a fiery form accompanied by a black dog. Others have observed this spirit appearing in the form of an old man with a similar canine by his side, while still others have reported seeing an old man and old woman with a dog. Grandmother Tika said that *Pujen* appeared to her as a naked man who was fiery in color and appearance.

Middle World Rituals

Bear Rituals

There are two types of bear rituals in the Ulchi culture. The first, known as the "Play of the Bear", is the most sacred festival, although the most infrequent. Its primary objective is to persuade the Bear spirit to speak positively of the people to the Master spirit of the animals, thus increasing the willingness of that being to provide future game and fish for the people.

Every so many years, a bear cub was found and taken from the forest back to a clan settlement, where it would be cared for by a host family. The bear would be raised like a member of a human family for the next three to five years. Many times, a puppy would be raised alongside as a companion to the bear cub. This puppy was specially chosen for its markings. The fur was completely black with a white marking on its chest or forehead. The family took care of the bear as if it was a great honored guest.

The bear was allowed to wander throughout the village and could gain access into any or all homes if it wished. It was treated as a member of the clan and would be given food when entering a home.

The best foods, fish, and accommodations were provided for the bear. At the end of three years, the clan that had raised the bear would set up the festival in a location within their own settlement.

Traditionally, the Ulchis did not live in villages but in clan settlements that contained between four to eight family groups. Each clan had a large geographical area that provided them with game and fish, and each knew the boundaries of the other clans. If a family was having a difficult time finding food in their area, they could always ask to hunt or fish in another's area, and permission was always granted.

The festival marked a time when people from surrounding areas would come together after many years of being apart. This was the only ritual that drew the entire Ulchi people together in one place. It served as a time when young women and men would meet in hopes of forming marriage alliances. The festival was held in late February or early March, before the spring thaw, and would last from ten to fourteen days. People would arrive on dogsled from all over the area. The host family was responsible for providing shelter and food for all of the visiting guests.

TOP • BEAR BEING
LEAD THROUGH
SACRED GATEWAY
LEFT • VILLAGERS
WATCHING PROCESSION
RIGHT • WOMEN PLAYING
BEAR RHYTHMS ON
UDJAJU (LOG DRUM)
BOTTOM • BEAR
BEING LEAD THROUGH
RITUAL HOME

TOP LEFT• BEAR ARRIVES AT
SACRED PLACE OF SACRIFICE
TOP RIGHT • MEN CARRYING
BEAR'S BONES AND SKIN TO
SACRED MAUSOLEUM
MIDDLE • RITUAL OFFERING
TO BEAR'S SPIRIT
BOTTOM • BEAR'S SKULL
WRAPPED IN SACRED STREAMERS
OUTSIDE MAUSOLEUM

When all the clans had arrived, many playful competitions between the families were begun. There were games such as rope pulling/ tug of war, archery contests, eating competitions, etc. Both men and women of great skill competed with one another. It was also a time to barter or trade for beautifully created clothing such as dresses, boots, and coats; wooden carvings; and other goods needed for daily life. The settlement became a large festival of music, art, food, and sports competitions for this two-week period.

The women would gather in the main home to prepare the special foods for the ceremony, in which the bear would be ritually sacrificed with great honor. The men would make the sacred wooden streamers that hung on the poles and marked the sacred path that the bear would travel to the place of sacrifice. There were many preparatory details that were taken care of by all.

When the time to begin the ceremony arrived, the elder women would start beating out the sacred rhythms on the *udjadyu*, or log drum. Other females, of all ages, would take wooden streamers in each hand and perform the Dance of the Taiga (*karpa*). This dance served two purposes. First, it cleaned and prepared the way for the sacrifice of the bear. It also reenacted the path that the bear would take to the spiritual land in the next world.

As the dance was taking place, the men placed a leather collar with two long chains on the neck of the bear. Holding one chain in the front of the bear and the other behind, the men led the bear upon the prescribed path, marked by the poles containing wooden streamers, through the village and along the hills to the frozen water of the Amur. There a small hole would be cut through the ice and would serve as a watering hole for the bear. After drinking the water of the river, the bear would be led back along the path and into the village, through the home of the host family, and on to the place of sacrifice. The sounds of the log drum and the dancing continued until the bear reached that final destination. The elder clansman of the host family would then call to the Spirit master that the "sending of the Bear spirit" would commence. The best archer was chosen to dispatch the creature. He would shoot the first arrow into the sky, announcing that the bear's spirit was on its way. Then the second arrow was shot into the heart of the bear. The killing had to be quick and painless. Once the bear was dead, the participants began to weep and cry. It was permissible to remember those family members who had passed over into the Lower World.

At this moment, the Ulchi say, the spirit of the Bear flew into the heavens. First, the spirit flew into the Blue Lake, at which time the bones of the animal were restored. Then the bear skeleton traveled to the Yellow Lake and dove in, at which time the muscles and meat were returned to the skeletal frame. Next, the bear flew into the Red Lake, where the fur of the animal was reattached. Now the bear was complete and whole. The bear continued its journey to the Master of animals. Upon arrival, the bear would speak to this Master spirit: "I have arrived as an emissary of the Ulchi people. Please help these people when they go hunting for your children. Please send them whatever you can spare. They are very good people who know and obey the laws of nature. I know them. They raised me. I lived with them for many years. They loved me and treated me like a member of their own family. They fed me and gave me the best of food. Please be kind and generous to them when they call upon you." Having made this request, the bear spirit would disappear from the spirit world and be reborn upon earth.

Back at the settlement, the body of the bear was being prepared. The bear was placed on a bed of wooden streamers on the ground. Then the fur was removed, and the meat was ritually cut from the bones. All bones were collected and placed off to the side. The meat was boiled outdoors in preparation for the great feast. As men began to cook the meat, the bones were gathered and carefully wrapped in wooden streamers. All the bones, except for the skull, were taken to a wooden mausoleum, built especially for the bear. One had to be careful about collecting all of the bones. If a bone was missing, the bear could not reincarnate upon the earth. The bones were placed in the wooden mausoleum and the skull was smoked and hung on a large pole decorated with wooden streamers. Everyone ate the bear meat. Young boys would pick a few hairs from the bearskin as an amulet of strength for themselves as they grew into manhood. If a dog had been raised with the bear, it was also dispatched. Its spirit would travel with the bear and continue to be a guide and friend.

In the Ulchi tradition, this is the only rite where an animal is sacrificed. The last traditional bear festival was held in the 1930s. The Soviet police got news of the impending ceremony and arrived to take the bear away. The bear was handcuffed and led out of the village. In early 1992, a Japanese group of ethnographers commissioned the Ulchi people to conduct a bear ritual one last time. This was recorded on film, and, although the festival only lasted a few days, the traditional elements were preserved and documented for posterity.

The other bear rituals involved hunters, who occasionally went out in search of this type of food source. Special rituals and offerings were made to the Master spirit of the taiga. The preparation, collecting of bones, and so forth, followed the same pattern as the "Play of the Bear". The meat was distributed among the people, and the skull was smoked and hung in a tree or on a pole.

Commentary

Grandmother Nadia:

When the bear meat was entirely eaten, then all of the bones were carefully collected and buried in the same place. The old men would chant magical invocations as they smoked the bear skull over the fire. These invocations would cause the meat to grow back on the bear's bones and cause fur to reappear over the entire body.

• • •

ADAWU POKTONI: WAY OF THE TWINS

Twins were seen as part human and part spirit, living their conscious lives between the layers of this world. Although humans reside in the realm of the Middle World, these special people could naturally access the invisible membranes of the spiritual landscape.

Hunters and fishermen would always go to the mother or one of the twins to ask for happiness and success in their endeavors, and after hunting or fishing, they gave the best meat or fish to these individuals. They believed that if they gave the best food, their future hunting and fishing expeditions would be fruitful and prosperous.

A mother of twins was referred to as a "taiga woman." Such women would enter a state of trance and begin to dance prior to the return of bear hunters. They would inform the people how the hunt had gone before the hunters arrived back at the village. They would speak about the journey of the hunt: where the hunters had traveled, where they had walked, where they stopped to rest, and what hindrances, if any, they had on their trip home.

These taiga women would begin to dance the *Khondari / Karpa*, or Dance of the Taiga, by taking fir branches in their hands and stroking and cleaning their bodies with them, or by using the rattles. They would shake and shudder as they entered a deep trance state. They would also have other journeys to the spiritual world of the Bear spirit during their lifetimes, and these events were unplanned and spontaneous.

Besides dancing the rhythms of the hunters' road and the paths of the animals, the taiga women and the twins themselves would, at times, conduct healings. They were also thought to have the gift of clairvoyance and were consulted by people, from time to time, about future events. When these special people passed into the next world, their burials were conducted in a manner different than those of ordinary people.

75

Commentaries

Grandfather Misha:

When twins were born, the old men would construct a little house called kori. Even within this house, no harmful spirits could penetrate. The house was small, about a foot long and wide. Inside the house was placed the afterbirth and natal strings of the twins. Outside the house, they hung the wooden streamers. They would make food offerings as well. This little house was so beautiful. When people saw this house, they knew that twins had been born, and the people gave respect to the kori. The kori house was placed on the ground in the taiga. Each clan territory was so large that these kori homes were situated near the clan's main residence. There was always a special place for these homes in the taiga.

··

Grandmother Nadia:

During the autumn hunting season, the taiga woman will know if a bear has been killed or captured by one of the hunters. She will instinctively feel the event taking place. She knows if it is a male or female bear and whether it is young or old. She can see the people involved in the hunt and the landscape and circumstances involved in the capture or killing. She enters a trance-like state and starts to sing and dance, which signals the people to prepare for the hunters' return. Through her song and dance, she tells the whole story of the bear's life and how it was dispatched. Her song tells of the hunters' journey, where they traveled, any hindrances they encountered, and how they came upon the bear. She sings of the mountains they crossed and which roads they took. Then the people would quickly prepare for the great festival by preparing special ritual foods, carving sacred wooden streamers, and setting up the special place where the head of the bear would be taken and preserved. The skin and muscle would be removed, and the skull would be taken and placed in a sacred tree in the taiga. Everyone would dance, play the drums, and eat great amounts of food. The secret among the taiga women is that they all report having unusual dreams where they are wandering through the forest and meet the Bear spirit disguised as a young man. They become as man and wife and later on give birth to twins in the earthly realm.

• • •

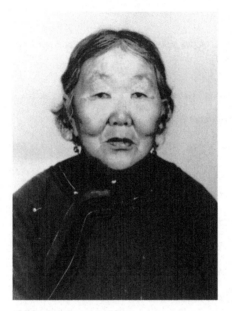

GOGA DUVA, CA. 1979

Grandmother Nadia's mother, Goga, gave birth to a set of twins a few years after Nadia was born. This twin lived only a few months, but from that time on, Goga was recognized as a taiga woman. Although Nadia was not a twin, this special Middle World path was passed to her by virtue of the fact that her mother was a taiga woman. Grandmother Nadia spoke about a conjuring that she received from Grandmother Indyeka, in which Indyeka traveled along the Twin's Road. Obviously, children who are not twins but have twins in their family have a special affinity or access to this spiritual layer of knowledge.

WAY OF TWINS RECITATION/SONG

GRANDMOTHER PANUKA LONKI

Village of Bulava
Recorded 1975

I have got a good disease because I gave birth to twins

The disease is from the mountain

The disease is from the taiga

The end of three mountains have appeared

At the end of one mountain, Labrador tea sounds

At the end of the second mountain, the wild celery sounds

At the end of the third mountain, the fir tree sounds

Men, nine men are beating on a musical beam

Oh, it is very pleasant

Oh, it is very joyful

And I'll beat it too

My savens, my assistants, will lift the tall father

The father meditated in the forest

I'll go along nine mountain ranges

Red Labrador tea grows

Blue Labrador tea grows

At the foot of these mountains

In the blue mountain lake

Ducks that come flying in spring

Ducks that fly away in autumn are bathing

Dabbling

Different beasts come to the mountains
    to make balance for themselves
And they wash themselves here in the lake
The Red Lake is from Red Labrador tea
The Blue Lake is from Blue Labrador tea
From here I'll climb up through the forest
Passing nine mountains and leaving seven valleys behind
I am walking quickly and widely like a bear
I am turning my head left, and I am
    turning my head right
I am climbing up with my hair tousled
I have climbed up one mountain
And now a pair of rocks is appearing
The tall father
Throw nine sacrificial foods
From here climbing, I'll climb up three mountains
Red Labrador tea spreads out
Blue Labrador tea spreads out
And now walking from here I see nine young men
They are playing with a stuffed seal,
    dragging it here and there
And stabbing it with spears
And now I am climbing up and climbing up
I am running fast to my cherished place
I'll take fir branches into both of my hands
And waving them, I'll climb up into the forest
Nine women are carrying skins
Having pulled out a tobacco pipe

From a woman on the end who carries a skin

I'll run away

Saven protector

Appear here and there

So I'm climbing up into the forest

The tall father

Going to the ends of the mountain to throw sacrificial food

Speak well

Advise me well

Falling and crawling

I try to go

I see a motley shelter

One side of it is covered with fir tree branches

Out of this shelter, an old trembling woman has appeared

And here between my dragon pillars is a large forest

We'll rub ourselves with different branches

We'll fumigate ourselves with these branches

There are two stone pillars

At the first pillar is a white dog

At the second pillar, there's a black dog

I haven't brought you any food

I'll give you shavings from this mountain ash

I'm throwing edible roots and red bilberries

Now I have reached my place

My homeland I have reached

My homeland I have reached

In front of the motley shelter, there's a little
  shelter covered with coniferous branches

On the side of it, there's a little shelter
covered with shavings
And here in the central part of it
A taiga tiger has rolled over it
Its shadow speaks as a tiger
A litter from three bear skins is in the shelter
A litter of three skins is in the shelter
In the center of the shelter is a Masi idol
It looks like a tiger
I have got my sufferings from it
My savens, protectors
Speak well
I beg you to throw off my sufferings
On the three-layer litter
I'm jumping
From here different unusual berries
Different galantines were given to idols
Jumping on my way
The male's way
I begin to climb down to the house where a man lives
I'm climbing down to the house built by a man
Having come to the house
I see a spear that sticks out of the door
It's a spear that sticks into my side
Its nine arrows have stuck into my body
Entering the house, I see an old trembling
woman on a plank bed
She's shamanizing there, and her head is shaking.

There is Labrador tea

A lot of Labrador tea

I have entered the house to fumigate it

With Labrador tea and with fir tree branches

It has been so

Now I have entered my man's house

Nine musical beams are sounding

Savens

Feel sorry for me

I have just returned to my place

To my birthplace, I have returned

This shamanic conjuring by Panuka Lonki describes the topography of the Middle World realm, her experiences as she travels, and her encounters along the way with spirits and ancestors. She ends her song saying that she has reached her birthplace in this parallel world, identifying herself as belonging more to the land of Bear spirits than the human world.

. . .

WATER RITUAL AND RETURN OF THE SALMON

This ritual follows the seasons of the salmon's return to the rivers. In this ritual, all prayers are addressed to *Temu* in the hope that, in the future, the Water spirit will send fish to the nets of the fishermen. Safety while traveling upon the water is also requested. If the ritual is properly performed, *Temu* will appear to the participants.

The ritual begins with the carving of the sacred sticks that serve as a doorway to the world of the underwater beings. The name of the water ritual is *Vaysi Nyalau*, which means "to cast into the water." These sticks are carved from willow trees that grow near the banks of the Amur. Trees growing near a riverbank have an alliance to the underwater worlds. Their roots are described as antennas that penetrate into these otherworldly locations.

Food offerings to the water kingdoms are very specific. Tobacco, berries, rice, millet, fish (except sturgeon), and a sacred grass called *vaysi* (Allium Ursinum) are placed in a little white boat made from birch bark. *Vaysi* is a type of onion wild crafted in the taiga regions. This ritual boat, or *oto*, is carved in the shape of a duck or fish.

IVAN ROSUGBU (SECOND FROM LEFT) AND GRANDFATHER BORIS DJAFU (THIRD FROM LEFT) MAKING OFFERINGS TO THE WATER SPIRIT, AMUR RIVER

The sacred sticks are wedged into the river bottom, close to the bank, about eight to twelve inches apart. Prayers and requests are then made to Master spirit of the water. The prayers usually follow this pattern: "*Temu*, please find these offerings that I send to you. Please don't be offended. Send us the tiny fish; send us anything that you can spare." People must never ask for the bigger fish or take more than they need for themselves and their family.

After the prayers are made, the birch bark boat, laden with food offerings, is launched between the sticks out into the water. Then a cup of water is given to the spirits. This is the only ritual where vodka or other alcoholic beverages are never present. Alcohol is taboo for all rituals involving water spirits.

After the ritual boat is sent upon the water, a person must watch and see how the boat fares. If it turns over, spilling its contents quickly into the water, this is taken as a good omen, indicating that *Temu* has accepted the gifts. If fish, seagulls, or other seabirds quickly arrive at the scene to devour the contents, this too signals an acceptance of the offering. How nature responds to any type of ritual must be observed and noted.

Once the ceremony is completed, a small bowl of water is taken from the place in the river where the ritual was performed. This bowl is taken back to the family's home and added to the large rain barrels that contain fresh water for daily household use. The mixing of this special water into the household supply insures good health and happiness.

COMMENTARIES

GRANDFATHER MISHA:

In the spring and fall, we asked the most powerful spirits, the water spirits, to assist us in the catching of fish for the upcoming season. We would only ask for the small fish, the little ones. If we caught a large one, then it was given to us by the grace of the Water spirit Temu. We used all parts of the fish and would fashion their skin into coats, boots, hats, or rattles. If someone died in the water, we would make a special ceremony on the bank of the river. That place on the shore where we had performed the rite became a special place. You could never again travel to that spot on the shore without permission. It was dangerous to go to an area where a death occurred.

••

HANGING FISH TO DRY ON TRADITIONAL RACKS,
CLARA ROSUGBU (TOP IMAGE, RIGHT)

GRANDMOTHER NADIA:

Respect and caution are necessary when approaching the Water spirits. So much of our daily lives revolved around the water with all of our fishing, hunting, and traveling to and from other villages.

When we sent the offering boat out into the water, we would carefully observe how the boat would overturn and how the offerings were consumed by the Water Spirit. This would tell us whether or not the spirits were pleased with our sendings. We could gauge how to behave ourselves in order to be cautious.

•

GRANDMOTHER KAPA ICE FISHING ON THE AMUR, CA. 2011

The Water spirits are possibly the most powerful spirits on earth. Beneath the waters is an underwater kingdom where the spirits live. This is a separate land with its own houses and people.

•

In the spring, when the ice breaks up and begins to flow down the river, we go and place our offerings on large sections of the ice flow. In this way, our offerings are taken to Temu in his ocean dwellings. Never point your finger at the water. This is forbidden!

••

Grandmother Tika:

Make an offering when walking along the shore of a river, lake, sea, or even the ocean. Never give alcoholic beverages to the Water Spirit! It is forbidden! The strong energy of alcohol is completely forbidden. It is also good to give vaysi, tobacco, and rice. Now I see the younger people (people around the age of 40) always giving these offerings/presents to the Water spirits.

•••

WATER RITUAL

GRANDFATHER MISHA

Portland, Oregon
1995

Temu

Please find my offerings

I have come to you before making such an offering

The river is so very deep

This is the land where underwater people live

Father

This is the first time that I call you here

I send you these offerings

Please find them

What is this? (a spirit appears)

It is very black

Why is it this way?

Speaking to the spirit

Please forgive me

Do not be offended by what I do here

Mother

Please carry away these offerings

Master Spirit of the Water

I traveled to the top of the white house

The golden house

I make these offerings here

I came with these people to give offerings

Completely find this food that I offer myself

I have carried it to your shore

When we come to fish, please help us

Please send us the little fish

Seal Master

Search for our offerings for your children

We haven't forgotten you

How will things be when you accept our offerings?

Please give us your good protection

People of the underwater kingdom

We make offerings to you

We send these foods to you

Please help me, water people

People of the ocean

The master of the fish people is a seal

A powerful master

When I travel to your land to fish

I travel to your home, Seal Master

I walk to your dwelling

I don't know if I'll be pulled inside

Mother spirit; don't pull me under the waters

Be well

Don't be offended by what I do here

I am surprised

I stand at the top of a mountain

The river is so long and wide

It cuts the land in half

Can I cross?

Is this permissible?

SUMMER FISHING ENCAMPMENT WITH DRYING POLES FOR FISH, CA. 1930

Be well, spirits

I give you these offerings in a traditional way

It will be well

Don't be offended if I make a mistake, water people

[those who have died by being drowned]

Mother of the water people

You are the master

So I have finished here

I have carried these offerings to you

You know me, Water Master

I turn round and round above the ocean

I turn around the Seal Master

Be well

Grant me your good protection

What is this?

I am so surprised (a spirit appears)

I make these offerings to the people of the water

To the underwater kingdom

Temu

Master Spirit of the ocean

Mother, Father and all of your children

Seal Master

Shaman, this shaman

And to your daughters

What kind of shaman?

I don't know

Temu

People of the water

Don't be offended by the noise I make here

I cry for you

So I am finished

Everything will be well in the future

Please accept these offerings

Be well

These people are surprised

I have searched for them

Don't be offended if these people make a mistake

Mother of the water people

Be well

Grandfather Misha, in a sending ceremony, launches the boat of offerings into the great river

Don't be offended

Please find these offerings of food and tobacco

Eat what I have offered you

Please hear my words

Please listen well to all that I have spoken here

I beg you

I traveled under the water to the kingdom of Temu

Maybe this was permissible

• • •

FIRE RITUAL

The Spirit element of Fire creates a bridge joining the world of the living to ancestors and deceased family members. The fire element is also a doorway used to navigate from the Middle World into the variable invisible dimensions. There are various types of rituals to *Pujen*, as prayers and offerings were given to this spirit daily.

Pujen was also referred to as "mother" or "female parent," as women are the masters of fire inside the home. Taboos demand that the fire is never turned or rearranged with a metal poker or sharp object, as the use of these objects could be injurious to the spirit. A wooden stick with a blunt edge is preferable. An old tale tells of a young bride who, having entered her husband's new home, was in haste to start a fire. She created the fire within the hearth and, not finding a proper stick, used a metal object to turn the burning logs. She went outside but soon heard crying and moaning from within the house. Having reentered the cabin, she saw a young woman, cut in half, writhing upon the floor. She had severely wounded the Fire spirit of her new home. The tale ends here and says no more of what happened to the bride.

Hunters, who lived and worked outside the home for months at a time, would pray and ask for help from this spirit for success in their upcoming hunts. They might give thanks to the spirit of the forest, human ancestors, or ask for protection of the family left behind during one of these trips into the taiga. After a meal was prepared by fire, the best portions of the dinner were given first to the fire. The firewood was stacked in a specific way. The wood was laid out in a square fashion, or what is referred to as a crisscross fire lay.

GRANDFATHER MISHA CONDUCTING A FIRE RITUAL, BAINBRIDGE ISLAND, WASHINGTON STATE, USA, 1995

Fire portals are the primary method when sending foods and material goods to departed family members residing in the Lower World. A journey to the land of *Pujen* is traversed by the shamans from time to time for the living. This outdoor ritual is considered a dangerous rite which requires great caution and skill.

Food offerings of tobacco, rice, fish, and so forth are given to her, and copious amounts of vodka are offered. Whether it is a hunter, common person, or a shaman making an offering, the end of the ritual remains the same. The fire must be allowed to naturally burn out. Using water to hurry this process along is taboo. Water would harm the fire, as would any metal object. If she felt harmed by any mistaken action, a tragedy or mishap would occur in the family of the offender.

COMMENTARY

GRANDFATHER MISHA:

I always make offerings to the Sun, Moon, and Pole Star for the Fire ritual. How well a fire burns is indicative of how the Fire spirit receives an offering. After making the proper sacred food gifts, one must watch the fire. If it quietly dies down, then this is a good sign. This means that the spirit is happy and sated. Perform the Fire ritual in the spring and fall or on the New Year. The Fire spirit can reveal information to you or become very angry. Never sit behind a shaman for any ritual. This is forbidden! You can either sit to the side or in front. This is permissible.

• • •

FIRE RITUAL

GRANDFATHER MISHA
Bainbridge Island, Washington
1995

> *I've come here from afar*
> *Spirits, I have come here from afar*
> *I have traveled from afar*
> *Forgive me for what I am about to say*
> *I am a small person*
> *I am a small person*

Once I had three tongues, but now I only
have one from which I sing
I have become small and weak
I have traveled far
I have come not only to sing my song, but I have
come to show these good people what I know
I have come to share

At this point in the ritual, Grandfather breaks free from the earth and begins to fly into the heavenly realms and describes what he is experiencing and what he sees.

Don't be angry
Don't make noise at me
I am just a small person
I have just come here to sing and show what I know
Don't be angry at me
Don't think I've come here to be a shaman
I have only come here to share what I know
Guardian spirits of the Earth, of the Sky,
of the Waters, of the Taiga
Don't be offended by what I do
Don't be angry with me
Don't punish me here
Don't punish me at home for what I do,
to show, to share what I know
Take pity on me, great-grandmother shaman

Altaka Olchi appears to him in his vision.

Forgive me, spirits of the Sun, of the
Earth, of the Stars, of the Moon

Don't be offended
I've tried to do what you've taught me to do
To do as the elders have instructed me to do
Don't be offended by what I do here
I have tried not to defile your places
> *or desecrate your rituals*

Now he sees the spirit of the Fire. The Fire spirit can appear as an old grandmother or grandfather. Either way, the Fire spirit is always accompanied by a dog.

Old grandfather
Don't loose your dog on me
Don't send your terrible dog to bite me
Take pity on us here
Think of us here

Then the Fire spirit says to Grandfather Misha:

There are those among you that are not
> *taking this ritual seriously*
Who mock and laugh at me
There are two people
Two older men
One is bald, and the other has grey hair and a grey beard
Have them stand before me and have them
> *ask forgiveness for the group!*

Grandfather Misha then asks the group if there are two people who match this description. This event is being held outside at night, so it is difficult for Grandfather Misha, as well as the rest of us, to clearly see the physical makeup of the participants attending the ritual. There are two such people in the group, and Grandfather Misha takes these two men in front of the fire and has them ask for forgiveness from the Fire spirit. Then Grandfather Misha continues his singing.

Spirit of the Fire

You give us light

You give us food

You grant the continuance of our people

Thanks to you we grew up, and we live

We will continue to live

Guardian spirits of the Earth, the Taiga,
*   the Heavens of the Blue Star*

Forgive us

Forgive us

Think of us

I've tried to obey all of the laws

I've tried to do everything that I have been taught

Forgive us and take care of us

Forgive me

I am a small person

I am learning

I am learning

All of my life I am learning

· · ·

Forest/Taiga Ritual

Hunters and gatherers conduct specific types of tree rituals. When going into the taiga to procure small animals, berries, herbs, firewood, etc., a person is entering a geographical area controlled by specific land spirits. Offerings to the Master spirit of the place are necessary and required. One must gain permission to take away anything from the spirit's home. The largest tree in the landscape is usually chosen, but a person may also intuitively feel that the Master spirit of a particular area may be residing elsewhere and may choose any tree in that particular geographic setting.

Offerings are made, and requests for the needed provisions are asked of the spirits. If the spirits are agreeable, the hunter's arrow will find its mark. The land spirits will surely share their resources if the person asks and makes a food sacrifice in the proper way. Hunters never ask for specific animals. They ask the spirits to send what they can spare. They ask for the small animals or anything that will feed their family for one more day.

There are many cultural taboos concerning the acquisition and distribution of meat from the animal people. Large game animals, such as deer, moose, or elk, cannot be stored or hoarded by the family of a hunter. On their return, the hunter will take a large portion of the meat, but the rest must be given to poorer families.

Although the Ulchi are skilled hunters, their primary source of protein is fish. Berries, herbs, woods, and other types of material gathering follow the same ritual. One must ask permission to take these necessary goods from nature. An offering of a little food or tobacco is given. They will always walk along with a little bit of food or tobacco in their pockets. Whether traveling to the water, a friend's home, or strolling in the forest an Ulchi remembers that they are a guest in this world and that spirits must be propitiated at all times.

CHAPTER 5

Lower World

T he territory of the underworld is known collectively as *Buni* or the land of the dead. If a person died in a water accident and their body was never recovered, the deceased would travel to the underwater kingdom within *Buni*, known as *Dorkin*. The topography of the Lower World—including both *Buni* and *Dorkin*—mirrors the elements found in the other worlds. Some legends say that when it is daytime in the Middle World, it is night in the lower regions, and vice versa. If it is springtime on the earth, it is autumn in the Lower World. Other stories and personal accounts from shamans who have visited this realm speak of ever-changing weather patterns, with rain, sunshine, windstorms, darkness, and light all occurring and transforming within minutes. Some say that this place always remains dark and that light never penetrates here.

No matter the belief, this world is rarely discussed in any fashion. In Ulchi tradition, it is a taboo to talk or even think about this region because doing so might bring about premature death. The only persons who seek access to it are the *Kasa* shamans, the psychopomps, and even for them, this is a wild and frightening world. What information we have about the Lower World is largely based on the laws and taboos associated with the territory, rituals for the deceased, or the beliefs surrounding reincarnation.

Indeed, a person's death is essentially considered a change of residence for their soul. During the final memorial rites, known as *Humahu* (pouring water), the soul is at last escorted into the land of *Buni* by the *Kasa* shaman. The soul may not arrive in the land of the dead without the aid of a great shaman knows the roads that lead into this realm.

Some of the concepts associated with the Lower World include the following:

1. All deceased people become younger in the kingdom of *Buni* than they were at the time of their death.

2. People live for a very long time in *Buni*. During that time, they will meet with everyone they lived with on earth.

3. A person will spend thousands of years in the village of *Buni* and then die there. After their death in *Buni*, that person will be reborn on earth.

4. If a woman has lived a good and productive life during her most recent earthly incarnation, she will be reborn as a man. If a man does this, he will be reborn as a woman.

5. If a person has lived an average life and has not succeeded to their greatest potential, that individual will be reborn as a dog.

6. Bad people are reborn as grasses.

7. Murderers and suicides are never allowed into the kingdom of *Buni*. They turn into destructive spirits and

remain earthbound, bringing harm to members of their clan.

8. True heroines and heroes are reborn as great people.

9. Each person has three lives upon the earth and three lives in the world of *Buni*.

10. If the deceased's ritual is conducted poorly; they will live poorly in the next world.

COMMENTARIES

GRANDMOTHER NADIA:

My father once said to me, "In the land of Buni, this is what should be given to the people as far as different types of food from the yellow earth, and this food, araki, and water must be given back to the yellow earth. When people die, when people travel to the land of Buni, the body does not travel there. Only the soul goes to this land to be with the members of their clan. When a person dies, their soul is traveling and searching for water to drink and drink and looking for food to eat and eat. They find the food and water that has been given to them." My father's words really stuck with me.

··

GRANDFATHER MISHA:

My father said, "The Lower World is the place that our spirit travels to after our time on earth is finished. In this place, we will have our own life exactly as we have our life here. There is earth and everything surrounding it is the color yellow. This is the world we travel to after we die. The water in this place runs black, and of this water, we drink and feed ourselves.

· · ·

Major Spirits of the Lower World

The spirits who inhabit this lower region are the snakes, reptiles, amphibians, and insects. The snake and the frog occupy the highest ranking. Snakes (*mui*), frogs (*buraka*), and lizards (*kolinga*) hold a unique position, as these creatures are the foremost healing spirits for the diseases that are inflicted upon the female members of the clan. As idols, the snakes are carved or decorated with either stripes or circles. A shaman will braid a snake made of fabric and sew it to a patient's sleeve. Snake spirits also have the special ability to cure chronic lower back pain. Two- or three-headed snakes are found as major helpers in a shaman's retinue of spirits, and such a snake is seen by some shamans as the Master spirit of the drumstick. Insects such as bees, flies, or mosquitoes were forms that a shaman would transmogrify into when journeying between the worlds. After shape shifting into one of these diminutive creatures, a shaman could seek out a wandering soul. This allows them to remain inconspicuous to the spirit inhabitants within the invisible landscapes.

Rituals of the Dead

When people depart this world for the land of *Buni*, they cannot travel there without the assistance of their living relatives. Their relatives and friends must provide for them during the year(s) that it will take for them to walk down the road to *Buni* village. The sending ceremony begins inside the home, where the body of the deceased lies in state within the communal living area. Relatives and friends must watch and guard the body around the clock until the beginning of the third day, at which point the deceased is taken to a village cemetery for burial. During this time of observation, everyone must sit together; no one may sit off to the side or alone. The body is laid out in an open casket so that all may come and observe while paying their respects to the deceased. The coffin must be the correct size because if there were to be any extra space, the Ulchis believe that the deceased family member could abduct a living relative to take them along on their underworld journey. While the body is in the home, a rope is tied around the ankles to prevent the spirit of the deceased from wandering throughout the environment and disturbing the living. As the mourners watch throughout the day and night, they will quietly speak to one another or construct various articles of clothing or hunting tools to be given to the deceased for the descent to *Buni*. The earthly possessions of the deceased are hung above the head of the corpse.

The deceased is buried in seven layers of their own personal clothing. Each layer is cut in half between front and back. The seven back layers are placed in the bottom of the coffin before the body is placed within, and the remaining top seven layers are placed above the body. Since the soul travels in and out of the body from the top of the head, a hat of lynx, mink, or fox is placed upon the deceased's head to protect it from harmful spirits. The journey to Buni can be long and arduous, so it is of utmost importance that the deceased has proper clothing that will serve them throughout the various seasons of the year: spring, summer, fall, and winter. Moreover, it must be clothing that they wore in life, not new clothes. The clothing must have the energetic imprint of the deceased; otherwise, they will not recognize it along the road to Buni. This also holds true for the various objects of daily life that are placed in the coffin for the journey, although newer offerings can be given during the monthly memorials that are held for a year after a person's death.

Before the body leaves home, the thread ritual is performed. A long, white thread is tied to the middle finger of the deceased's right hand. The other end of this thread travels out of the coffin toward the direction of the rising sun. The closest living relative pulls on the thread until it breaks, and then the two pieces of the thread are measured against one another. If the piece held by the living relative is greater in length, it is considered a good omen, signifying a long life for the living person.

Commentary

Grandmother Nadia:

I remember when my mother died that I performed the thread ritual, and after it was complete, I discovered that the piece left in my hand was much longer than the piece remaining on my mother. The elders told me that this was a good omen and that I would live just as long as my mother. We continue to perform this ritual. When I was a child, I remember seeing people taking this whole thread around the whole house to protect the living relatives. In doing this ritual, death would not make a mistake and take one of the living relatives. This also insured that the living would not have a tragic death but live their own life and find their own death, not a strange death.

• • •

A silk covering is placed over the face just before the body begins its final journey to the gravesite, where the ritual of burial, or the sending, begins. At the cemetery, a new string is tied either to the top of the hat worn by the deceased or to the forefinger of the right hand. Offerings such as cosmetics, needles, and thread are placed inside the coffin if the deceased is female. Effigies of items such as axes or bows and arrows are placed inside for men. Family and friends may also place in the coffin other articles of clothing, such as scarves, hats, gloves, and blankets, or anything else that was quietly constructed for the deceased while the observation of the body took place in the home. The ropes that were placed around the ankles of the corpse are removed before the lid of the coffin is closed, and the string that is attached to the hat or hand is threaded through a hollow wooden tube. The coffin is then lowered into the grave alongside the wooden tube containing the string attached to the corpse. This string extends up through the tube to ground level.

Once the coffin and tube are situated, the grave is filled with dirt and completely covered. The thread is attached aboveground to a small ritual board, carved with traditional designs, that has a hook on the top. This ritual board is partially buried in the ground next to the grave, and the string is then attached to the hook on the board. In the center of this ritual board is a hole into which a cigarette is placed. The cigarette is lit and, as it burns, it is watched by the members of the funeral entourage. If it burns evenly, this indicates that the deceased is satisfied, but if it burns unevenly or too slowly, this is an indication that the deceased is displeased with the sending. A small larch tree is then planted in the center of the grave. This allows the soul to travel back and forth between the other worlds and the land of the living until it makes its final departure to the village of *Buni*.

FAMILY, RELATIVES, AND FRIENDS GATHER TOGETHER IN BUNI VILLAGE FOR DECEASED DUVAN CLAN MEMBER, BULAVA VILLAGE

Two fires are lit at the gravesite. The larger fire is for the deceased, and the smaller one is for the family members attending the ceremony. A suitcase full of the deceased's belongings is brought to the gravesite. Relatives and friends add farewell gifts. Some of these items are placed upon the fire, to be sent to the deceased, who will find them—as well as the items that were placed in the coffin—along the side of the road that leads to *Buni* village. Ritual food, water, and vodka are given to the fire to make sure that the deceased does not go hungry along the way. The participants also enjoy the last meal with the deceased, as a portion of the ritual offerings is shared among all who are attending.

The only thing removed from the site after the ritual is the suitcase, which is brought back to the residence of the clan. It will be used again when the deceased's supply of items such as tobacco, vodka, and various types of clothing is replenished later by family and friends.

After the first ceremony, the relatives and friends of the deceased will return to the gravesite each month at the New Moon. The suitcase, full of new items, will be brought back to the gravesite, and these items will be placed in the fire for the deceased. The ritual of sending water, food, clothing, and sundry items to the dead is carried out monthly for one entire year. Each time, the deceased is given a tobacco offering in the form of a cigarette, which is placed inside the hole of the ritual board. How well it burns—or whether it does not burn—is noted by the relatives. These tobacco offerings placed in the ritual board serve as spiritual barometers that help to gauge the quality of life or the hardships being experienced by the deceased on their journey.

At the one-year memorial of the death, a *Kasa* shaman could be called to finally escort the deceased to their next residence, in *Buni* village. The shaman would speak to the relatives about the deceased's travels to the underworld and inform them whether the deceased was happy or unhappy about the offerings that had been given along the way during the twelve months of sending ceremonies. The *Kasa* shaman could also relay information to the family about any concerns that the deceased might have concerning their living relatives. After the one-year anniversary was complete, it was forbidden to travel to this gravesite. The living were not to return, as to do so might interfere with their loved one's new life in the world of the ancestors. This tradition was the norm, although, depending upon the amount of grief that the living relatives were experiencing, the monthly offerings could take place for two to three years before the final sending was complete. This was rare but would occur from time to time.

COMMENTARY

GRANDMOTHER NADIA:

At the site, we would give so many clothes. First, we would give the deceased water and then food. There were pillows and shoes on top of the body. We would all share food at the gravesite, but if any food was left, we could not take it home. We had to place it on the larger fire for the deceased to be consumed.

•

There must be enough offerings; otherwise the deceased will have a difficult time on their journey. Our people have a great respect for our funeral traditions so that our relatives can make their journey to Buni village successfully.

•

The deceased will remain with the living for one year and then begin their transition into the Lower World.

•

At the gravesite, if the larger fire burns well, then the deceased is satisfied, but if not, then they are in trouble and are not getting what they need along their journey.

. . .

I remember speaking to Grandmother Nadia about this from time to time. I would say, "I hear your ideas about the Lower World and *Buni* village. You speak of a beautiful land full of friends and family members, yet you also have so many rules about staying away from ill people or taking their objects after death, etc. If the land of the dead is so wonderful, why is there so much fear about it?" Grandmother Nadia said, "It is not that we fear this land, we are just not in any hurry to get there."

COMMENTARY

GRANDMOTHER NADIA:

I made the funeral arrangements for Grandfather Misha as we put his clothes inside the coffin. We used white clothes in seven layers cut in half. It is a long walk to Buni; that is why we put in so many clothes. At the funeral site, first, give water and then give food.

·

We used to bury our dead above the ground before the Russians outlawed the practice. My house was near the cemetery, and when I was young and coming home at night, I would hear the sounds of the dead coming from that place. It sounded like the whispering of voices chanting "huri, huri, huri." I was always so frightened at this. When we had to bury our dead below the ground, I didn't hear the whispering from the graveyard anymore.

·

Old people say that after the death of a relative, they still feel the person around for about one year's time.

・・・

Special Funeral Rites for Twins and the Mother of Twins

As twins and their mothers were seen as semi-divine people among the Ulchi, special funeral rites were conducted for them. They did not travel to the land of *Buni* but instead returned to the taiga to be reborn as bears. With the help of a shaman's singing, they departed for the land of the taiga people. These songs also served to ease the mind of the mother who had borne them, if they died before her. The shaman was obligated, in the name of the mother of the dead twin(s), to lay out the course that the soul of the deceased had to take to the kingdom of the bears and to overcome along the way extreme and complex obstacles. Those who knew how to sing *adawu poktoni* or "the road of the twins" would act in the name of the twins' mother, who may not have known the appropriate ritual text or how to perform it.

BIRCH BARK CONTAINER WITH SKY DRAGONS

In the singing of the recitation, the shaman's drum was not used. The singer held in their hands only fir boughs, which they waved periodically, bowing down as they were controlled by the actions of their spirit helpers and protectors. The bodies were placed in a wooden mausoleum, sitting upright in a fetal position, and were wrapped with white cloth and wooden streamers from head to toe. They would be wrapped with the streamers exactly as the body parts of the bear were wrapped after a bear feast. Rhythms were beaten out on a wooden log drum, both at the funeral and on the first anniversary of the death.

Commentary

Grandmother Nadia:

When I was a child, I remember seeing a funeral for an old woman who had given birth to twins and she herself was a twin. She had no clothes, and her body was wrapped completely with the white wooden streamers. It was very frightening and unusual as a young child would have experienced it, of course.

•

When a shaman died, she was buried in the same way as the mortal people, but many wooden streamers were placed in the grave. It was forbidden to bury a shaman's costume or their spirit totems with them; otherwise, the spirits would torture the people who remained among the living.

• • •

Special Rituals for Those Lost at Sea or in River Accidents

When a tragic death occurred during a water expedition and the body was not recovered, it was believed that the person's soul traveled to the underwater kingdom of *Dorkin* or *Temu*. The souls who resided there were called the *Dorkini*, or people of *Dorkin*. The ritual conducted after such deaths involved the male relatives and friends of the deceased. Women were not allowed to participate due to the potency of the Water spirits. As propitiating these spirits was a frightful undertaking, great care and caution were observed. The area of beach directly in line with the place in the water where a person had lost their life became the ritual location where offerings were made, and prayers and requests were given. Once this ritual was complete, it was forbidden for any person to set foot in this area. Grandmother Nadia told me that when a person lost their life on the river, it would be forbidden to travel to the site for a long time. She remembered so many times in her early life when her mother had forbidden her to even swim in any part of the river after a water death because harmful Water spirits were very active and were seeking out another unwitting victim.

KASA RITUAL FOR DECEASED WOMAN WHOSE BODY WAS NOT PRESENT, CA. 1930

RITUALS FOR THE DECEASED WHEN THE BODY IS NOT PRESENT

When a body was unrecovered due to a water accident, eaten by a predator in the taiga, or cremated because death had resulted far from home, a *Kasa* shaman would perform the last rites by creating a specific type of effigy, like a straw doll, for the person. They would take a complete set of clothing, shoes, hats, gloves, and other items

111

and place them flat on a surface and begin the final rites. Once the rites were complete, this effigy would be buried in a coffin, and the regular monthly rituals would be conducted by the family members. Because the buried clothing of any individual held their energetic life force, the traveling soul could maintain its connection not only to the family but to the yearlong offerings it would receive while traveling to the land of the dead.

COMMENTARY

GRANDMOTHER NADIA:

If a person's body which had drowned was not recovered within a year or two, a small straw doll was constructed. The doll would be dressed in the clothing material of the deceased and buried in a special ceremony.

. . .

KASA RITUALS FOR THE DECEASED

There are two forms of the Kasa shaman ritual. The first is performed at the one-year anniversary of death. Upon arriving, the Kasa shaman will undertake a journey into the lower realms. They will begin to tell the story of the yearlong journey that the deceased took to the village of Buni and will recount the spirits, situations, and feelings the deceased encountered along the way, as well as how the soul responded once it entered the outside gates to the village. The deceased will then make their requests, through the Kasa shaman, to the living relatives, who thus learn what the soul needs in the way of provisions, goods, or other items. It is also the time that the dead can speak to their relatives for the very last time, by way of the shaman. As the ritual is concluding, the relatives and friends in attendance are expected to eat great amounts of food, which are quickly transferred to the deceased employing a type of sympathetic resonance. The Ulchis say that at the moment when the feast is occurring, the deceased is standing at the gates to the village of Buni, waiting to cross over and end the

ALTAKA OLCHI, BULAVA VILLAGE

yearlong journey to this land. The Kasa shaman will then lead the
soul into the village and return alone to the land of the living. This
final, one-year memorial service also includes presenting new clothes,
shoes, tools, and utensils to the deceased, who is seen as moving into
a new residence. The offerings represent a type of housewarming gift
and include items necessary for this new life.

The other form of the Kasa ritual can take place at various times. A
platform around six feet high and four feet wide is constructed. On
either side of the platform stand two tall, young saplings, and tied
across these trees and to the trunk itself are multiple sets of metal
spirit cones and bells. This ritual is used to create a bridge between the
family with their deceased relatives and to convey information from
the land of the dead. The ritual begins inside the house. The shaman
makes all the proper offerings to the spirits who reside within the
family dwelling. After the house spirits are propitiated, the shaman
moves outside to the platform. Some family members sit in front of
the platform, while others help the shaman to climb onto the wooden
structure. Once situated upon the platform, the shaman grasps the
trees on either side and shakes them back and forth, causing the metal
spirit bells to ring. The shaman then begins a rhythm with the bells
while calling to the spirits to assist the shaman's flight to the Lower
World. As the deceased members of the family begin to arrive, the
ritual takes on a question/answer format.

Commentaries

Grandfather Misha:

I saw this type of Kasa rite made by three powerful shamans during my youth. These strong shamans would stand on the platform shaking the trees. This is called a Harkume or a Harkowu yiyee. These shamans sang of what kinds of pains and illnesses the deceased person had during their lifetime and what illness finally took their life away. They sang about the person's entire lifetime. They knew everything about their life on earth. The shamans saw everything, and even their clan's history and pains. The shaman would also sing about the living clan members and what had happened and what was now happening in their lives. They spoke of all of the fortunate and unfortunate situations of the living clan members. That is why the shaman stands between two trees. They would stand between the two trees singing and shaking the trees with their hands

As they sang and shook the trees, the sounds of the different yampas (metal spirit belts) also added their metallic clanking voice in harmony to the shaman's song. The voice of the yampas was so loud as to be almost a deafening sound. The yampas swayed on the trees just like they swayed on the shaman's waist. Those shamans shook the trees as they sang, and those trees bent left to right and front to back along the platform. The shaman stood on the platform about six or seven feet above the earth. Then two, three, or four men would catch the shaman as he fell backwards and unconscious off that platform.

Those men were prepared and quickly rushed over once they saw that the shaman was about to fall. Then the men would carry the shaman into a small house nearby. This was a small dome-shaped house made from hay and other grasses. Once they carried the shaman into the grass house, the men would place the shaman down on a grass bed. One man would hold a yampa over the head of the shaman and ring it and play it. Another man would take the sacred streamers and cleanse the shaman's body to insure that any negative energy would be cast off. In this way, they revived him and brought him back into this world. The shaman stayed in this grass house for a while to rest and recover. He was so tired and spent after this ritual.

We called that grass house a Hogduwa Tuambuwu. Then an offering of health and happiness was made outside the grass house. We made offerings to the altar and to the base of the tudja. Then the shaman would return inside the grass house and sing. He would sing for all of the people who have died that they live well and have protection. He would sing for the entire household, the beds, dishes, plates, Great Moon Mother, the cabinets, walls, rising sun, altar, the living family members, and their children.

The journey to the land of the dead is a very frightening road. A small shaman can never take this kind of journey.

··

GRANDMOTHER NADIA:

If a Kasa shaman is called for the one-year memorial, the singing takes place in the evening. The shaman will describe how the journey of the deceased is progressing as they are accompanying them along to Buni village. The shaman will describe the experience of the deceased, which could be frightening and horrible. The shaman will describe the Lower World and talk about the deceased's history and past. The shaman will then speak of whether the deceased was met well or poorly when they arrived at Buni village, describing the landscape of the Lower World. The shaman will tell the living about anything else that the deceased may need or if any ritual mistakes were made and what needs to be corrected to insure a proper and happy passage for the deceased into Buni village.

·

Before Grandmother Tika passed, I asked her about a Kasa shaman to preside over her one-year anniversary. She said to me, "I am going to live in the stars after my death, so I don't want any shaman to make a conjuring for me and drag me down to Buni village.

•

Before Grandfather Misha passed, he said that if Grandmother Yetchka was around, then have her make the ceremony for him, but if not then he would find his own way to Buni. Grandfather would sometimes comment that he would not travel to Buni but take the road of his grandfather's—whom he called father—Path of the Thunder shaman and ascend into the heavenly realms. I had a great dream about him a short while after his death. I saw him and his deceased wife, Loga, sitting on a favorite bench in my village, looking out across the Amur River. They looked happy to be reunited once again.

•

When a shaman makes this kind of Kasa conjuring, a prophecy is also given. Only the most powerful shamans can do this, and not the little shamans. When a shaman begins to sing outside, all of the people sit in a semicircle in front of the shaman's platform and never behind. After the ceremony, the grass house was left untouched to naturally decay once the ritual was complete. No one touched it because it still retained the energy from the land of the dead. If a living person came in touch with it, then it could bring death to that person. The shamans do not like to make the Hogduwa Tuambuwu structure because they are afraid to construct them, due to the residual negative energy that inhabits such a house after the Tuandame (ritual for the dead). People can find illness or pain if they come into contact with such a structure. That is why when they were made; they were created in a proper place in the taiga.

• • •

Kasa Ritual to the Dead

Grandfather Misha

Sonoma County, California
1996

Grandfather Misha, while singing to the spirits during this ritual, contacted the deceased parents of the man being questioned below. Upon meeting these spirits and listening to their story, Grandfather Misha had to ask questions of the living man to confirm whether or not he (Misha) had found the correct family members in *Buni* village. All questions and answers follow a yes/no format.

Grandfather Misha: (speaking to the living but listening simultaneously to the information provided by the dead): *After the death of your parents, you did not lack for money or other things to live a good life?*

Man: Yes.

Grandfather Misha continues to sing to the spirits once this first question is answered.

G.M.: *You are their only son?*

Man: Yes, correct.

G.M.: *You have no sister?*

Man: Yes.

G.M.: *Did you remember to perform the monthly ritual services for your parents after they died?*

Man: No.

G.M.: *Was your father a strong man?*

Man: Yes.

G.M.: *Was your mother tender-hearted, strong, and of average height?*

Man: Yes.

At this moment, this section of the ceremony came to an end. Grandfather Misha lost consciousness and fell backward off the platform, and was caught in midair by four men. While this ceremony is conducted, men are always required to stand by and catch the shaman when they fall off the platform. The men then carried Grandfather Misha back inside the home. When he regained consciousness, he continued the ceremony.

The drum is used very sparingly in this type of conjuring. It is played a little in the opening House Spirit ceremony, not at all while on the outdoor platform, and a little when returning inside the house for the final section. Grandfather Misha began to sing a short song of thanks and praise to the men who had caught him and carried him back inside the dwelling. He then conducted a ceremony giving a special blessing to these fellows. He used the drum for the blessing ceremony. When the blessing was complete, he turned his attention to the Master spirit of the house and the great Guardian spirit of the altar. The question and answer ritual began again.

G.M.: *Did you see or take a bear cub out of the woods when your father died?*

Man: I saw one, but I did not take it.

G.M.: *You found the soul of your father.*

The questions asked by the shaman depend upon what the shaman is seeing and experiencing during the ceremony.

Unlike a healing ritual, the Kasa ritual places the client in the position of having a direct conversation with the shaman during the ritual.

After these questions were asked and answered, Grandfather Misha, performed a special healing for the four men. He and the four men moved to stand together in front of the door and made an offering to the Door spirit together. Then Grandfather Misha asked permission from the Master spirit of the house to continue the ceremonial work inside. For a long time, this spirit would not grant the request. Grandfather Misha begged and begged the spirit, saying, "I don't want to do this, but I am just teaching people. Please forgive me for doing the work. Please do not be angry." Grandfather Misha also called to his deceased mother and father, asking for help. He called to his parents, saying, "Help me to travel on this road. I do not know which road to take." Then he instructed the people to go and make their own personal offerings to the altar spirit. Finally, Grandfather Misha received permission from the Master spirit of the house to proceed with the ceremony. He went back outside to the *Kasa* platform and sang to the spirits:

I do not know which road to take

I beg you for this is a different road

This land is not my own

I am stronger in my own land

I'm going outside

I am going to perform the Kasa ritual

That is what I am going to do

I am afraid

Mother, Father, help me to travel this road

I turn to the door

I walk over to the two shaman pillars outside

I bow three times, touching my head to the

ground to the master spirit of the home

I don't know whether I'll find this road

I'm a little person

I might die

I'm speaking with you, my mother and my father

Please, I do not know why I am standing here

Please do not be angry at me for this

My body is dark blue

My body has already been taken away

I cannot sing

I cannot speak

I do not know which road to take

Let's go ahead

Let's take a step

Let's travel to the edge

I stand on the edge of the mountains

On the edge of the cliff

I am flying

If you cannot hear me

I hope you hear me soon

If you do not know me

I hope you know me soon

I am going on the road of the taiga people (animals)

There are many here

I do not know this road

I am afraid to touch the big road

Master of the taiga

I've been singing for a year
I don't know what you think
Who is the master of this place?

The question/answer format reappears at this portion of the shaman's song.

G.M.: *Your father died first, and then your mother died a few years later?*

Man: Yes.

Grandfather chooses the road to the man's deceased father and continues the journey.

On the road of the father, I am passing now
I see the distance between the mother and the father
It is great in length
You do not know what to do when traveling
*   through the mountains, the ponds, the rivers*

Grandfather Misha asks permission from the Mountain spirit.

Help me well
Do not make a mistake, please
Our road is a single road
The road of other people is another
Lead me well along this road
Protect me
Show me the road well
I do not know the laws of these people
I do not know this land
I do not know their traditions and customs

I am walking

The deceased mother of the man appears and says, "Live well."

The question/answer section resumes between Grandfather Misha and the man.

G.M.: *Please tell me how they are buried. Is the ground flat or rounded?*

Man: Flat.

Grandfather now attends to the roads of the other people present in the ceremony.

I am going on the path of other people

Lead me well upon this road

Protect me

Show me the road well

I do not know the laws of these people

I do not know their traditions and customs

I don't understand things here

I beg you

Please help me to go through on the road of the unknown

I do not even know the language of these people

I beg you

Please help me well

Please let these children (people) live well

Please let them know happiness

I am just asking here

I am singing with the voice of the golden bird

I am flying

GRANDMOTHER NADIA TYING WAIST STREAMERS ON GRANDFATHER MISHA
FOR KASA RITUAL, SONOMA COUNTY, CALIFORNIA, USA, 1996

Please protect me well

Please protect these people well

I beg you

Please help me

Grandfather bows three times.

Everyone who is here

Please protect them

I beg you to help them

Please do not be offended with me and
      anything you have heard or seen

I am turning three times like the wind

I see a light

The people probably see it also

I am turning to the left

I am turning to the right

I am turning

Master of this house

I make an offering to you

I bow to your corners

I bow my head to your doors

I do not know your language

I do not know your laws

I do not know your traditions

I do not know your customs

Master of the door

Spirit of the threshold

Please do not be offended that I have stepped on you

The master spirit is powerful

Grandfather asks this spirit to help protect the people.

I am singing

I am singing

I am singing

Door

Threshold

I bow before you

To the four corners, I sing

Do not in any way harm them

I scream here with screams

I beg you

Do not toss these people in the turning

Please take pity on these people

Please take pity upon these children

Grandfather begins to work with the threshold spirit and the four corners, asking them to protect the people.

It is very difficult to step on you

(addressing the threshold spirit)

All the steps that led up to you are sacred

The ceremony concludes with final offerings to the spirits.

CHAPTER 6

• • •

Rituals for the Home, Travels, Hunting, and Tree Ceremonies

The primary spirit of the home is called the *Masi*. This spirit is female, and her name comes from the combination of two Manchu-Tungus words. In the Ulchi language, *ma* translated is "strong" and *asi* "wife." The House spirit, or strong wife, is the primary protector of the family. The other spirits that occupy the home include the spirits of each corner of the house and the threshold deity. All of these spirits are addressed separately through prayers and offerings.

The home altar, or *mali*, is located on the southern wall of the home, along the path the Sun travels each day. The altar is decorated with the various clan deities that protect the family. These idols, called *savens*, are made from wood and vary in size and shape, ranging in height from twelve inches to five feet. The figure that occupies the center of the altar is always the *Masi*, which is usually portrayed with the face of a bear. Atop the head of this *saven*, smaller spirits, such as mountain spirits and birds, are also represented. There is no specific form for the *Masi*, as this idol can differ from one household to the next. On either side of this central figure, other wooden idols may be placed, including such spirits as *Kuljamu*, *Buchu*, birds, snakes, etc. The clan spirits of each family vary, and the family's idols are passed down from one generation to another.

The monthly house ritual, described below, is the most common and most frequently repeated ceremony in daily life. Although usually performed at the time of the Full Moon, it can be conducted at any time, if family members are ill or have fallen on bad luck, to restore balance and harmony within the clan.

House Ritual

This ritual is known as the *Kesi Guliyi*, loosely translated as "giving of thanks." It is a time to express gratitude and to offer prayers for health, happiness, and fortunate circumstances.

On the evening of the Full Moon, the ritual foods of tobacco, berries, rice, millet, and fish are placed in the wooden offering dish. This vessel, along with a cup of vodka or sometimes water, is placed on the altar. The ceremony is then performed by the eldest female of the family group, followed by the rest of the family members in descending order by age.

The house ritual begins with the petitioner making offerings of vodka or water to the *Masi*, the corners of the home, the threshold, including Heaven and Earth. The prayers that accompany these offerings are spontaneous and from the heart and spoken in a quiet, almost inaudible voice.

To make the offerings, one holds the cup of liquid in the left hand and dips the middle finger of the right hand into the cup. The liquid is flicked out (*chicturi*), first to the center of the home (to the front of the petitioner) and then to each of the corners: south, east, north, and west. Then the solid food offerings, called *chuvachi*, are then given to Heaven and the Earth.

One then approaches the idols that reside on or to the side of the altar. The middle finger of the right hand is once again placed in the cup of vodka, and a little vodka is fed to each spirit by placing the liquid on its mouth. It is taboo to give vodka to spirits associated with water, so if any type of water spirit resides on the altar, an offering of water is touched to its lips instead. Then the various foods in the offering dish are fed to the savens in a similar fashion, by smearing the foods onto their mouths.

ULCHI HOUSE, MID 19TH CENTURY

Once the feeding process is complete, members of the family share in the little portions of food and vodka or water that remains. If a fire is burning in the hearth, offerings are also given to the Fire spirit. After all of these ritual steps are complete, the petitioner bows three times to the center of the altar.

There is also another special place for giving offerings inside the house. This is a small ventilation window called a *chanko*, which is located in the eastern section of the home. This small eastern window is also given offerings including bows of respect following the ritual to the house altar.

A small portion of food will be left on the altar until the following day when it must be given to the family's sacred tree. In this way, the remaining food and liquid are sent to the *Ba Enduri*. Once again, prayers for health, happiness, and fortunate circumstances are made. This ritual to the sacred tree must be performed in the early morning hours before the Sun is directly overhead.

The house ritual is also performed similarly when a person comes to stay for a while in another's home. The guest will give food and liquid offerings to the altar of the host family at the time they arrive, whether day or night. They will also feed the House spirits of the host family. Cultural taboos dictate that socializing with their host can only commence once this ritual is completed.

Food offerings that remain overnight are given to the host family's tree the next morning. The host begins the tree ritual by thanking *Ba* for allowing the visitor to arrive without incident. The host then makes prayers for their own family and offers the food to the base of the tree. The guest concludes the ritual by thanking the spirits for a safe journey and asking that their family be protected, safe, and happy while they are away.

This ritual is repeated the night before the guest returns home. The morning of the guest's departure is marked with a final ritual to the tree, in which they ask for a safe journey home while expressing thanks for the time spent with their family, clan, or friends. The only variation from the previous ritual is that the guest leaves a large glass of vodka on the House altar, and this must be entirely consumed by the host the following day. Once the guest has left, their bedding must not be disturbed for the next few days. Moving or washing the bedding of a guest too quickly would be considered offensive as if the host wished that person a hasty departure.

Commentary

Grandmother Nadia:

When the night of the Full Moon arrives, and everyone has gone to sleep, this is the best time to conduct your own personal ritual because you won't be disturbed or interrupted by other people.

. . .

House Placement, Cleaning and Driving Out Harmful Spirits

Every month, during the house ritual, a family is required to spiritually cleanse their abode. The mistress of the home will light the sacred herb *sankura* and carry it from one room to the next, fumigating the corners, doors, and threshold. The family may use a drum in conjunction with this smudging, as they travel around to different sections of the home. When the rooms have been ritually cleaned, the front door is opened. With the aid of a drum, harmful or mischievous spirits are driven out and over the threshold and onto the road. Each family is required to keep their own household spiritually clean and clear from destructive spirits.

Commentary

Grandmother Nadia:

Before you build a home, it is very important to investigate the energy of the land where it will be constructed. Some people's homes could have negative feelings within them. The "soul" of the house could not only be harmful but frightening as well. People who live there could find that they are always sick or ill in some way and that one after another of the inhabitants of the home would die. That is why we always go out and search for a special territory before we would build a home. We spent a long time

BULAVA VILLAGE, KHABAROVSK KRAI: IN SPRING (TOP), AND WINTER (BOTTOM)

searching here and there, saying this is a fortuitous place or this is a negative place to build a house.

•

Never have tree limbs over the roof of the home. It will cause the roof to rot and not be able to breathe. It also blocks energy from the cosmos coming into the house.

•

For those unfortunate people who found illness and bad luck in their surroundings, they could also employ a powerful Kasa shaman to come and clean their homes of these unwanted and destructive forces Later, after the shaman has cleansed the home, the people would find that their lives became healthier, happier, and well because the shaman exorcised the destructive forces from the environment. The shaman would thoroughly search for all of the harmful spirits.

•

Even in my village today, many people still ask the shamans to come to their home and perform this ritual. They say, "Please help us. Please give a conjuring for our home.

•

I remember that Grandmother Tika and Grandfather Misha never liked to do this type of ceremony. They would tell people who had requested this service from them that they could not do it. Both of them would say, "I cannot do this. I have no strength to do this now" or "I cannot, and I do not want to." Later, they both would remark to me the same types of observations, saying, "That home has very negative energy. Harmful spirits sit inside that place. Who knows what destructive energy might attach itself to me if I go and work in this place. Then I would lose all of my strength, or perhaps my spirits will also lose their strength. Sometimes it is even our spirits that protest and do not want us to go there. I never saw this type of house cleaning done either by Grandmother Tika or Grandfather Misha.

•

I remember a story about a woman who had moved into an old house at the edge of my village. That house had been sitting empty for a very long time. She moved in, and her health began to fail. She called in a shaman who discovered that the home was being occupied by a harmful spirit who had lived there in past times. It was a former occupant of the house who had committed suicide. No wonder no one wanted to live in that old place. Well, the only remedy for her was to leave and find a new dwelling if she was going to survive. There is no "fixing" of places like this. They will always bring unhappiness or even death.

•

Now, it is up to each person to energetically/physically clean their own home and keep harmful forces at bay from the family. As in all of the rituals, a Kesi Guliyi is made at the altar. Sankura is burnt, and the smoke from this plant is used to drive out all of the destructive forces from the home. People must help their own house. That is why, in our tradition, our homes are kept clean and orderly. Any cracks in the walls or by the doors or windows are quickly repaired because even a small opening could be an entryway for something harmful to enter your home. If you live in a dirty, fouled, and messy home, your life will be the same.

•

Now, if a person needs healing, then they might call the shaman to their home. The shaman would arrive and make offerings to the altar and then begin the singing (yiyee). The shaman or the shaman's assistant would also clean the house by smudging with sankura. They would use the smoke to clean the walls and the corners of the house, and everything unhealthy would be expelled. The harmful spirits did not like the smell of the sankura and would quickly fly away from the home. Only the strongest shamans would go to another's home to perform a healing.

.

Spiritual house cleanings for others is a very difficult and dangerous ritual to perform, according to the shamans. This is why most of them refused to undertake this ritual. They worry and are fearful that they might encounter harmful and destructive spirits. In the past, there were many shamans who made prophecies. Even Grandmother Indyeka would not perform this ritual. This is why a shaman or person must spiritually clean their own home. If they don't have a drum, then they can beat out a rhythm on a metal cooking pot or pan. Destructive spirits do not like the sound of drums or clanking metal. You can also use a candle to purify the house by taking it through all of the rooms. Once you have energetically cleared the environment, you open the door and drive those harmful spirits outside.

.

House spirits are different because each family is different. There are families who are very good and others that are evil. Each family lives by their own rules and in their own way, so of course, their spirits would be very different. This is especially true where families have unfortunate circumstances because they have lived in an evil way and violated the laws of nature by killing someone or taking their own life. Their soul will not travel to the next world in the way most people do because that soul is discontented. It will stay and hover, twisting around itself, and bother the family members and people who live in the Middle World. You have all these nuances when it comes to a particular spirit or spirits of a household or family. That troubled soul will always be a part of that family's spiritual foundation and reality. Special rituals would be conducted by a family if they had a troubled soul among them and offerings would be made to appease that spirit. Those spirits could never be reincarnated because they are like vampire spirits and they transform into Busawus. Their troubled spirit hovers constantly, and they are always bothering the living.

. . .

Spirit Visitations in the Home

One evening, I remember telling Grandmother Nadia that, from the corner of my eye, I had recently observed the image of a cat wandering about my home. It appeared as a type of shadowy creature. She told me that it was either a cat spirit that had lived at my home before I moved there or a cat of mine that had died many years ago. "Either way," she said, "when a spirit visits your home, you must feed them because they are hungry." As she was telling me this, we both heard an unusual sound coming from the kitchen. Grandmother Nadia said the spirit had returned and we must immediately go and prepare offerings for it. We went into the kitchen and created a small offering dish with fish and berries. After the preparation, Grandmother Nadia instructed me to leave the offering in the kitchen until the next morning.

We returned to the living room to continue our talk when, all of a sudden, we heard a cacophonous noise of clanking crockery issuing out of the kitchen. We looked at one another wide-eyed in amazement and went back to find that the ritual dish was overturned and one foot away from where we had placed it. She remarked, "The spirit was very hungry." These telekinetic events in one's environment are very commonplace among the Ulchi. Spirits of relatives, ancestors, animals, or guardian beings may come and go at different intervals, and when they arrive, they must be treated like honored guests. Foodstuffs are prepared for them and placed in the part of the home where they seem to be most active. Food has its own spirit and must be kept safe and protected from harmful spirits. Grandmother Nadia remarked, "You know that if you leave your cupboards open at night, then the spirit of your food will fly away."

Later, we continued our nightly discussion until we heard new sounds coming from the kitchen. I asked her what this might be, and her response was: "It sounds like the electric people to me." "The electric people?" I asked.

"Yes," she replied. "You must remember that everything is alive. The stove, the microwave, the refrigerator work all day long and they too get tired, and sometimes you'll hear them just take a big sigh. They work very hard and maybe that noise from the kitchen was one of them. Remember that there are all types of spirits in your home, although not all people can see them." Then she went on to illustrate this point by telling me the following story of her friend's visit to her abode.

VERA DUVAN WORKING IN HER GARDEN, BULAVA VILLAGE

Commentary

Grandmother Nadia:

When my friend Rosa came to visit me in my home, we would spend the day catching up on all of the news. At all of her visits, we would spend hours and hours talking together. At one of these visits, Rosa turned to me, saying, "What is that small child doing near your window? See how this child is turning round and around?" I said to Rosa, "Who is turning?" Then Rosa replied, "Look, look at the child now crawling on the floor. I think the child is happy that I came to your home today." I didn't see the child, and then Rosa stood up from the couch and approached the window and began to turn in circles around the invisible child. She was laughing and so very happy. I said to Rosa, "Is it true what you see?" She replied, "Yes." Then my youngest daughter came out of her bedroom and joined us in the living room. I asked her about this spirit child. She replied, "Of course, momma, I always see this child, and I am never afraid."

So at night, it is important to leave food on the plate in the kitchen for these visitors because they are hungry. Leave the same food that you eat, but never give them meat. This is taboo. If you don't leave a plate in the kitchen, then it is permissible to leave the food on the altar.

• • •

I remember that when Grandfather Misha first came to my home, he would talk to three spirits who occupied my living space. Later, he asked me about these two men and the young boy and how they fit into my family structure. I told Grandfather that I didn't see the people he was talking about, and he commented that they were my spirit helpers who came to visit me from time to time. Grandfather never made a distinction between the living and the spirit world when it came to good manners and conversation. He would spend his time at my home conversing aloud to spirits whenever he was aware of them.

RITUALS FOR TRAVELING

Before one traveled away from home, a small ritual was conducted at the house altar to insure health, happiness, and a safe return. A shaman's song might also be sought out by people who were about to make a long and arduous expedition. The shaman could foretell the exact circumstances and events that the person would encounter in their travels. If fortunate circumstances were seen to surround the journey, the person would proceed. If not, the journey would be either canceled or postponed, especially if it involved traveling to a foreign region.

I remember one year when Grandmother Tika was scheduled to come to the Pacific Northwest. She had her passport ready, and bags packed two days before she was to leave the village. On the day of departure, Grandmother Nadia arrived to pick her up for the fourteen-hour boat ride from Bulava to the city of Khabarovsk. Grandmother Tika did not go with her, however. She announced that during her morning discussions with her spirits, they had told her to remain home and not travel. She had been excited to take the trip but remained behind so as not to offend her spirits, as well as to heed their warnings.

COMMENTARY

HUNTER SITTING ON HIS SLED WITH PART OF HIS DOG TEAM, 1928

GRANDMOTHER NADIA:

When starting off on a journey, make a good road to travel. This will help you to have a good life. When you travel on a road, ask for a good life and all happiness, and it will be this way. Carry with you a few seeds, rice, cookies, or tobacco in your pockets, and as you walk down a path, drop this food along the way for the little animal people or birds. They will find this small offering of thanks. Even when Grandfather Misha and I would fly from Russia to America, we would be on that plane so far above the earth. We would watch the Cloud and Star people as we traveled. We would take a little bit of the food that they gave us to eat and silently gave our thanks dropping food on the floor beneath us to all of the Sky spirits. I am sure those airline people would look around our seats, once we landed, and think that we Ulchi were not very tidy people.

. . .

Hunters' Rituals

Grandmother Nadia speaks about her father, Dumbin:

When my father was about to start on a hunting trip, he would wake up early and make an offering to all of the spirits who lived in the rafters of our home. The spirits lived in the southern part of our house because it was forbidden that they live in the east, north, or western sections of the home because the House altar was always located in the south. He would climb up into the rafters and make an offering to all of the spirits. Once completed, he would go outside and make an offering to our protective tree and only then would he begin his journey into the taiga to hunt.

I also remember when he would go hunting in the sea. He would travel along, and when seeing the seals, he would ask them, "Are you married or are you a bachelor?" He would never go after the married males, only the ones who were on their own.

. . .

DUMBIN DUVAN IN MILITARY UNIFORM DURING THE RUSSIAN CIVIL
WAR, 1921. DUMBIN FOUGHT FOR THE ARMY OF THE WHITES.

TREE RITUALS

Various rituals are also conducted at the sacred tree, or *tudja*, of the family or clan. Each family's tree is usually found close to their house. It is chosen by height and strength and is usually a Siberian larch because of this tree's properties and availability in the natural environment. Before the Russians arrived in the Ulchi territories, the family's sacred tree would be located either inside or at the edge of the forest. This proved disastrous to the old clans, as the Russian immigrants, through either ignorance or disregard, would indiscriminately cut down obviously marked family *tudjas*. Soon the family tree was located closer to the home to keep it safe from the newcomers.

This tree serves various functions as the outdoor protector of the home and family as well as the "telephone" to all of the spirit worlds. This is a place where one prays to the Cosmos spirit, where offerings can be sent to deceased family members in the Lower World, and where one may communicate with spirit masters in the Middle World. Rituals to trees are always performed in the morning, before noon. It is taboo to perform a tree ritual in the evening or night hours.

In these rituals, prayers and request of spirits are made at the base of trees. Sometimes a fir branch is used as a type of altar cloth in front of the tree. The offering dish (*oto*) is placed atop the branch. Two sticks, six to twelve inches in height, are stuck into the ground approximately twelve inches apart, exactly like the sticks in the water ritual, although the type of wood from which they are constructed may vary. These sticks are "spirit gates" that open a passage between the natural and supernatural worlds.

If a woman is of childbearing age, she must use an additional ritual item when performing any type of outdoor ceremony. This is a wooden stick or branch that is placed a few inches across the ground in front of her. Since the outdoors is the domain of the spirits and the spirit gate is open, this stick is used to provide an extra protective element, keeping unwanted energies from entering her body. The petitioner begins by kneeling in front of the tree, facing south or east. The vodka/water offering of *chicturi* is given. Instead of the four corners inside a home, the four directions are always honored in outdoor settings. Then a small portion of vodka/water is poured from the cup with the right hand to the base of the tree. This is poured in a sideways direction to the left. Pouring any liquid offering to the side is always done for spirits and living people. Pouring liquid away from oneself is only done for the deceased who live in the land of the dead.

Once the prayer is complete, the food offerings are thrown between the two sticks to the base of the tree. If the spirits accept the offering, birds, dogs, cats, and other creatures will soon gather to consume all of the offerings. One finishes the ritual by bowing. People bow three times after finishing any ritual, although women bow differently than men. Women bow from the waist, with their hands together in front of their hearts. Men bow with their hands flat on the ground, touching their foreheads to the earth.

COMMENTARIES

GRANDMOTHER TIKA:

When giving offerings in your home and to your tudja, always give vaysi, tobacco, and berries that you have wild crafted from the forest. Give also Monti (similar to Chinese dough buns), but never give any meat or sturgeon to your tudja. Always give offerings, first to the altar inside the house and then later outside to the tudja. It is okay to give araki (clear alcoholic beverage). If you have no rice, then this is all right. Just give araki.

••

GRANDFATHER MISHA:

My wife gave birth to twins. I think she is helping me while I am visiting the United States. When my wife is ill, I travel to the sacred tree grove in the taiga and ask help from these spirits, and quickly her illness subsides without the intervention of doctors or medicine. Because she is the mother of twins, she knows and sees everything.

•

First, you must make offerings to the tree and then later to the Earth. Do this ritual well and with a good heart! If you find an area and a tree that someone else is using for ritual purposes, then do not make your ceremony there. It will defile and ruin someone else's offerings or sacred place.

GRANDMOTHER NADIA:

As you make the ritual offering, you think and hold the image of the other people whom you are also petitioning for in your mind.

• • •

GRANDFATHER MISHA PLAYING A UDJAJU (LOG DRUM), CA. 1960

Three Tree Rituals

Grandfather Misha

Bainbridge Island, Washington
1995

So tree

Old man

Ancient one

You've stood here for many years

I know

I can see

I come here to bring you my offerings

My modest offering

Please accept this modest offering

This is what I have to give

Please forgive me if there is something that I do not know

Please forgive me if I have offended you

I don't mean to offend you

Accept this offering

I ask you for the safety and happiness of myself

I ask for all of those people who are here

Who are attending

Who are around me

Keep us safe

Please forgive us if we make a mistake

We bring you this offering

I ask that you accept it

I bow my red forehead to the earth three times before you

• • •

Grandfather Misha

Seattle, Washington
1995

> *Guardian spirit of this place*
> *Don't be offended*
> *Guardian spirit of the taiga*
> *Don't be offended*
> *Guardian spirit of this sacred tree*
> *Don't be offended*
> *Receive my gift*
> *Please accept my gift*
> *I ask for happiness for myself*
> *Don't be offended by this work I do here before you*
> *Please accept my gifts*
> *These gifts that I bring you*
> *Accept them well*
> *Spirits of the tree*
> *Please accept my gifts*

Grandfather Misha pours a little vodka at the base of the tree, saying:

> *Guardian spirit of the Earth*
> *Please accept my gift*
> *Don't be offended by what I do here, spirits*
> *This is your region*
> *Your place and territory*
> *We recognize this sacred place*
> *This sacred place that many have gathered*
> *   so they may learn the ways*

Please don't be offended, great tree, that

I have made you a ritual place

You are a tudja!

(Grandfather Misha now gives tobacco to the tree, saying)

Great spirits receive my gifts

Give me health and let me live a long life

Great spirits of the taiga and great spirits of the mountains

I bid you farewell here

Don't be offended by that which we do here

I ask forgiveness from you for these good people

• • •

Grandfather Misha and Grandmother Nadia

Seattle, Washington
1995

Grandfather Misha speaks:

Spirit of this place
I have come here for the first time
I ask that you bring me happiness
*   and success in my hunting*
I brought you this offering
I've offered it with my rhythms and my song
I sang to you
I've sent out the rhythms on this log drum
Here I have the ritual dish
In it find fish, berries, rice, millet, tobacco, and sacred grass

Grandmother Nadia speaks:

Don't be offended by what I do here
I ask you to help those that have gathered
*   beneath your branches*
I petition you to help all of those who
*   have gathered here today*
Protect Grandfather Misha while he is here
Help the relatives and friends of these people also
I know you see me here
I give thanks that you are aware of me

• • •

GRANDMOTHER NADIA AND GRANDFATHER MISHA, BAINBRIDGE
ISLAND, WASHINGTON STATE, USA, 1995

CHAPTER 7

Nature of Spirits

In Ulchi cosmology, spirits can be divided into two primary families: those whose existence springs from the invisible realms parallel to the mortal world and those that have previously taken human, animal, or other corporeal form in the Middle World. Those who are deceased or removed from physical existence now serve as heavenly protectors, guides, or harmful spirits. Spirits exist in each of the three worlds and may be categorized into groups such as animals, plants, minerals, ancestors and deceased shamans, and elements (fire, water, wind, and earth). Regardless of their type, all spirits are referred to by the term *sava* or *saven*. This term can apply to a spirit in nature, a denizen of the invisible world, or an idol, amulet, or design through which a spirit manifests on the earthly plane. For the Ulchi, the spirits are classified by their strength rather than their form.

Spirit contact with the human world is both a fixed and a dynamic reality, never ceasing. In daily life, people must be constantly vigilant in remembering that the spirits are always around them, watching, listening, and noting their actions. Whether in a passive or active relationship with spirits, one must always remain aware of these invisible forces. Contact with them can occur for short periods of time or continuously throughout a person's life. Contact with the spirits can be accomplished through appeals and prayers, which in the Ulchi tradition have no prescribed verbiage; instead, the words used are spontaneous and from the heart. The specific form of these requests may involve speaking, listening, dancing, singing, and drumming, and can take place during meditations, rituals, otherworld journeys, visions, dreams, or experiences in daily life. When contacting spirits, one must respectfully appeal to them as one's protectors and present offerings and gifts. In some cases, these offerings may be presented to an idol or at a shrine housing the specific spirit with which contact is sought. When the appeal is directed to the greater spirits who reside in natural settings, no residence or idol is constructed. Rather than embodying an amulet or shrine, these higher forces, which dwell in the natural environments of the mountains, oceans, sky, and forests, are said to be omnipresent in territories in which they exist.

For the shaman, the protective and helping spirits either are family ancestors and clan spirits or emerge from the invisible dimensions or worlds—Upper, Middle, or Lower—and they have their own ranking among themselves. Spirits also have their own families, work, and interests. They are complex psychological beings whose behavior and affective states mirror the human condition. They are also said to behave like hooligans and can be very lazy in their relationships with the human realm.

The shamans do not believe that one can completely control a spirit, so when calling upon one of these beings for help, the shaman asks, begs, and cajoles them for their assistance. Prayers or rituals include asking the spirits for forgiveness, often using words similar to these: "Please forgive me, spirits, if I offend you in any way. I am a small person, and I do not know everything. If I have forgotten anything, please pity me. I come and ask you for help. If you can help me, I would appreciate it. I would appreciate anything that you can do for my family or me. Please forgive me if I make a mistake."

There is no expectation that the spirits will comply with a request. If a person finds that a request has been granted, there is great surprise and joy. If not, self-examination of one's actions or deeds is necessary. If no error can be found, the request can be made again. People's thoughts are also accessed by these supernatural beings. If someone worries or exhibits cognitive distortions such as polarized thinking, catastrophizing, or personalization, harmful spirits that feed on negativity will be encouraged to enter into that person's life. The mind—both conscious and unconscious—is the doorway to the world of the spirits. Good action, behavior, and ideas attract benevolent spirits. Wrong actions, destructive affect states, and ideas call to the harmful ones. The spirits may seek to punish a person for speaking badly about them or showing disrespect, but in their parental role, they are kind and understanding of ignorant people. They can be benevolent and forgiving of mistakes made by humans.

The cultural laws and taboos of the Ulchi have been handed down from one generation to the next for thousands of years. It is the duty

GRANDMOTHER LILIA DECHULI (FOREGROUND) AND
CHILD AT THE BULAVA VILLAGE MUSEUM

153

of all parents to instruct their children in the ways of the world and the ways of the spirits. Spirits, like humans, are very complicated, elaborate beings and are to be approached, examined, and understood on an individual basis. A shaman spends years developing a relationship with each of their spirit helpers, and over time, the virtues and attributes of the spirit are slowly revealed and incorporated into an enduring partnership.

Commentaries

Grandmother Nadia:

If you believe in the Ulchi spirits, then they will help you, and if you don't, they will not help you. Harmful spirits do not like the work of a shaman. A shaman may speak in an angry or shameful way in discourse with a client. What the client may not understand is that those punitive remarks are being addressed towards the harmful spirits that are surrounding them. This reveals to those negative spirits that the shaman is strong and means business and that the shaman is on their way towards a confrontation or battle among the offending spirits in the invisible worlds in hopes of driving them away from the client. The shaman behaves in such a way to engender shame in those spirits and not the client.

.

A human may live one hundred years. This is a very long life. The Enduri Ba, the Sun, Moon, Mountains, Seas, Thunder, Stars, Clouds, and the Earth are eternal. Most other spirits live a much longer life than humans. Their normal lifespan may be two or three thousand years.

..

GRANDFATHER MISHA:

My father always told me that you must never speak or address the spirits of the heavens in vain, and I asked why. My father said, "See how the heavens twist and turn and tumble about, and do you see how the Clouds are changing from one form to another? Do you see how the lightning flashes? You are very small, and the heavens could take you in an instant for that reason. Never, oh never, address them in vain! Never speak poorly of the heavenly spirits. Maybe that is why, once a year, we carefully make an observance and give offerings to the spirits of Heaven." My father was a great and powerful shaman who traveled with the Thunder above the heavens to the higher heavens.

·

Families that have murder or suicide in their line do not live a good life. Those spirits do not travel to Buni village, and stay on earth and bring harm to those living members of the family as well as to other people. Special ceremonies could be made to appease those harmful souls who become vampiric spirits.

·

The elders say to live this life well, be humble and don't desecrate any sacred sites. Be kind to other people and never offend them. People who die quickly when their time comes and do not suffer have lived a good life. Humility is important, and that is why you always hear us saying to the spirits not to take offense at us, or forgive us if we are ignorant and make a mistake in Nature.

• • •

IDOLS AND AMULETS

Idols and amulets are containers in which particular spirits will take up residence. They are not mere symbolic representations of the powers of Nature or the invisible worlds. They are both "homes" for the spirits and material manifestations of them. Just as a human body has a spirit, the idols and amulets are the physical bodies of the spirits. Amulets and idols can be carved from various materials, but wood is considered the most "alive" or "potent" of all materials. The type of wood used and the particular design chosen will vary dependent upon the type of *saven* that is being constructed.

The designs of the various spirits follow strict patterns that have been handed down for thousands of years. The earliest recorded images of these designs can still be found in the region's ancient petroglyphic sites. In the construction of idols and amulets, the images must be created exactly as they were made by the ancestors. There can be no improvisation or error on the part of the artist when creating a traditional piece. Any mistake by the carver could result in either a punishment from the spirit or the spirit's refusal to inhabit the carving. If the image is incorrect, the spirit will not recognize its "home." It will refuse to enter or may become offended in some way. Because of these laws, very few skilled carvers take up the task of creating traditional amulets and idols.

COMMENTARY

GRANDMOTHER NADIA:

The ritual sculpture of the peoples of the North, and in particular the Ulchis, is one of the most interesting. Our idols have not been completely researched by outsiders because our elders hold fast to the secrets. It is very interesting. Most academicians cannot make heads or tails of it, particularly what the connection is between our art and philosophy of life. Without a complete comprehension of our animism and our conception of the world, it is impossible to evaluate our sacred art work.

• • •

Besides the traditional designs, there exists a category of special amulets whose creation is ordered by individual shamans. In a healing ceremony, a prescription for a cure may involve having the client procure such an amulet. Specific amulets are carved for specific ailments. The shaman will see the type of spirit that must be constructed, as well as the various design elements, the size, and the species of wood required for the piece. Shamans will either create the amulets themselves or send clients to other carvers whom they trust.

HEALING SAVENS FOR VARIOUS DISEASES, ARTIST MAXIME KYALUNZIGA

People can share and trade some types of amulets with one another. If an amulet is effective in curing a stomach ache, it may be permissible to loan it to a friend or family member who has the same illness.

Clan idols or larger totems can range from three inches to eight feet in height. These spirits are not worn on the body. They are placed on the family altar or carried in a small bag or in a pocket. These idols are passed down from generation to generation and usually bear the image of the House spirit, Mountain spirit, hunting and fishing spirits, etc. New family spirits are added from time to time.

Shamans have special idols created for their spirit helpers. These can be made from wood, metal, cotton, leather, fish skin, or other materials.

Since amulets and idols are living beings, great care must always be given to them. They must never be placed in small containers or closed up in any way. They must have access to air and light, and they must be fed at various intervals. At a minimum, the spirits will be fed during the monthly Full Moon/house ritual. Additional feedings will

GRANDMOTHER YETCHKA ROSUGBU OBERTALINA
AND PERSONAL SAVENS, BULAVA VILLAGE

vary in frequency, depending on their purpose. These other feedings may occur when a person asks for specific help from a spirit amulet. They may also take place when the person intuitively feels that the amulet is asking for food, water, or alcohol. One behaves toward the spirits as a good and faithful friend. A person is expected to spend time talking and cultivating contact with the spirits, whether they are embodied in carvings or omnipresent in the environment.

COMMENTARY

GRANDMOTHER NADIA:

In the past, the larger clan idols were kept outside next to the family's tree. The monthly ritual to the spirits took place outdoors. The tree ritual and home ritual were combined in this way. If a person were on their way to make a water offering, they would remember to stop first at the tree and make their offerings to the clan spirits. People knew each family's ritual trees and sacred places of nature. They respected these areas and remained away as to not disturb someone else's sacred place. When the Russians began to populate the Amur region in great number, the idols were brought inside. These foreign settlers were ignorant of indigenous traditions and taboos. The Russians were known to have disturbed and desecrated many of the sacred sites. Now the tree stands close to the house, instead of being in a grove, where it can be guarded and protected from other people.

•

All families would choose a special place in the taiga, alongside a sacred tree, to place their large family idols. Every month, they would go there to make a ritual with offerings. Even after a water ritual was performed, they would travel back into the taiga and make offerings to their family savens. Even when my family made a water ritual, it was obligatory to finish up by going to our family idols. Now things are not the same. There are many people wandering through the taiga. In the rafters of our home also lived our idols. The rafters are seen as the cleanest, purist, most sacred part of the house. I remember in my childhood we had so many large savens and how my father always went there to feed them. Some of these idols were wrapped in wooden streamers, while others wore clothes made of sable or deer skin. He made so many offerings to them and addressed each one in their own particular way. My father would make offerings to them by putting the food to their mouths.

•

About those savens that live in Nature, there were different reasons why people made these spirits. The main reason was that these spirits were connected to their clan. People would go and give respect and make offerings to these idols. I remember walking through various territories like the village of Kolchom as well as other places. I always saw these savens standing on the earth. I remember in my own territory of Bulava there were so many scattered throughout different places in the taiga. They were placed there by different family clans. All of the villages

LEFT • MAXIME KYALUNZIGA AND TRADITIONAL MIDDLE WORLD SPIRITS
RIGHT • RAISING THE TIGER TOTEM
BOTTOM • MAXIME CARVING THE TIGER TOTEM

LEFT • MAXIME ADDING FINISHING DETAILS
RIGHT • GRANDMOTHER NADIA SINGING DURING THE CEREMONY FOR THE TIGER SPIRIT
BOTTOM • TIGER TOTEM IN THE PROCESS OF BEING CARVED

were the same. Every family clan would erect these savens in the taiga.

•

We only had three or four Russian families in our village until the 1960s, and later many more Russians began to move into our territory. I remember in about 1967 when I saw an old paddleboat arrive on the shore of my village. They had emptied out the gulags and sent the former prisoners to many villages along the Amur. This was when our village had so many Russians coming to live in our territory. Up until this time, we had so many savens that stood in the taiga because every family placed savens in their own territory.

•

I remember a story of another Russian man who did not respect our savens. He needed to make a fire, so he took some of these idols and threw them into the flames. He defiled the spirits, and later his penis became very swollen and full of great pain. He had not been with a woman. He quickly understood that our spirits are great and have much power. Some of my people taught him how to make offerings and how to beg forgiveness from the spirits. He was told to speak to them and ask them for forgiveness because he was an ignorant person and did not know what he was doing when he used them for firewood. He gave the offerings and prayers, and later his penis became small, and he regained his health. Another Russian man had burned idols also because he was lazy and did not want to search for firewood also. The results were the same. His penis became very swollen, but later this man died.

•

Another time came when I was 19 years old, and I had just graduated from college. I took my mother, Goga, to live with me in the village of Solontsy. We allowed a Russian family to stay in our home in Bulava while we were away. This Russian family had discovered the Duvan clan spirits that lived in the

BEAR FACE EMBROIDERED ON CLOTH POUCH, ARTIST NADIA DUVAN

rafters of the roof of our home. The family took them and used them for firewood. After that, they all died. The first to die was the husband, then the wife, and then the children. Some died due to diseases and others to tragic accidents. When my mother and I returned home to Bulava, we found that our clan savens were destroyed. We were both sad and broken hearted.

•

We no longer place our savens in the taiga. Many of the Russians who live in our village respect and follow our traditions. Many of them make an offering to the spirits before they go into the taiga to hunt or to the spirit of the water before they fish. They are mostly old men. They are the early immigrants to our land, and they remembered the stories of their fathers. The younger Russians do not respect our traditions, and because of this the Ulchi people no longer place their clan spirits outside in the taiga. These ignorant people, who do not understand or respect our traditions, could make a mistake and be injured by the spirits.

• • •

TOP • SAVENS IN BULAVA VILLAGE MUSEUM
BOTTOM • GRANDMOTHER TIKA AND PERSONAL SAVENS
OUTSIDE HER HOME, BULAVA VILLAGE

These wooden idols have their own lives, families, and histories. They can even experience a type of "soul loss." If a person has been neglecting their personal or family idols, these spirits may become offended and fly away. A shaman may be asked to take a journey for a spirit idol. The shaman will travel to the invisible environments where the idol has chosen to take up residence. The spirit will inform the shaman about their experiences with their human hosts. The shaman, as intermediary, returns informing the caretakers about the content, discontent, wishes, or desires of the spirit idol .

Idols or amulets that are accidentally broken are given their own type of funeral. All the broken pieces are gathered up and wrapped in three layers of white cloth or wooden streamers and buried in the ground.

If a shaman dies, their amulets and idols are either taken by the family or passed on to family friends. Sometimes people are afraid of keeping these powerful spirits in their homes. This was true in the recent passing of the shaman Grandmother Tika. People were offered the spirits, but everyone refused because Grandmother Tika was a great and powerful shaman. If the new owner made any mistake, tragedy and misfortune could be visited upon the whole family. For this reason, Grandmother Tika's idols were taken to an ethnographic museum in Vladivostok for safekeeping. Many shamanic idols have ended up in various museums throughout Russia, and stories abound about their curses. One incident I heard about involved some museum washer women who, while cleaning up in the late hours of the night, played with the items, pretending to be shamans. As in other cases, tragedy visited their lives, and they died in strange and unusual accidents.

THE SPIRIT HOUSE

The *meu*, a protector of the clan, can take the form of an outdoor spirit house that can vary in size. In this form, it is always placed near the clan's dwelling. It can take the place of the family *tudja*, where offerings to the spirits are performed outside. Small spirit idols associated with the particular clan are placed inside the *meu* to stand guard over and protect the living.

Sacred Cloth Amulets

This ancient type of cloth amulet is usually written with ancient Jurchen or Chinese characters. This amulet will be hidden by the owner and will remain secret from those outside the clan. It is also given the name *meu*, as it serves the same protective function as the spirit house.

Commentaries

Grandmother Nadia:

I remember going to Grandmother Tika's house during the fall of 1995. She reached into a drawer and pulled out a piece of red cloth with Chinese characters written upon it. She said to me, "I have never shown this to anyone." I asked her why she was showing it to me, because usually, it would be something that you would even keep from your husband, and she replied, "It is a very sacred thing that used to belong to an old Manchu gentleman, and it's a great taboo to show it, but understand that our power is written here within the characters. These characters are very sacred." There were several layers to the cloth. And then Tika said, "Yes, I can show it to you." Once again, I asked her why she was showing this to me. Am I special in some way? She said nothing, but once again it reminded me how most of the time a shaman never finishes what they are saying. You will sit and talk with them for years, and you'll think that you'll never get to the end of a story.

•

It can be a spirit house or a piece of material or even an iconographic image. No matter the form, a meu is considered the main protective spirit of the family or clan. We had a spirit house, like the Djafu family, because my father's mother was a Manchu shaman. The concept of the meu was a gift from the Manchu people.

••

GRANDFATHER BORIS DJAFU

GRANDFATHER BORIS DJAFU:

My father was an Isachula (psychic) shaman. His name was Ivan Djafu. Our clan is from the ancient Manchurian peoples. My father always saw everything. We had a little spirit house nearby our own home, and before his death, he went out and destroyed that little house.

Two times each year, we made offerings to that spirit house. He destroyed this spirit house because he wanted to protect us if we made a mistake in the rituals or forgot to give offerings. He destroyed this just before his death to protect us in the future.

We called the house our meu. On Ulchi/Chinese New Year, we would carry out the rituals.

167

This spirit house was made for the protection of the family. We made a tudja in the taiga from a larch tree. We made offerings and prayed there twice a year. The women and children stayed inside the house, and only the men could go to this place.

• • •

KOLYA U (LEFT IMAGE), AND MAXIME KYALUNZIGA (RIGHT IMAGE)

Master Artists of the Spirits

Many shamans in the villages will send their clients to specific artists when the prescription for a cure involves having a spirit amulet constructed for the patient. The two major artists whose work is considered the most beautiful and powerful are Maxime Kyalunziga and Kolya U. Other artists who continue to practice the ancient style of woodworking are Nikolai Djavgada, Ivan Rosugbu, and Anatoli Dechuli. The shaman will see what spirit image needs to be constructed, either during their healing work or through dreams. Sometimes it can take months before the shaman understands the exact form that the spirit chooses to take within the ritual carving. Once the shaman is clear about the image of the healing spirit, they will describe in detail to the client what the amulet should look like. It is then the client's duty to travel to the home of one of the artists to give the exact details to the master carver.

Although there are various skilled woodcarvers among the Ulchi people, very few take on the burden of constructing the healing amulets. Each woodcarver is keenly aware that working with the spirits can be dangerous. If an artist makes any type of mistake during the carving process, the spirit could become angry and focus its displeasure upon the woodcarver and their family members.

When the amulet is ready, the client will take it back to the shaman for the next ceremony. This involves a different type of singing ritual, called *ewu*, which calls the soul of the spirit to take up residence in the body of the amulet. Only after the amulet has been awakened with this new life can it begin to heal and protect the patient from the specific malady.

COMMENTARY

GRANDMOTHER NADIA:

I was sick for a very long time, and when I entered my middle age, I had a leg that was in constant pain. I developed this at the Institute because I was a dancer and I studied ballet on hard wooden floors for many years. I had also had an accident in childhood to my leg, so my dance instruction just compounded the problem, which Grandfather Misha found out when he performed a yiyee for me. My leg was hurting so much that my older sister Shura said to me, "Nadia, turn to the old ones. What if they help you? In my childhood, they helped me a great deal. I suffered greatly from rheumatism, and at that time there were no doctors in our villages. The only one who could help me was an old grandmother shaman. I received a spirit amulet with a hanging foot made of larch. Every month, when I hurt, I made an offering to this spirit. It was almost unnoticeable, but I healed. It was very slow, but it happened.

She advised me to turn to Grandfather Misha. I was in my twenties. I said, "Okay." I was young, and I was skeptical. The Soviet schools taught us to be that way. They forced us to forget our culture and traditions. But I thought, my god, it can't do any harm. I turned to Grandfather Misha, and he worked on me for three months. I went to him, only telling him that my leg hurt and that I had gone to the doctors and they said they couldn't help. This was my first healing with Grandfather Misha. I just said to him, "Please try to help me."

During the yiyee (shaman song), he retold me in exact detail my entire childhood, although I didn't tell him anything about myself. He saw that when I was ten years old, I had turned my leg when I almost drowned. He said, "Did that really happen?" and I said, "Yes, it did." Then he said, "You also turned it as a result of dancing on hard floors," and I said, "Yes, this is true." Grandfather Misha said, "Because of this, it is a weak point that with years shows up as an injury."

By the second session, I had become more familiar with shamanism and what the healing savens were all about. I asked him, "What type of saven do I need and what types of offerings and food shall I give it?" I thought if I could get a saven really fast and start feeding it really fast, I'll get better much faster. He said, "No, I don't see, I don't know what spirit helper you need." I started to learn about all of the different types of savens and what type of illness each specific saven would help. So I said to him, "Grandfather, is it my leg or the joint or which saven shall I use?" He just said, "No, because you need something very different." He searched for three months, and at the end of the third month, he gave me a description of what type of saven I needed. It has the head of a bear with one paw, the right paw hanging down. I still wear this saven, and I feed it every month, and I ask for happiness. I go outside to my sacred tree and make my offerings, and this is what I teach my children to do.

· · ·

TIMES FOR FEEDING THE SPIRIT IDOLS

Traditionally, spirits are fed when one is performing the monthly house ritual, traveling on a journey, or going to hunt, fish, or gather plants and herbs from the environment. Propitiating the spirits is a daily occurrence no different than feeding yourself or your family members. The larger spirit rituals are much more elaborate in their elements. The idols are given new clothes, ornaments, and greater amounts of food and drink that correspond with the seasons of the chase and the return of the salmon. These are the demarcations of the cycles of life that occur annually and coincide with the New Year's festival and the spring and fall water rituals.

COMMENTARIES

GRANDMOTHER TIKA:

You must always feed your spirits; otherwise, they'll act like hooligans!

· ·

GRANDMOTHER NADIA:

Spirits are omnipotent and can easily change their places in space and take the form of any animal. They like to be close to people because, like people, they experience cold and thirst, and for this reason, they require food offerings. If homage or food offerings were not made, the hungry or ill-tempered spirits would settle in a person's body, torturing and tormenting, or else they would steal the soul and take it someplace far away. Some spirits and Busawus were evil and crafty.

· · ·

Spirit Parties

Grandmother Tika would have special parties for her idols. From time to time, she would bring out all of her carvings and place them on a table. She would wash, feed, and speak to them throughout an entire day. She might present them with new clothes made of leather, fur, wood shavings, or cloth. She would ask them to tell her the news of the other worlds, about their lives and the lives of their friends and family. Before sunset, she would return them to their special wooden box and move the box back into one of the sacred corners of the home.

Commentary

Grandmother Nadia:

One day, while working in my home, Grandmother Tika flew into my house feeling very panicked. She was in the middle of one of these "spirit parties" when she discovered that a wing from her Buchu ponga saven (spirit idol used to tell fortunes) was missing. She asked me to return with her to her home in order to help her find the missing piece. Upon arriving, I observed all of her spirit idols on the table. I noticed that a small piece of wood was slightly hidden next to the table leg, resting on the floor. I bent down to examine it, and when I picked it up, I recognized it as being the missing wing. I said, "Look! I've found it!" Grandmother Tika was very relieved. I picked up the Buchu idol's wing and reinserted its missing part back inside the carving. At that very instant, a great sharp pain entered my knee which caused me to collapse. I was in such pain. I asked Grandmother Tika what she thought was happening to me. She replied, "The Buchu spirit was very angry and offended about losing its wing." I said, "I

can understand, but I am the one that found it and returned it!"
Grandmother Tika replied, "Oh well, it must be punishing you.
Don't blame me! It's not my fault. My Buchu spirit is just very
upset."

. . .

BULAVA DANCE ENSEMBLE GIVA PERFORMING THE BEAR DANCE.
DANCE STICKS ARE ALSO USED IN TRANCE DANCING.

Although Grandmother Nadia had helped the *Buchu* to recover its
missing wing, it was so upset at losing it that it chose to strike out at
the first person it came into contact with. It would have been impossible to have anticipated these consequences, but the results left an
indelible mark in Grandmother Nadia's mind. If Grandmother Tika's
Buchu had ever gotten into trouble again, Grandmother Nadia would
have been reluctant to help.

Traveling Savens

Shamans can also send their spirit idols on journeys to other geographic areas, to act as scouts or messengers. This account by Grandmother Lilia Dechuli describes such an occurrence.

Commentaries

Grandmother Lilia Dechuli:

I went to my window and saw an old woman sitting in my backyard in the snow. I recognized her as being the shaman Grandmother Daya Djan from Ukta village. I thought to myself, "Why is Grandmother Daya sitting in the snow? She must be cold, so I will go outside and bring Grandmother into my home before she freezes."

I went out to my backyard, and when I arrived at the spot where I saw the grandmother sitting, I found a spirit idol. I was most confused, but I brought the saven into my house anyway. Three days later, Grandmother Daya arrived from Ukta village. I told Grandmother Daya the story and showed her the saven. Grandmother Daya said, "This is my saven! It came in advance of me to clear the way and let the people in Bulava know that I was coming.

••

Grandmother Nadia:

You need to remember that savens are alive and animate. They can dematerialize and materialize wherever they wish. They can travel here and there and return in the blink of an eye.

• • •

TAKTU, TRADITIONAL STORAGE HOUSE, BULAVA VILLAGE.
TAKTUS ARE USED TO STORE MEAT, FISH, AND FURS.

A Child's Toy Spirits

Traditionally, dolls that were constructed for children usually took the form of spirits. They were miniature representations of the same idols that were placed inside the home. Whether bears, tigers, or land spirits, these small carvings were the "action figures" among the Ulchi youth. The children would make clothes for them, have tea parties, or engage in other imaginative games with their spirit dolls. As living beings, these dolls served to protect children as well as introducing them to and instructing them on the invisible powers and inhabitants that surrounded their world.

Spiritual Clothing, Household Objects, and Equipment

Their clothing was traditionally constructed from animal fur, fish skins, and various types of cloth. Most of the cloth and thread available in the past were received in trade from the Manchu people of Northern China, who traveled in merchant junks up and down the Amur River, exchanging their goods for furs or ginseng roots from the local people.

175

When clothing was constructed from animal fur, great care and caution were taken by the seamstress to not offend the spirit of the animal that had sacrificed itself. Wearing this type of clothing connected the human to the spirit of the animal and imbued the wearer with the spiritual virtues associated with that specific creature, as well as providing protection from unwanted or harmful spirits. Women were the main creators of clothing for the family, and they followed various rules and taboos in the construction of garments made from the skin and fur of the animal people. The skills and taboos involved in making clothing were passed down from mother to daughter, generation after generation. Ritual songs also accompanied the work as raw skins underwent various stages of preparation, including curing, stretching, and softening them to make them malleable enough to sew into a jacket, pants, or a set of new boots.

Fish skins are durable and pliable and made the best waterproof material available to the Ulchi. This material was used to construct jackets, boots, bags, quivers, hats, gloves, and a host of other items. All rain gear was made from fish skin. A jacket constructed of this material might take seventy or more skins. The primary fish skin used came from the salmon, although some shamans would make their drum bags from the skin of the pike fish.

Whether made from fur, leather, fish skin or cloth, most items of clothing had various spiritual motifs and patterns embroidered or appliquéd on them. The origins of these motifs can be traced to the early designs found in ancient petroglyphs throughout the region, dating back to the Neolithic age. Grandmother Nadia said that these are the blueprints or organic patterns in all of Nature, regardless of whether specific images are representative of animals, plants, or spirits residing in the mineral kingdom or invisible worlds. Motifs included the Tree of Life, the Sun, birds, spiral dragons and serpents, tiger and bear faces, frogs, deer, water, butterflies, fish, and various plants found in the region.

Hunting or fishing tools and objects used daily in the home were carved with the same motifs, serving the same dual purpose. To sew

TOP • ULCHI WOMAN USING WOODEN MALLET TO SOFTEN ANIMAL SKINS, CA. 1930
MIDDLE LEFT • TRADITIONAL FISH SKIN ROBE, FRONT
MIDDLE RIGHT • TRADITIONAL FISH SKIN ROBE, BACK
LOWER LEFT • SOFTENING THE FISH SKIN
LOWER LEFT • PLACING DESIGNS ON THE PREPARED AND SOFTENED SKIN

LEFT • TRADITIONAL BIRCH BARK HAT
RIGHT • ULCHI CUT PAPER DESIGN

or carve a spiritual design on an object not only called the strength and energy of the design into the item but served to keep harmful spirits at bay, preventing them from spoiling or infecting it. Hunters would wear elaborate designs upon their clothing to protect themselves from unwanted spirits while on the winter chase, as well as to provide luck for themselves during their endeavors in the taiga. Marriage gowns contained the Tree of Life motif, full of images of small nestlings. As the unborn souls of children were seen as small birds prior to their incarnation as humans in the Middle World, a new bride would wear this design on her day of matrimony in order to be assured of giving birth to children. The everyday clothing of the people was also embroidered with various protective designs, but these were less elaborate. To wear or possess a design was to invite that particular spirit into one's life, as these motifs had a magnetic quality that combined the virtues of the spirit with those of the human wearer, and affixed them onto the individual.

Shamans also used these materials and motifs when constructing ritual garments and other items. Their shamanic vests, skirts, gloves, boots, and hats contained the images of their spirit helpers. If one of their main spirit helpers was a lynx or a bear, just having a piece of fur from the animal would suffice to energetically connect them with that spirit.

Paper Amulets

People can also cut these images out of paper and use them as a medicinal treatment for various ailments. One time, while Grandmother Nadia and her daughter were in the United States, the daughter began to complain of a toothache. Grandmother Nadia took a piece of paper and cut out a stylized image of a frog. She instructed her daughter to hold this paper image up to her cheek in the area of the offending tooth. Within twenty minutes, the ache had almost completely subsided, and it finally went away. Once the ache had been absorbed by the paper frog, Grandmother Nadia took it out into nature and placed it in a location that was far from the beaten path, where it could remain undisturbed while it slowly decayed naturally.

CHAPTER 8

Shaman Autobiographies & Memories from the Elders

Knowledge about the individual shamans and elders, who contributed to this book, and their shamanic lineages, was assembled from many sources. This information was collected either from their own personal accounts or the memories of family members and friends. Some individuals were very forthcoming about their lives, while others were shy, modest, or secretive, giving very little detail. As a rule, the shamans and elders never talked too much or too long about their personal histories, so what is contained in this biographical section are bits and pieces gathered and spliced together from various talks and discussions over many years. Where information as to births, deaths, and locations is available, it has been included in this section.

The two Goldi (Nanai) shamans who appear in this book are Indyeka Djaksul and Linza Beldy. The Goldi tribe, who live just south of the Ulchi people, speak a similar language as the Ulchi, although there are variations in the dialect. The style of shamanizing within these two tribes is similar, except the Goldi include more elements of

Manchurian shamanism, due to their proximity to Northern China. Grandmother Indyeka spent most of her life in the Ulchi territories, working with the local villagers. Grandmother Linza, who passed away during the writing of this book, was one of the last practicing Goldi shaman of her village. Before her death, she met with Grandmother Nadia and provided her with insights on the shamanic path that were similar to those of the Ulchi.

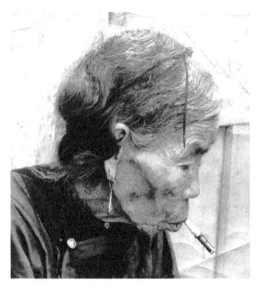

Grandmother Altaka Olchi

Born 1886, Mongol village
Died 1979, Bulava village

Memories

Grandmother Nadia:

Most of her life was spent in Bulava. Her maiden name was Rosugbu. Her husband's name was Pavel Olchi, and her relatives were Sagda and Saida Rosugbu. Saida was the grandfather of my husband. Grandmother Altaka had three daughters. She was a powerful Kasa shaman. She had a coarse but beautiful voice when she sang. Her daughters' names were Kuma, Buyaga, and

Nura. Grandmother Altaka gave conjurings for all of the people in Bulava village.

I remember how she sang for me so many times when I was a child. I especially remember a time where Grandmother Altaka came to give me a healing when I was about ten years old. Grandmother Altaka had fashioned a salcha grass saven in the shape of a pig to take away my illness. Once the healing was complete, I saw this grass pig run all over the floor and then across the room. I told my mother and other relatives what I had witnessed. They said to me, "Very few people can see the spirits move about." Then they spoke to my mother, saying, "This is a wonder. It is very interesting that your child has seen this. Not everyone can see this." I know that Grandmother Altaka's savens, especially the silver ones, are being kept safe by her grandchildren.

Grandmother was a great shaman. She is probably one of the greatest shamans of the Ulchi people. I remember the elders saying that one must never offend a great shaman.

Grandmother Altaka was my mother's best friend. I was a little girl at the time. Grandmother Altaka would always come over to my house to visit my mother. If I ever felt ill, my mother and father would call Grandmother Altaka to come over to my home and give me a healing. I was five or six years old when I remember her coming to help me. She would come to my house to visit and then eat and drink with my family and even stay the night. My father always gave a large odi (shaman's payment) to Grandmother Altaka. He was never greedy and always a great and generous man to all of the people.

My mother, Goga, and Grandmother Altaka were loving friends, and because of their fondness for one another, Grandmother Altaka always sang for me and helped me. Now, as a child, I was always a little afraid when Grandmother Altaka would give me a healing. Her voice was so big and powerful, and she smoked tobacco all of the time. I remember sitting next to her while she sang, and I just remembered that she had big lips and a very coarse voice. I remembered our healing times together where I would sit next to her for a while; then I will go and lie down for a while and sleep, then I would wake up and sit and watch everything that was going on in my home. Sometimes I would be very frightened just sitting next to her.

··

Grandfather Boris Djafu:

Peter Dechuli and I went and took some red araki (alcohol) with us when we took a Russian woman named Tatiana, who was visiting our village from St. Petersburg. Grandmother Altaka gave her a healing ceremony. This was in the year of 1963 or 1964.

Grandmother Altaka said to her, "I see in your home that there is only one young woman, and inside the house are so many cabinets, dressers, tables, and chairs." Grandmother Altaka went on to give her an accurate description of everything in that house! She saw everything correctly. Tatiana was so surprised at the description of her home and said to us, "I am amazed that this old person can see all of this. How can this happen? She sees everything so clearly and accurately, and this now makes me truly believe in the talents and skills of a shaman.

··

Grandmother K.V. Duvan:

My mother, Minka, had been diagnosed by the doctors with a serious form of schizophrenia, but she didn't want to be hospitalized. She turned to Grandmother Altaka, a strong shaman, for help. After the conjuring, the sickness passed.

···

Grandmother Tika Valdu Anga

> Born 1915, Mongol village
> Died 1998, Bulava village

I never gave birth to any children. I have lived in the villages of Mongol, Ukta, Marinsk, and Bulava. My father's surname was Valdu, and I am the seventh shaman of my clan. My shamanic lineage is continuous. I wore a shaman's coat, and had many savens and used three different shaman's caps.

The first shamanic equipment that I saw in my dream was the shaman's cap. When the dreams began for me, I saw two savens that I was instructed to acquire, a Buchu Masi and a Tiger Masi. The Tiger Masi was my home's main spirit. These were the first shamanic elements to arrive. Then I had to learn/begin to sing/find my shaman song. I really had to work for that song.

I was young, around seventeen or eighteen years of age, at this time and knew I might become a shaman. My father was born a great shaman, and his name was Yakov Valdu. When you first become a shaman, they tie to your arms and legs the wooden streamers."

MEMORIES

GRANDMOTHER NADIA:

Grandmother Tika Anga (maiden name: Valdu) was one of the most powerful shamans of the Ulchi people. She was a seventh-generation shaman. Tika's personal shamanic path began at the age of eighteen years of age.

Grandmother Tika's story of becoming a shaman talks of the hereditary path. Having received the call while still in her teens was a difficult experience. Having a father who was a sixth-generation shaman was fortunate. He instructed her during this time, this tutelage being invaluable. Her father took care to help initiate her by performing special rituals, even instructing her from the dream worlds while still alive. In generational shamans, spirit helpers that have served your relative shamans can serve you also, along with your new spirits.

When Tika performed a conjuring, she takes the spirits that she wears around her neck and brings them from under her clothing to the outside of her shaman's vest where they can be seen. She makes an offering to each spirit amulet. Tika has three main spirit helpers that she used during a journey. First is the silver amulet in the form of the spirit Ajaha. This is her main spirit. The next amulet is made from silver also and is a large shamanic front piece representing the three worlds. Her third spirit amulet was made of deer fur with the images of snakes and heavenly dragons.

• • •

GRANDMOTHER INDYEKA DJAKSUL

Born 1911, Niszney Khalbu village
Died 2007, Sophisk village

My father had three children: my brother, my sister, and myself. I was twelve years old when my family moved to Sophisk village. I was married at the age of twenty-one and moved to the village of Mai with my husband, Djaksul. He was an Ulchi. My father was from the Samar clan and my mother from the Tumali clan. My husband and I had nine children. Their names are Nadia, Lena, Andrei, Sergei, Yura, Dima, Nikolai, Alexsai, and Eugeni. Ponga Valdu was a great shaman. She was my aunt. She was my mother's sister, and she sang for Nadia Duvan when Nadia was a little child. I had another aunt, from my mother's side, who was also a great shaman. Her name was

MEMBERS OF THE GIVA SINGERS ENSEMBLE: GRANDMOTHER LILIA
DECHULI (FIRST FROM THE LEFT), CLARA ROSUGBU AND VERA
DUVAN (SECOND AND FIRST FROM THE RIGHT), CA. 2013

Taluka Tumali. My grandfather, on my father's side, was a very great, powerful shaman. His name was Depekai Taypakay.

My husband and I worked in the village fish cooperative. He died in my forties, and I married again. My second husband's name was Peter Valdu. He was born in 1922 and died in the 1980s. We lived together in Mongol village, and three years later we moved to Marinsk, but we didn't like living there. We had one child together, and her name was Tonya. We had a second child, but that child died. Peter worked in the village administration offices for the fishing cooperative. He was a very educated person. After WWII, he returned home a highly decorated soldier. During that time, I worked at the fishing cooperative. From 1972 to1975, I worked as a guard for the water plant.

I really began my shamanic path when I was fifty years of age. My son died and a little while later my house burnt down, which cause me such great stress that I fell into a deep sleep that lasted seven days and seven nights. My relatives thought that I had died. Nature had taken away everything, my family home, my husband, my son.

Before I took the shaman's road, I was also ill for two months. Five different shamans sang for my soul, but it was only the fifth shaman that was able to help me. I didn't want to become a shaman for a long time, but maybe that is why I became a hunchback. All of my body and bones were so ill, and for a time I became insane and senseless and understood nothing."

Memories

Grandfather Boris Djafu:

In Mongol village lived Indyeka Djaksul. When people need help, they go to her.

I am seventy-four years old as of October 11, 2001. I understand that all people are children of Nature and shaman people are true children of Nature. That is why everyone says, "But I understand nothing, hehehehe." A shaman always sees what you are doing and what you have done. All of your crimes, everything! She tells you what she sees, and everything is true!

••

Grandmother Nadia:

Her shamanic gifts developed earlier when she was around forty or fifty years of age. She would always say to never offend a shaman, or they can curse you. Indyeka was a very quiet person and spoke very rarely about herself or her shamanic path. She knew that I sat around and studied with all the shamans in the different villages, and encouraged me to try the shamanic ways.

• • •

GRANDFATHER MISHA DUVAN

Born 1903, Kadi village
Died 1997, Bulava village

I was raised by my grandfather, grandmother, and great-grandmother. I was very small when my parents died, so my grandparents raised me. They taught me how to catch fish and hunt. My grandfather died in 1917, and hard times came after his death. My grandmother had to make things to sell to find money to feed both myself and her other grandson. I called my grandparents Mother and Father.

After my grandfather's death, we bought a bear cub. An old Ulchi man named Olengu brought it to the village. We bought it and kept it and fed it all the time with fish. After three years, we sacrificed it at the Bear Festival. This is the most interesting festival of our people, which is held at the end of winter. We first let loose a strong dog upon the bear to tease him. People from different villages were invited to the feast. Lots of people came.

When the bear was killed, they played on the udjadyu (log drum). My grandmother played on the udjadyu and imitated the way the bear walks. After she played, she lost consciousness. She was revived with sankura and fir branches. The people smudged her body with the smoke of these plants. When she became conscious once again, she began to sing and to cry. I began to cry also, but people stopped me from doing so. They said to me, "Let her cry alone." When the bear meat was boiled, everyone got a piece.

I had an elder brother named Chita. He was a shaman. He could make tigers obey him, so I could say that he was a powerful shaman. After my grandfather died, Chita married one of his younger wives. Ulchi men could have two or three wives.

My grandfather (father) was a great shaman. He could make the Thunder obey him. Many people wondered at his ability and also envied him. I find my own road high up in the skies. I have flown up between the red, blue, and white clouds in the sky. There is a clean, blue, and beautiful place. There I have found my father's house. My father is a greater shaman. I am not so good. I cannot rule the Thunder, but I do my best to help people. When I was younger, I could work harder and longer hours, but now I am old, and my voice is not as beautiful and strong. My father was not ill, and nobody knew what caused him to die.

.

My Journey to Kadali

Grandfather Misha singing his autobiography

Detu is where the tundra begins.
My clan is from the Negidal peoples.
My mother and father are from this clan.
They journeyed from the Yako territories where
the Negidal, Evens, and Evenki live.
They traveled along the Amur River and arrived
in the Ulchi territory of the Duvan clan.
We are not from the Duvan clan.

My great-grandfather was from the Gurka
 clan, and my mother's people were Negidals
 and from her line were great shamans.
My shamanic lineage is a straight and strong road. My
 father's lineage is also complete with shamans.
My father was a great thunder shaman
 and visionary/psychic.
He could play the thunder.
I had an older sister, but she was killed
 when lightning struck her.
I also had a brother who was attacked by
 a tiger, but my brother lived.
He became a tiger shaman.
The Negidal shaman, my mother's relative, was the one
 who could cut through an iron cable by pointing his
 finger at it, making a gesture of cutting it with a knife.
My father's side traveled and lived in the different
 territories of the Orochi and Yako lands.
He saw everything with great clarity and remembered
 everything well. All the blue waves of the sea and
 the red sea. Oh, my clan is a very ancient people.
My father's clan stayed and rested with the Orochi
 people and later stayed in the Yako territories.
He journeyed in a boat and traveled and
 traveled and traveled for many months.
I was born at midnight on September 15, 1903.
That was a powerful night full of thunder and lightning.

They took my navel cord and placed it into

a kamchu (birch bark container).

My family members took this kamchu into

the taiga and hung it in a birch tree.

• • •

Grandmother Ama Echa

Born 1910, Udan village

Died 2005, Bulava village

"I was born in Udan, but I grew up in Auri village. I told fortunes and was taught the history and legends of my people. These stories I passed down to my children and others in the village. No one carried out any special ceremonies concerning my shamanic initiation, and that is why I have only taken half of the shaman's road. A great shaman should sing a yiyee for a person's beginning path to becoming a shaman. I was about fifty years old when I first met Grandmother Yetchka Rosugbu Obertalina. She had come from a very powerful shaman clan, so that is why she became a shaman.

"I had five children and fourteen grandchildren. My maiden name was Kuysali, and I am the sister of Goga Duvan, Nadia's mother."

Memories

Grandmother Nadia:

I would always see my aunt Ama and ask her to pongachi (divine) for my children. She was a well-known psychic and had many clients from the village.

• • •

TOP • GRANDMOTHER AMA ECHA
AND HER OWL PONGA SAVEN
BOTTOM • GRANDMOTHER
DALIKA AND GRANDMOTHER
YETCHKA, DUDI VILLAGE

Dalika Kotkin

Born Unknown, Unknown
Died Unknown, Dudi Village

Memories

Olga Bedly:

Before the death of the great shaman Alexander Kotkin, he arranged that all of his spirits fly to his wife. Slowly, day by day and year by year, Dalika grew into a shaman. She then began singing her visions to the people. As an Isachula, she sees everything correctly. Her spirits always speak the truth. She is a powerful Isachula.

She is a shaman because her husband gave her this talent. All of Alexander's spirits completely flew to Dalika, and after he died, she slowly transformed into a shaman. She does her work for people here in the village.

..

Grandmother Nadia:

I remember traveling to Dudi village to see Grandmother Dalika and Grandmother Yetchka. Grandmother Yetchka lived in Bulava for a while but later moved to Dudi village. She moved in with Dalika, so these two shaman–grandmothers lived with each other until they died. I had many talks with the elders of this village, who told me tales of Grandfather Alexander Kotkin. He had passed his talents down to his wife, Dalika. Grandmother Dalika told me that she just does Isachula work, but most of the other elders said she was a strong shaman.

...

GRANDMOTHER LINZA BELDY

Born 1912, Unknown

Died 1999, Naikhan village

I began my singing at ten years of age. When I was fifty years, I began to use the drum and sing for my family, my husband, and my children. Now I just continue to sing for people if they need a healing.

MEMORIES

GRANDMOTHER CHIPAKA PASAR:

Linza was married once, but her husband died in WWII. Now we (Goldi people) have no Kasa shamans. Linza is not a Kasa shaman. She can only treat and heal people and tell their fortunes. She finds people's souls and brings them home to their bodies. She cannot wear her yampa due to different illnesses and pains in her hands and feet. Linza sang for my granddaughter when she was seventeen years old, and she was helped. Linza is not my relative, but I help her, and that is why I have brought her to my home to live with me. She has been with me these past two years (1997-1999). Linza now gets ill, but she continues to sing and shamanize.

..

Grandmother Nadia:

I remember my first meeting with Linza. I was sent on behalf of Grandmother Indyeka. Indyeka had just lost her eldest son in a river accident, and no one could find his body. She was so full of grief that she could not use her abilities to go and seek out the location of her son's body. She asked me to ask Grandmother Linza for a conjuring to see if she could help. On my first meeting, Grandmother Linza gave me a singing, saying, "I will just sing for you. I am just checking things out and guarding your shamanic road." I was quite surprised that Linza talked of my shamanic path as I didn't tell her of my shamanic interest or road, as we had just met.

This was the first and only time I had met Linza Beldy, and yet I found a kind of urgency from her about the shamanic information she gave to me. Perhaps Linza's spirits felt that I would be the person to pass her information down to or perhaps she knew or felt that I had taken the shamanic road. It is common for a shaman to pass down their secrets to a trusted individual or another shaman prior to their death. Linza died three months after meeting with me.

...

Grandmother Nadia Duvan

Born October 20, 1950, Bulava village
Died April 12, 2016, Khabarovsk, Russian Far East

I was born at six in the morning on October 20, 1950, in Bulava village. My father was a very old man when I was born. He was born in 1886, and my mother was born in 1902.

I remember when I was eight years old; I began to have flying dreams. In those dreams, I was flying through the heavens, and below, the earth was a deep and beautiful red. The mountains that rose above the floor of the red earth would be the places that I would land upon from time to time. I would land on these mountaintops and fly off skipping to the next mountaintop as I made my way across the whole of the mountain range. I flew all across this territory. I always remember wondering what kind of territory this was because I have never seen such a place on the earth in my life. This red land was such a beautiful land. I was so amazed, and later I remember that at ten and fourteen years of age, this dream returned again. I remember asking my mother about it, but I was young at this time. Then I had this dream again when I was sixteen, twenty-five, and then again at forty years of age. One time, my daughter Ksusha, who was about eight years old, came to me and told me of the same dream. Why did we see this land? I remember my mother never speaking of such a place. My mother was always a good teacher, imparting important information to me about our traditions, cooking, and cleaning, and speaking for hours of our legends and history.

When I was about six years old, I remember many different people going to our village school, but at this time I only spoke Ulchi. I did not know the Russian language, and at that time, there were no Russians in my village.

When I was born, Bulava was a small village, and we called our village Bulawu, which means "a shaman's staff." Bulava has grown, but my family home still stands in the old part of the village, called Old Bulava.

In the past, the territories that stretched from Auri village to Bulava were the clan territories of the Olchi and Duvan families. When I was young, I knew all of these facts because my mother would speak and teach me these things. My mother enjoyed talking about our clan's history. I also remember her saying things like "this is forbidden" or "that is taboo." Those lessons still echo in my thoughts to this day. I can still hear my mother's voice.

I remember so well the lessons she gave me as to the traditions involving the deceased. She would say, "Don't walk too near the gravesite of a person who has recently died. Their soul may be wandering all about these days, and that soul may try to snatch you away! When you walk near the home that they lived in during life, walk around and don't get too close, even if you have to take a long way coming back home. It is forbidden for children to come too close to a deceased person's home. Never even look at the house! Never even go to that house! If a person has died due to drowning, this is even a bigger taboo! Young children and young women must never go near their former home."

I remember that if a person had died in the river, we were not even allowed to swim there for at least a week. My mother would say, "Never take gifts from a family whose family member has died due to some kind of tragic accident. It is forbidden because the energy of that tragedy might attach itself to you and create illness or bad luck." That is what I remember.

I remember my father always making offerings to the spirits, especially at the New Year's celebration. I remember my father climbing to the ceiling of our home, where savens were kept, and he would spend a long time there speaking with all of them.

When I was about six years old, I had a husband, so to speak. The family named Urongin had a son named Valentin. He and I were supposed to be man and wife when we were grown up. Later I asked my parents why I had to have him as my husband, and my mother replied, "It is our tradition." My mother went on to explain to me that her children (my sisters and brothers) were born and born and born, but they all quickly died and died and died. She said, "This is a special tradition where you ask for the health of newborn children. If you give birth to a son or daughter, you quickly find a spouse for them. If you do, the two children will grow up healthy and never find illness. This is the law, and it is a way of protecting children."

NADIA DUVAN, AGE 3

So, here I was married to Valentin although I had to wait for a very long time before we would truly be man and wife. I saw Valentin from the time when he was five years old to about the age of fourteen. He and his family would visit my home from time to time, but they always came to celebrate New Year at my house. Valentin's mother and my father would always conduct the New Year's rite together. When we were children, Valentin would try to boss me around when I played with the other boys and girls. He would tell the other boys to leave me alone because I was his wife. I didn't like this, and I ignored him. As an adult, I chose my own husband rather than marrying Valentin.

I remember the same big ceremony in the autumn and the springtime. Before my father would go on a hunt, he would conduct the same elaborate ritual. Our savens that lived in the rafters were about fifteen in number. They ranged in size from about eighteen inches to eight feet in height. They were dressed in animal skins, cloth, and fish skin clothing. He would be with them for the longest time, making offerings. There was a ladder that he stood on that rose into the rafters. Young women and children were forbidden to do this type of offering for fear they could lose their strength.

In the evening—and we had no electricity, only lamps—my mother and father would sit around the fire in our hearth and tell me legends and fairy tales. I only remembered that most of those stories had frogs and mice as the main characters. I sat on their laps, close to the fire, listening to these stories.

My father was a strong and serious man even when he was old. All the people in my village remember him this way as well. He had two wives at the same time. The first wife was named Pulmaka Rosugbu, and the second wife was my mother, Goga Kuysali. She was the younger of the two wives.

I was born late to my parents and was the only child living in the home. By the time I was born my older sisters and brothers were young adults who had already moved out to start their own lives.

The first wife gave birth to fifteen children, and my mother gave birth to thirteen children of which only my older sister Shura, my older brother Serge, and myself lived. My sister Leda is the only child alive from the first wife, and I am only child alive from Goga. My mother gave birth to a set of twins a few years after I was born. They only lived for about one month. Grandmother Indyeka gave me a conjuring once and saw this twins' road.

When I was a child, I was always sick, but perhaps it was due to my mother being an old woman when I was born. My parents called in the shamans to help me during this time. The first shaman that helped me was Grandmother Ponga Valdu. She was a very tiny woman in stature. She came to me from Mongol village. Later Grandmother Altaka Olchi came and sang for me all of the time. She came at least four times per year, but in some years she came each month until I was about fourteen years of age. I always had great fevers and lung problems. My parents called other shamans into my home to help me as well. My parents would always give great presents to the shamans. They gave meat, fish, plates, fishing nets, material, and silver coins in payment for their work.

When I was still a child, I remember my home was always full of guests. My mother, Goga, would always have a table set out with

NADIA PARTICIPATING IN VILLAGE FESTIVAL, AGE 11, BULAVA VILLAGE

many different types of food. This was a time in our village when women never went outside of their home to do work in an office, factory, or collective. All the women were in their homes, so other women would come over to visit, gossip, and talk with one another.

My family home was on the edge of the village, but my best friend Rosa's home was right in the center. I went to her house every day. She was a few years older than I, but then again I never liked children my own age. I always wanted to be with the older people. It would take me thirty minutes just to walk to her home, and even in fall and in wintertime, I would make that trek. Rosa's home had two wives also. The first wife had no children but loved Rosa very much. Rosa's mother, the second wife, was named Achinda, and her father's name was Ilka Duvan. Ilka was a wonderful man and a great hunter and fisherman like my father. Inside Rosa's home sat the two wives, and there was always eight to ten women visiting there when I came over to play with Rosa. It was like a "women's club" in the village. They would just sit and smile and talk and eat with one another all day long. That's how it was in those days.

My mother, Goga, never listened to my father. She liked freedom, and she had a big personality. She would organize many events in the village because of her inexhaustible energy. Our home was always beautiful and clean, and our family was considered well off by Ulchi standards. As I grew up, I had a poorer lifestyle. My mother was a beautiful dancer and drummer as I remember her performing at the village healing ceremonies.

My father, Dumbin, was a great hunter. When he would come back from a hunting trip, he would give presents to everyone in the village. He gave large portions to meat to everyone, especially the poorer people. If he caught a lot of fish, he would give the fish away also. Sometimes he would travel by boat to hunt on Sakhalin Island. It would take many strong men to row in a boat such a distance. They would hunt and fish and be gone from home for a very long time. I never saw very much of my father because he was always gone on some type of expedition, even in the wintertime. He was around our home mostly in the summer.

The times I liked best would be in the month of March when he would return from one of his hunting trips. He would bring back so many furs of sable, fox, squirrel, and mink. There were about twenty-five to thirty of each of these furs except for sable, and there could be fifty of them. Those foxes were such a deep red color.

Those furs would be taken to a special office in the village. I would sit down with my father, and he taught me to divide the furs into three different piles. The piles were the best, the medium, and the not-so-good pile or the ones that were a little bad. When we worked together, dividing the furs, we would hang them up.

Later he would go to the Russian fur office and sell them, and return home to give my mother the money who immediately would go on a shopping spree. She would buy cabinets, chairs, and once she even bought two black leather couches. The small one was for me, and the larger one was for the adults. My mother always loved those shopping sprees! I think she loved to travel, going hither and yon looking for items because that was the most fun of all. I remember one year when my aunt, who married the linguist O.P. Sunik, came to my home from St. Petersburg. She brought me about ten stuffed elephant dolls.

At that time, there were about three families in the village that were considered well off, and they were my family, Ilka Duvan, and Fedor Dechuli's family. After my father died, Ilka always helped my family. Ilka was a little younger than my father.

After I finished school, I traveled to Solontsy village to work. I was the director of a village club in the village, where I taught dance. I also taught dance in the village school. I worked there for about two years before I traveled to study at the Institute in Khabarovsk. It was a four-year program in ballet and other Western classical dance. Once I graduated, I moved to Takhta village in the Ulchi region. I worked there for a year, and then by 1976, I got married.

NADIA, AGE 14, BULAVA VILLAGE

I missed Bulava, so I returned there with my husband, Maxime Kyalunziga. We lived there together with my mother, and even then she would speak of the legends and traditions of my people. She spoke all of the time about my culture, even when I was an adult, and of course, I remembered these stories because they were the stories of my youth. I would sit quietly and listen to all that she said. I was never bored because they were always interesting stories.

MAXIME KYALUNZIGA

Now, when I was young, I had been a member of my village's traditional dance troupe named Giva. It was founded in 1956 by Peter Dechuli. Peter and Boris Djafu urged me to continue training in dance, so I went to study at the teacher's dance college in Birobidjan with my friend Mado. Later I returned to Khabarovsk for further training. I returned to Bulava and became the director of Giva until my retirement.

It was in the early 1970s when I began to record the deeper information from the elders of my culture. While in college, I had spent a long time reading all the books and articles about my people. I spent a combined time of seven years in various colleges, and one could always find me in the library, just sitting and reading. I read the works of all of the great ethnographers. I just spent my life in the library, reading about my own history. My mother would always talk about her peoples traveling up from Manchuria a long time ago.

She had said that her clan name was originally Jurchuli, which later became Dechuli. The first time I had heard about the Jurchens was from my mother, and that is why I searched long and hard for more information about these people—who they were and where they lived and all of their trials and tribulations with Chinggis Khaan. I understood why they ran away and left their homeland, moving north to the lower Amur region.

Later I found great pains in my hands and legs. My second daughter, Ksusha, was born at that time. I had such great pain in my head and all of my body. My older sister, Shura, told me to go back to the shamans and ask them to check things out for me. She said, "Who knows, maybe they can quickly help you." I went to Grandfather Misha, and he gave me three conjurings. We did this once a month for three months. He sang first for the pains in my legs and knees, and in his vision, he said to me, "In the past, when you were fourteen years old, you cracked your kneecap." He saw this is his conjuring. He went on to say, "Little by little; your soul flew away because it was frightened."

GRANDMOTHER NADIA VISITING GRANDMOTHER
YETCHKA IN HER HOME, DUDI VILLAGE

I was so amazed because he was correct, and I wondered how he knew about this incident in my youth. When I was young, I had gone skiing

NADIA IN HER MANCHU CLAN ROBE

on the frozen river. My elder sister, Shura, was angry at me and tried to persuade me to stay home. She told me that it was dangerous and crazy and that I might return home dead. I did not heed her advice because I liked to ski. It was November, around five in the evening, and was growing dark outside. I couldn't see well, and I hit a small patch of ice and flew off my skis and landed on my knee. A young boy, my same age, helped me home. When I arrived, I didn't care about the pain, and I quickly changed my clothes and went back outside to play. My sister was very mad and called me crazy, but what can you say. When it is early evening time, and the Moon is shining brightly on the snow, and looking out at the frozen ice on the river, it looks like glass, it is so beautiful, and besides all of the children were outside playing at this time.

Grandfather Misha explained all that had happened to me, and I thought that shamans could see everything. It was from this time forward that I really began my in-depth studies with the shamans and elders of my village. I began at the time to see Grandmother Tika concerning the pains in my hands, and she helped me with her singing and spirit prescriptions. Then the dreams begin to enter my life to take the shaman road."

· · ·

DUVAN CLAN HOME, BULAVA VILLAGE

Clan Histories

Valdu Family

"This is a story from long, long ago about the clan, the Valdu clan. The Valdu clan came from the city of Gaydi. The Valdu clan came from the Mongol people. They were born in Mongolia. There was much fighting, so our clan traveled downstream. They rowed and rowed and rowed for a very long time. The water flowed and flowed and flowed. They journeyed along the river, and then they stopped. They arrived at a tributary; a little mountain river called an undani. They traveled on the river that led toward the mountain, and one part of the family decided to stay there. Other people arrived later. Many people came and came. One part of our clan traveled toward the sea, and the other part of our family stayed in Mongol village.

"An old man named Neykunu lived in Tualan. Tualan was a small fishing village. He had arrived from the sea territory. Our lake has a large mountain river, and from here is where the old man had traveled to this area. Later he lived in Tuali. He lived there his entire life, and he was from the Valdu clan. A distant relative, another old man, named Gayolonga, lived in Mongol village and had seven sons. After that, seven families appeared, and we were born from one of these families. We took care of each other. The older brothers and younger brothers took care of each other. One of the brothers, an old man, named Hosembu, was my grandfather.

"These words were addressed to Pusandi Valdu. Pusandi is my father's brother and my uncle. Another younger uncle is named Chomo Valdu, and his father was Saldangi, and his grandfather's name was Detungi, and his father was Choka Pusandi, and his father was called Kapati, and his father's name was Chopo. The father of Chopo was named Gentungi, and the father of Kilo was Navsaka. Enough! That is all that I remember this legend. The grandmother of my husband told me this story."

• • •

"This is the story of how and where the Valdu clan appeared. Our Valdu clans are not real Ulchi people, so how shall I tell you correctly about the clan? There was a clan in the upper reaches of the Sungari River. We lived in a city called Vali. Long ago, the city existed during the reign of the Manchu Emperor. They lived in this city. Nobody knew any legends. No one had legends to tell. In that Manchurian location on the Sungari River, the people were called Manju. There was a great war in that region of Manchuria. Who fought with our clan? It was the Mongol clan who lived in Mongolia. They made war with us. The Emperor of Manchuria sent our clan to the war. We went, and other clans were sent. Some of our clan members went to the war, and others just

GRANDMOTHER TIKA ANGA WITH THE VALDU CLAN DRUM

remained in Vali. People could not stay and survive in this location, so we decided to run away.

Later, after we ran away, five men from the same mother and father traveled from Sunsina through Manchuria, along the Sungari River. So they ran away. Where shall we go on the Sungari River? Two men traveled downstream, and three men traveled upstream. The people who traveled upstream went to the Tatar Sea. The two men who journeyed downstream traveled to the Amur River through the Sungari. They traveled for many years through the Sungari. The land was called Na Khalbu.

There is another territory called Undani. Undani is on the other side of Na Khalbu and is located at the mouth of a mountain river. In that place, two boats with two families arrived. One boat traveled to one side of the river, and the other boat traveled to the opposite shore. These boats stayed there, and from this time, these two boats (families) were divided. One of the boats that traveled to the mouth of the mountain river founded a village.

So, the people traveling down the stream came to Tualan. This place was located near the village of Mai, which is a short distance from the village of Auri. They came here as fishermen. Who knows how many years they lived there or how much time had passed. People who lived there were very strong and had great eyesight. They could see clearly from a very long distance. They were Valdu.

So, a long time passed, and in that place, Mongol village, one family lived, and their name was Sugdali. They lived peacefully with the people already there and decided to come together and unite into one clan. They became relatives in spirit. These people together came to Mongol village. This is the legend about the Valdu clan that I tell you now. We remember it, and we pass it down to the younger people."

• • •

VILLAGE ELDERS, CA. 1960

KUYSALI CLAN MEMBERS, SUKIN KUI (MIDDLE), CA. 1920

KUYSALI CLAN

GRANDMOTHER NADIA:

The Kuysali clan lived in the Kurile Islands and traveled to Sakhalin Island. There were three brothers, but they called themselves Kui, not Kuysali. They were Ainu. They decided to escape from that territory. There had been a smallpox epidemic that broke out on the island, so they were searching for new lands in which to hunt and fish and make a new life. One brother stayed in Sakhalin, and one brother traveled to Tir, and the last brother journeyed up the Amur to the village of Udan near Marinsk. Udan was later completely covered by the rising waters of the Amur River. There was a great flood, but after the waters receded, no one came back to rebuild in that place. They decided to search out the territory for a new home.

They traveled down the river until they arrived at the village of Auri. My mother and her three brothers lived in Udan for a long time but moved to Auri after the village was destroyed by the rising waters. My mother, Goga, and her brothers traveled from Udan to Pulsa and later landed in Auri village. It is in Auri where my mother met my father, Dumbin Duvan. After her marriage to my father, the family traveled south, up the river, to Bulava village.

My mother, Goga, and her sister Ama talked about the Kuysali clan. Their father was named Sukin, and the clan was very rich. In their territory were many storage houses. One was for meat, fish, silk, and furs. Sukin Kuysali would sell and trade these goods to the Manchu merchants who sailed up and down the Amur River in their trading ships. Sukin was also a judge in the territory and was very kind and just in all matters that he decided upon. Grandmother Indyeka also remembered him. He had two wives. All the Kuysali who live in Bulava are the offspring of both of these wives.

· · ·

Dechuli Family

Grandmother Nadia:

My great-grandfather Kui (Goga and Ama's grandfather) was a shaman. The name of my grandmother was Pulmaka from the Dechuli clan. The older name for the Dechuli was Jurchuli. This side of the family was Jurchen in origin. Sukin Kui found Pulmaka, and she became his wife. A very strong son was born to Sukin and Pulmaka, and his name was Daga. My great-grandfather was a medium-powerful shaman. After he gave a healing ceremony, he would fly to the shaman's tree.

· · ·

Duvan Family

Grandmother Nadia:

The Duvan clan came from Sakhalin Island. They were part Nivkhi and Ainu. They left Sakhalin and traveled to De Kastri Bay. The top of the mountain in De Kastri is called Duva. The territory of the Duvan and Olchi stretched from Lake Kadi down the Amur to Auri village. The center of the territory is Bulava. The Dechuli family territory was from Pulsa to Marinsk. In the village of Auri also lived the Rosugbu, Djaksul, and Angin clans. In the village of Mongol were the Valdu and Mai. A long time ago, there were such territories. My father's mother was a great Manju shaman.

· · ·

DUMBIN DUVAN (CENTER) WITH HIS TWO WIVES (EITHER SIDE) AND 7 OF HIS 28 CHILDREN, CA. 1930

TOP • DUVAN CLAN NURSE MAIDS WITH 12 MORE OF THE FAMILY CHILDREN
BOTTOM • DUVAN CLAN EXTENDED FAMILY MEMBERS

TOP • MEMBERS OF PULMAKA ROSUGBU (DUMBIN'S FIRST WIFE) FAMILY
LEFT • PULMAKA ROSUGBU (SEATED) WITH HER FAMILY
RIGHT • GOGA DUVAN (DUMBIN'S SECOND WIFE)

CHAPTER 9

Legends and Foundations of Ulchi Shamanism

There are many oral histories that speak of the first shamans and the unique circumstances that brought them to this vocation. The oldest is the Legend of the First Shaman, which lays the foundation for the shaman's relationship to the mythic World Tree. Another legend tells of a woman becoming the first shaman and constructing the first shaman's drum. These oral histories about the ancestral shaman are retold during the farewell ceremony for the deceased.

LEGEND OF THE FIRST SHAMAN

People had lived on the earth for years and years when suddenly, one day, three Suns rose above the Amur River. The earth became so hot that the water began to boil, animals and fish began to die, and the rocks began to melt. The people called the most skilled marksman and hunter, *Khadai*, to come and help them. He traveled to the side of the mountain just before the sun rose, and waited for the three suns to once again make their appearance. As they rose, he picked up his bow and arrows and shot at the two offending suns. His arrows found their mark, and only one Sun remained in the sky.

Quickly, tranquility returned to the earth, but this cosmological event set another misfortune into motion upon the earth. The number of people increased more and more, but nobody died. Then *Khadai* took up the next task, opening the gates of the underworld to the land of the dead, *Buni*. People began to die, and their souls went forth to the kingdom of the ancestors, to be revived on the tribal celestial tree of souls.

The hunter, *Khadai*, returned home and saw that the people had died, but nobody had buried them to allow them to travel to the kingdom of *Buni*. The dead were confused as they did not know how to travel to the land of the deceased. They could not travel on their own. They needed a shaman's help, for only shamans knew the secret roads to the underworld.

Khadai went to sleep and had a wondrous dream. He saw in his dream a powerful and frightening mammoth. This ancestor taught him how to become a shaman. *Khadai* journeyed into the forest and saw the shaman tree. There were bronze mirrors and round copper bells hanging from its branches. On the top of the tree hung the iron horns (cones of a *yampa*), and the bark of the tree was made from frog skin, while the roots were nine gigantic snakes.

The ancestor spirit taught *Khadai* how to make the shaman's clothing. "Go to the forest!" the mammoth said. "Get the skin of a bear, a wolf, and a lynx and make them into a hat. Wear the iron horns and bells. Fasten the bronze mirrors to your breast and on your back. Make a belt from the iron horns and bells. The belt and the drum will carry you into the world of the dead when you wish. The assistant spirits, *Buchu* (a mountain spirit) and the iron bird, *Koori*, will help you to return to the land of the living." (In this legend *Khadai* is portrayed as male, but historically *Khadai* is also seen as a female huntress).

222

THE WORLD TREE

The World Tree is the birthplace of a shaman's soul. This soul is called *khargi*, and the shaman's life strength emerges from this transmogrified state of consciousness. The contour and shape of the tree is that of a human figure. On the ground, near the roots of the tree, the deer was born for the shaman. The tree is envisioned as a Siberian larch—because of its height and strength, the tree considered closest to Heaven—and the shaman's drum is constructed from such wood. Ulchi history speaks of the World Tree as growing on the top of a large hill near a lake in the center of the Earth. The shamans report that this Tree grows from the earth's surface to the upper reaches of space.

There are also celestial trees of souls specific to each clan. The souls of the ancestors, in the form of birds, sit upon the branches of these trees. Shamans will speak to these bird-ancestors to gain knowledge and instruction about the spirits of the world. These bird-ancestors can also be instrumental in fulfilling any request made by the shaman.

The life force of each human being is connected to a particular tree of a specific species. Each family also has their special tree, their *tudja*, which is connected to the health, welfare, and success of all the family members. Besides the World Tree, each shaman also has their special *tudja* on the earth. Since the shaman's life and strength are dependent upon the World Tree, their new life's vocation is explained and clarified near the location of their sacred tree.

In their oral history, the ancestor Mammoth spirit took *Khadai* away into the world of spirits, where s/he was reborn as a half-human, half-spirit being. This gave the shaman the ability to shapeshift into plants, animals, stones, and even thunderstorms. The new shaman soul was born and placed in a nest that hung on the World Tree. The strength and ability of the new shaman were connected with the specific location on the branch where the soul was situated. Some histories say that the life of each clan was also imbedded in the same tree.

The World Tree penetrates all levels in the three worlds: the Upper World, which connects to the Tree of Souls; the Middle World, which is the place of shamanic abilities, skill, and strength; and the Lower World, called the Tree of Ancestors, which is the place of the shaman's reincarnation.

MAMMOTH PETROGLYPH, AMUR RIVER REGION, KHABAROVSK KRAI

SHAMANISM OF THE ULCHI

The word shaman is a mispronunciation by early explorers of the original word, *sama*. Originating from the Manchu-Tungus language, of which the Ulchis speak the southern dialect, *sama* combines the two words *sa*, meaning "knowing," and *ma*, meaning "strong or powerful." The term *sama* (shaman) would be best translated as "strong knowing or knowledge."

There is no doctrine concerning the vocation and art of shamanism among the Ulchi. Shamanism is an amalgam of beliefs and techniques handed down to the individual from the clan as well as from unrelated members of the culture. Woven together with certain externally transmitted instructions are the individual's own interpretations and meanings gained from their personal experiences and contact with the spirits. This contact with the spirit world can take place in dreams or other involuntary or self-induced hypnogogic/hypnopompic states of consciousness. If a shaman's mother or father also practices as a shaman, the child will be taught their specific clan's approach to the vocation, yet this knowledge will be blended with the individual's experiential interpretation and the combined knowledge will be concretized into a hybrid form. A new shaman stands to inherit the shamanic tools of her/his ancestors because a shaman's tools are never buried after the shaman's death. Instead, they are kept safe within the family and are handed down to members of the younger generations who receive the shaman's call.

This was true in Grandmother Tika's life, as she was a seventh-generation shaman with an unbroken lineage. Ritual elements, such as Manchu/Jurchen clan spirits, were passed down to Tika, who incorporated them into her individual practice.

Grandfather Misha's people originated from the modern Sakha regions, formerly known as the Yakut territories. He was raised by his grandparents, whom he called mother and father, and was introduced to his practice not only by his shaman grandfather and shaman brother but by instructions from the great shaman Altaka Olchi. Misha's conjurings combined Yakut, Negadal, and Ulchi elements.

Each new shaman is taught the traditions of the art by their family members and elder mentors along the way. They then go on to pass this knowledge, along with their personal understanding of the shamanic art, down to those they deem worthy of these inner secrets. Their successors, in turn, will absorb this knowledge and combine it with their own interpretations and will pass this down to the next generation, and so forth. Each generation of shamans builds their vocation from previously constructed foundations, with the essential understanding that the process is organic, dynamic, progressive, and that it grows out of the past. They are entrusted with the solemn duty of passing all that they have come to understand to future shamans within the culture.

The shaman is not only the healer and carrier of tradition but the artist and poet of the invisible worlds. That which was noted by the early explorers who witnessed and observed shamanic rites would be best understood as the framework that gave rise to a shamanic performance. What remains unchanged even today within the tradition are the elements, background, and ambiance of the ritual surroundings.

CLASSIFICATION OF SHAMANS

1. Shamans who conjure for themselves alone

2. Shamans who tell fortunes

3. Shamans who work only with the souls of children

4. Shamans who work with the souls of children and adults

5. Kasa (psychopomp) shamans who lead the souls of the departed into the next world

Shamans can belong to one or more of these categories. Any shaman will conduct ceremonies for their own sake, and during a personal conjuring, they are developing their relationships to their helping spirits, performing self-healing, and practicing the skills of their vocation. Grandmother Tika told fortunes, healed adult clients, and was a *Kasa* specialist. Grandmother Ama told fortunes but conjured for herself alone. Grandfather Misha worked with the souls of adults and performed an ancient *Kasa* style of contacting the dead while performing the tree/platform ritual.

A person can be called to the vocation of shamanism during childhood or adult life. Sometimes a person is chosen at birth for this special talent. If a child is born with a cowl over their head, with special birthmarks or moles on their body, as a twin, or on the day of a special astronomical event, such as a lunar or solar eclipse, they may become a candidate for the road of a shaman. If a person comes from a family of shamans, the spirit of their bloodline may call them to take up this vocation. A person may also become a shaman in the absence of these specific conditions.

Ba Enduri, the Great Spirit of Heaven, chooses who will become a shaman. Whatever the circumstances of their life may be, a person is always chosen by the spirits, and their initial contact will come through dreams or unusual experiences in daily life. The spirits will teach the candidate all of the lessons necessary in becoming a shaman: how to call the spirits, sing, and take the shaman's road, and what tools and shamanic clothing they will need for this work.

The spirits are the primary teachers, and the relationship with them becomes the focal point of the candidate's life. Living shamans are

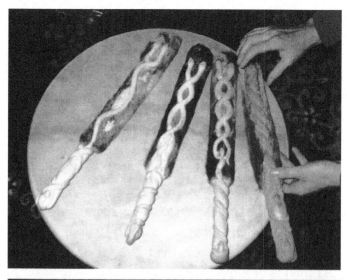

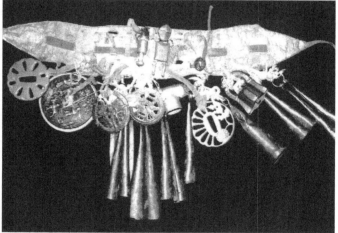

TOP • VARIOUS STYLES OF GESPU WITH ULCHI DRUM
BOTTOM • KUYSALI CLAN YAMPA

advisors, secondary teachers, colleagues, and initiators for a novice. Special rituals are conducted by the living shamans to help open the roads and secure the ways for a fledging shaman. A new shaman may also consult experienced shamans about dreams, visions, and other experiences that the novice encounters as they enter their shamanic vocation.

Spirits are not controlled or subjugated by the shaman as a rule, but sometimes a helping spirit may become fractious or disobedient, at which point a shaman must employ means to restrain such behavior. The spirits are in charge of the work. A shaman must listen and do everything that the spirits request of them. If the shaman fails to do so, illness can befall them and members of their family.

Novice shamans will spend a great deal of time getting to know their spirit helpers. They have entered a secret university taught by spirits and will spend their time in introspective solitude, away from family members and friends. Their curriculum involves working with their dreams, practicing the drum, and learning special rhythms for calling the various spirits. They will be given a unique melody and will be shown how to perform special rituals. They will be taught by these spirits throughout their entire shamanic career.

The beginning years of the vocation can be psychologically and physically difficult, and the comradeship of other shamans is thus very important to the newcomer. Novice shamans can explain any difficulties they are encountering to experienced shamans or ask questions of them. These elder shamans can sympathize, give hints, and tell them what to look for or expect when they begin to develop their skills in the world of the spirits. They will also remind novices that their ultimate understanding of this process will be imparted by their spirit helpers, not their shamanic colleagues.

COMMENTARIES

GRANDMOTHER TIKA:

If a person is to become a shaman in the future, then the shamans and old people will see this because they will recognize this talent from the moment that they were born on this earth. They will watch this child grow and say among themselves, "This child will probably become a shaman." Children who walk with a heavy step upon this earth will grow into shamans. Children who walk lightly upon the land will never be shamans, so those who walk heavily upon the earth will find their shamanic talents in the future. If you are a shaman, you will quickly recognize your path.

•

The novice shamans may not know how to sing or play the drum rhythms. The novice will begin by taking up the drum and drumstick and just begin as the spirits will teach everything.

••

Grandmother Nadia:

The art of shamanizing has been passed down to us from generation to generation; the roots of our oldest clans are buried in the depths of a thousand centuries. Our shamans are entrusted with the honorable mission of saving our people from natural, spiritual, and other catastrophes. They predict and control the weather, blessed the hunters and fishermen with success, drive harmful spirits away from people, and heal the sick. They are the wisdom keepers of the traditional laws and oral histories. Because the selection of a shaman can occur at any point in one's lifetime, from two to ninety-two years of age, this calling is usually accompanied by unusual dreams, cosmic visions, and estrangement from one's own life. Shamans walk the roads of the Sky; travel on or under the Water or the Earth.

There is a shamanic ranking, the most powerful being the Kasa shamans, who lead the souls of the departed into the land of the dead. The Dai (great) or Manga (strong) shamans work in healing and protecting both the souls of children and adults. As a mediator between spirits and ancestors, these shamans also have powerful and accurate clairvoyant abilities. The Bibe or Nuchka shaman is usually a term given to a beginning shaman. These ranks indicate the developmental stages of shamanism: beginning, medium, and strong shamans.

•

Each shaman differs in their approaches to healing. Some are very good when it comes to divining, and some of them are less strong in that area, but they all heal children in the same way. Children's spirits are always held and protected by the shaman in the North Star, a larch tree, or in the stony mountains. They would always keep the children's souls separate from the adult souls.

•

Shamans do not open their souls (divulge secret information) to just anyone, and getting close enough to them to have a deep personal relationship is very difficult.

•

A shaman can only pass down their knowledge to a person who has been chosen by Nature. A person who can see into the future or who has healing talents can be given secret knowledge.

•

A shaman is not a person with extrasensory powers. A shaman is a natural phenomenon.

•

I remember Grandfather Misha saying, "Just take up the drum and begin to play. Your spirits will teach you everything. They will give you your song and rhythms. Just remember well everything that the spirits teach you!

CHAPTER 10

• • •

Initiation and the Shaman's Path

A person does not make a conscious choice to take on the vocation of shamanism nor do they seek an established shaman to apprentice with, as this honor and profession will be determined by spirit visitations. It is important that the "shamanic road" be opened by living shamans in a series of up to six conjurings. These sessions/initiations may be given by one specific living shaman or may be procured through various shamans at different times during the beginning phases of one's shamanic vocation. The name for this type of initiatory session is a *Khasisi* ritual. I asked Grandmother Nadia whether there was a specific *yiyee* (song) that the established shamans sang to open the road of a new potential shaman, and she said each shaman would help to open the novice shaman's road in their own unique way.

When a beginning shaman is first starting out, it is wise for them to enlist the aid of more experienced shamans. This can be the most unsettling time for the candidate because with this period comes great confusion, fear, and trepidation. A person may encounter unusual dreams, auditory and visual hallucinations, or other events that may cause them to undergo a psychospiritual crisis in their everyday life.

Grandfather Misha was hospitalized twice in his life for these very conditions. There was a time when he left his village and stayed for many weeks alone in the taiga. He had been feeling very ill for a long time and was prompted by the spirits to make this expedition. No one was able to locate him during this period, and his family thought that he had possibly been killed or had died in some tragic accident. He traveled to a grove of trees and decided to spend the night there. During the night, the Tree spirits of the grove spoke to him. They told him that they were his new protectors and that this geographical terrain would become a place of great healing for him. He didn't divulge any more details about this experience, although it was a turning point in his shamanic path. The second time was when he was found wandering naked throughout the village in an agitated trance-like state, incapable of communicating in any coherent fashion. He endured this second hospitalization for two or three months, slowly finding the road back to his own health and sanity.

These psychopathogenic states, or sufferings of the soul, are the initiatory stages brought on by first contact with the spirit world. They are called *keselemi*, or tortures, and a novice shaman will undergo long periods of symptoms, such as dysthymia, anxiety, and various dissonant disorders. Usually, these adjustment periods can plague the shaman for many years.

Over time, a shaman will learn to manage these new cognitive and emotional states that impinge upon them from seemingly outside sources and events from the spirit world. Their personality will be altered permanently as they adapt to this new state of consciousness. When interacting with others, they will seem to be simultaneously attentive to the occurrences around them and preoccupied or distracted by their internal experiences. These so-called distractions are due to their discussions with spirits, which occur at various intervals throughout the day and night. Grandmother Tika would remark that she was a victim of sleep deprivation, as her spirits would come in the night and keep her from resting until the dawn of the next day.

During this time, they would provide news or insights concerning her clients or affairs of the village.

The shamanic path is not an undertaking that anyone consciously seeks because it is always fraught with various psychological and physical problems from beginning to end. This discomfort or illness can also carry over to affect family members. When the call comes, it is almost impossible to cast aside or reject because the only known antidote to one's sufferings is to accept the will of the spirits by taking up the art of shamanizing.

COMMENTARIES

GRANDMOTHER NADIA:

For an Ulchi, a shaman is a most respected person. A shaman is the bearer of the people's culture and language. If a person receives the gift of shaman hood and doesn't accept it, the person's external and internal life force will suffer. This majestic energy, visions in dreams and while awake, will force them to become a shaman. This is a mission brought on by the Dragon spirit in the sky. A future shaman who had been subjected to an attack of spirits cannot avoid their compulsion to begin their practice. Usually, a primordial involuntary connection with the spirits leads to the chosen one's being burdened with a psychological hell, evoking in this hell not only spiritual tortures but physical suffering as well. A real shaman suffers through paranormal phenomena with great intensity.

•

When other shamans sing for you, they help at the beginning to open the shaman's road for you. This is the beginning phase of an initiation of a new shaman. It is necessary to do this. The name for this is Khasisi. The word itself means "to catch up" or to "drive toward." The older shaman will sing/explain the road for the novice shaman. The novice shaman learns from the old shaman. When the old shaman makes a yiyee for a new shaman, the new shaman hears all the old shaman's song and advice that is being given. You will learn from the song. Sometimes a young shaman may go to an old shaman, pleading and saying, "I've lost my road, please help me! I cannot do this!" Sometimes the spirits speak so quickly that you "can't catch up." This is when you say, "Please slow down, spirits. I cannot take all of this information so quickly.

Now, for Grandmother Ama, the shamans only sang half of her road, and that is why she became an Isachula but never became a great shaman. For myself, well, Grandmother Indyeka gave me a yiyee. She sang a special song that opened my Masi and Ajaha spirit road. She called/gave me these two spirit helpers that came from the Cosmos.

Grandmother Indyeka sang for my road three times. Grandmother Tika sang for my road two times, and Grandfather Misha sang for my road one time. They found and gave me my spirit helpers and amulets."

.

When the novice shaman begins their work, they will find that first; they will develop the abilities of an Isachula/Nairigda (two different names for clairvoyant abilities).

.

I remember Grandmothers Tika, Ama, Indyeka, and Grandfather Misha saying so many similar things to me when I began my shaman's road. They told me not to be afraid. They said to sing and dance for myself and to sing for my family because in doing this, I will find my own power, my own road, and my own spirit helpers. They told me not to keep such energy inside my own body because the tension will build up inside myself. They said that if I don't release and channel the energy, that I would become very ill and that my own power would help me to discover my own road or shaman's work. If you have shamans in your family, a father or mother, and you begin to get the shaman's call, then your parent may ask or beg you to continue the work that they have started. Usually, the child will refuse, but the parent will continue to beg them to learn while the parent is still alive so that they can teach the child and help them at the beginning of their shamanic path.

••

Grandmother Ama:

Sometimes newer shamans become ill because they don't sing and dance or make a conjuring. If you don't sing and dance, you will never find your shaman's road nor find your spirit helpers. That is why you must sing and dance with a yampa. After this, you will feel better.

•

Grandmother Enka Dyatala was a great shaman grandmother. She said to me, "You have a straight shaman way about you, without any corners, and that is why I wanted to make a Khasisi for you.

•

If a person were called to their shamanic road, then all of the old people would teach and help. Those who traveled along this path must always respect the natural laws that are taught by the elders.

••

Grandmother Linza:

New shamans may find their own illnesses, and they need to sing, dance, and use the yampa to help themselves. In this way, they will find the shaman's road and their spirit helpers.

•

When I am ill, I never sing for people, because I don't have the strength or power so how can I sing? I was fifty years old when

I received the shaman's call. I got seriously ill, and I had sixty spirit helpers. I saw in a dream an old Chinese man laughing at me. That's all.

..

Grandmother Tika:

A shaman should sing the road for a new shaman at least six times. If you only have a singing for you one or two times, then you will not become an Isachula/Nairigda.

•

I received my calling when I was fourteen or fifteen years old. My father guided me along my path. In the beginning, my father wanted me to take this road, but I didn't want to, but I was forced. Being a seventh-generation shaman, I found spirit helpers who had served my shaman relatives in the past, along with my own new spirit helpers. When still awake, I would lie down to rest in the evenings. I began to feel a presence close to my heart that was woolly and furry. One day, I looked and saw it was a tiger! In fear, I ran away to my father and mother's bed. I spoke to my father, and he listened to me without uttering a word. One day, I see in my dreams that my stomach began growing. Before this, the tiger came nightly to my dreams, summer, and winter, and I slept with him like man and wife. I gave birth to two tiger children. I didn't want them. I didn't accept them. I was ashamed to think that I had given birth to animals. I gave them back to their tiger father. Later, that tiger keeps visiting me in my dreams and once again we were together like man and wife. I gave birth to three more tiger cubs, and I took their souls for myself, the souls of the tiger children. These three tiger children of mine are who I call to help me when I am conjuring. I ride upon their backs when I make a journey. They are flying tigers with wings. My father worked his shaman's magic on me so that I would become a shaman. He made a road for me, a road to the Sky, to the Taiga, and along the great Water. He showed and taught me things and protected me from accidents and illnesses.

Before I began my shaman's road, I experienced many tortures. I was very sick, and I suffered greatly to become a shaman. My spirits dragged me everywhere, and I suffered very much. If you obey the spirits' will, then you will become a shaman. I didn't want to be a shaman, but I had constant visions in my dreams. A voice forced me and dictated to me what I should do. Day and night, there was no peace, and I was afflicted with constant pain, so I had to become a shaman.

•

Several times, I had dreams of walking where there were obstacles and where I flew as if on wings. Throughout the Upper, Middle, and Lower World, there are dangers also.

••

Grandfather Misha:

Sometimes I wanted to sing, but I didn't know why. My words just appeared by themselves to me. I'll tell you how I became a shaman. Great shamans sang for me when I was ill, when I had diseases, and maybe that is why they gave me some power to become a shaman. I don't know what they did, so I am not a shaman. No one initiated me to the shaman's way, just Grandmother Altaka Olchi. She sang for me to the three levels of the world. She made an offering to the South, North, and East. These are the three parts of the world. She did not make an offering to the West because this is the direction to the land of the dead. I was good and followed all of her advice. So then she said to me, "If you do not follow all the rules to this ritual, then you will feel bad and ill and not live well. You will find diseases and torments and suffer greatly. If you follow these rules, then you will live a happy and healthy long life. When you make your offerings, place your staff near the tudja or tie it to the tree. You don't want to lay it on the ground." I remember the old shamans saying to me that I will become a great ponga (fortune telling), shaman. I have never given a ponga to any person.

.

Grandmother Altaka Olchi's daughter said to me that maybe her mother made me a shaman. Altaka sang for me and sukpungi (bit) the top of my head. She could not find my soul when she sang for me. She said I needed more singing, but she died before she finished her work on me to find my soul's road. She only did half of the work. When she was alive, she said to me to go outside and make myself a special tudja and then to make offerings to this tree.

. . .

The *Khasisi* initiations are necessary as a novice begins their shamanic vocation. Without the proper rituals, a candidate may only excel in their intuitive abilities and may not truly understand the deeper secrets of the shamanic road. Clairvoyant abilities must be developed and finely honed before the novice is capable of beginning their otherworld exploits among the spirits. Although in the Ulchi tradition, the spirits are the primary teachers, the aid of experienced shamans is necessary, as they help to provide through discussion a type of experiential road map to the invisible worlds and serve as the "opener of the ways" for the new shaman. As the beginner finds their spirits through their dreams, a more experienced shaman is called upon to open the road of that particular spirit for the candidate.

The elder shaman will divulge information about the spirit's road to the novice and instruct them as to any ritual or action that may be requested by the particular spirit.

Experienced shamans will also test the candidate while listening to questions being asked by the novice. The stages of shaman hood must contain specific experiences that take place both in ordinary life and in the dream state. If the novice does not have these predefined experiences or cannot describe the details of the secret invisible landscapes, their claims of "being called to take the shaman's road" may be in error.

There is a great difference between having spirit visitations and dream world journeys versus actually being called to take the shamanic path. The novice must describe certain hidden facts. If the candidate passes all of the tests, the elder shaman will serve as the initial go-between or host, making the proper introductions between candidate and spirits.

GRANDMOTHER ALTAKA OLCHI (SECOND FROM LEFT) WITH HER FAMILY, BULAVA VILLAGE

During a conjuring, a shaman may encounter deceased shamans who were helpers and teachers during their lifetimes as well as protectors of their soul during childhood. Grandmother Nadia is constantly aided by Grandfather Misha and Grandmother Tika while traveling in the invisible worlds. Even in death, they may occasionally send her down the wrong road or block her way. Their help and instruction are never ceasing, but, even as they did in life, they will test her skills from time to time. During one of her conjurings, I noticed a small female apparition standing in the doorway, and I asked Grandmother Nadia who this might be. She answered that it was Grandmother Ponga Valdu, who protected her soul when she was a child. This shaman grandmother still watches over her after all these years.

Chapter 11

Shamanic Tools and Clothing

Shaman's Pillar or Sacred Tree

The sacred pillar of the shaman is called *daro*, *toro*, or *tudja*. This pillar is either a larch tree or a type of carved totemic pillar. At the base of this pillar is found the encampment of the shaman's helping spirits, such as the *Masi* (house spirit), *Buchu* (mountain-sky spirit), and *Amba* (tiger) or other personal helping spirits. These spirits use the *tudja* to ascend and descend between the invisible worlds and the Middle World of the human being. Many shamans will begin their shamanic flight through the *tudja*, while others may begin by flying off the top of a mountain or directly ascending into the sky toward special stars. Each shaman begins their ascent in their own unique and individual fashion.

Drum

There are two types of drums used by the Ulchi. The older style is elliptical form. This egg-shaped drum (*umtahu*) is between 28 and 40 inches in diameter. The current style is round, and its diameter measures between 20 and 22 inches. Each Ulchi family possesses at least one drum. These family drums are passed down from generation to generation. Shamans may employ as many as three different drums that are used for specific healing ceremonies, funeral rites, or special rituals.

Whether round or elliptical, the back of the drum is constructed with a flexible set of four straps, allowing the musician to play both sides of the instrument. The front of the drum is struck with the drumstick, while the back is punched with a closed fist or tapped with the fingers while the straps are held. These leather straps represent the roads that a shaman takes to the invisible worlds of the spirits. They also represent the four directions: south, east, north, and west. These straps are connected in the center with a small metal ring. This small center ring is both the physical and soul of the earth while the rim of the drum symbolizes the universe. The straps, or shaman roads, originate from the center ring, the earth, and extend out to the rim of the drum, into the universe.

Although ancient legends may speak of the use of deerskin for the membrane of the drum, the Ulchis prefer goatskin. This type of material has a musically brighter quality. Heavier and thicker skins, such as deer or elk, give the drum a flatter, deeper, or lower tone. The skin is stretched around the rim and glued to the frame using sturgeon bladders, called *darpu*, which have been boiled and processed into a natural adhesive. Images of a shaman's personal spirits, animal helpers, and other designs may or may not be painted on the front or back of the drum face.

The drum is a living spirit that assists and protects the shaman during the journey. Prior to a conjuring, the shaman tests the "voice" of the drum. If this voice does not produce the specific tone required, the shaman will not journey to the invisible worlds. The shaman will exclaim that the spirit of the drum does not wish to be played or is angry or displeased in some manner. It can be a common experience that the people who show up for a conjuring are told by the shaman to go home and come back the next night, as the spirit of the drum does

GRANDMOTHER YETCHKA AND HER THREE
DRUMS, PERSONAL SAVENS (LEFT), AND
YAMPA (FRONT), BULAVA VILLAGE

not wish to sing and travel now. This does not occur frequently but can happen from time to time. Because this is understood within the culture, the people will depart, hoping that the drum spirit will be in a better mood, happier, and willing to work the next time they arrive.

As noted, shamans may own multiple drums, each designated for various types of conjuring. The drums are always stored in some type of bag and are only taken out when they are played. These bags are constructed either of leather, cloth, or fish skin.

Drums are cleansed by the smoke of the Labrador tea (*sankura*) prior to a conjuring and are often given alcohol offerings during the healing. The alcohol is usually placed upon the center ring, one of the four leather straps, or the rim of the drum. After a shaman dies, their personal drum(s) are kept safe by family members. These drums are later passed down to future shamans born within the family.

Within the Ulchi culture, a shaman is the only person to accompany themselves on a drum during a journey. The language of the rhythms mirrors the action that is occurring simultaneously in the spirit worlds. Not only does the shaman sing the narrative description of the journey that is unfolding, but the drum reflects or imitates the actions as well. If the shaman is climbing a tall mountain, the drumbeats may sound slow and difficult, expressing the arduous physicality of the ascent; or if they find themselves flying through the heavens, the rhythms will be light and quick as if soaring and floating. Meeting powerful spirits is accompanied by loud, abrupt beats, and resting on celestial clouds is quiet and steady. These drum rhythms, accompanied by the rich and complex narrative; make the shaman a complete improvisational artist

DUVAN CLAN DRUM AND GESPU

246

who expresses the feelings, apprehensions, actions, and geography of the spiritual realms.

There is only one section of the journey in which the shaman may not use the drum, and this is during the healing song. This is the part of the conjuring where the shaman will use either their drumstick or wooden shavings to clear the client's body of unwanted spirits and negative energy that have fastened themselves to the client. It then becomes the duty of the shaman's assistant to play a slow and steady beat in cadence to the shaman's healing song, if requested by the shaman.

COMMENTARIES

GRANDMOTHER TIKA:

My father passed on all of his shamanic tools to me. When first you become a shaman, they tie your arms and legs with wooden streamers. Some shamans would have two drums. One drum would be for children, and the other one for adult souls to conjure with against any type of sickness. If a drum breaks, it is either repaired, or a new one is constructed. Some shamans would make drawings on the drum head of a snake with three heads. They were the shaman's assistants. Mine has the image of the spirit master on my drum. When you beat the drum for the first time, you will recognize immediately whether the conjuring will be good. If the drum sounds bad, then the conjuring will be bad. If the spirit master of the drum takes pity on you, then the conjuring will work out fine.

..

GRANDMOTHER NADIA:

Most Ulchi households have a least one drum that can be used by any of the family members. When you are feeling a little ill or emotionally depressed, then go and pick up the drum and play it for a while. Playing the drum will help to heal you, and your soul will feel better and a little lighter.

•

From the very first strike, the spirits fly and position themselves on the rim of the drum. They ride along the rim during a conjuring.

• • •

Drumstick

The drumstick, called a *gespu*, serves multiple purposes. It calls in the shaman's spirits and is a primary tool for healing. A shaman may use the drumstick to touch various parts of a client's body for healing purposes, to capture spirits, or to drive unhealthy spirits from the physical body. The *gespu* has its own soul and is controlled by its indwelling spirit. The design of the drumstick may vary, but they are usually ten to fifteen inches in length. They are constructed from wood and naturally curve toward the end of the drumstick at an angle of ten to thirty-five degrees. A piece of fur, usually from the foreleg of an elk, is glued to the bottom. This fur runs under the entire length, from the end of the drumstick to where the handle begins. The top of the drumstick may have various personal spirit helpers carved into the wood.

Commentary

Grandmother Dalika:

In the past, when my husband was alive, I found great pain in my hand. My husband made a shaman's drumstick for me. On the top of the drumstick was carved a great snake, and the head of a bear was carved at the end of the handle. The snake on top was painted red. From time to time, here and there, my hand became healthy and well.

• • •

YAMPA

METAL SPIRIT BELT

The shaman's spirit belt is called a *yampa*. Its sound is used to protect and drive away evil spirits. When the shaman re-enters the human world after a conjuring, the noise produced by the metal cones hanging from the belt drives off any offending spirits that may have attached themselves to the shaman during the journey in the invisible worlds. Harmful spirits are frightened by the noise of clanking metal of all types (including pots and pans), and will quickly depart. These spirit belts vary in style and shape. The metal cones, made from iron or steel, are between seven and ten inches in length. There can be as few as five and as many as seventeen metal cones on a belt. There are usually odd, rather than even, numbers of cones. Along with the metal cones, other types of metal pieces are found on these belts. These include bronze pendants, pieces of chain, small metal bells, and so forth. The *yampa* can weigh as little as four and as much as twenty pounds. The metal pieces are placed at the back of the belt. The shaman plays the *yampa* while dancing. It swings back and forth on the shaman's hips in counter rhythm to the beats of the drum. The *yampa*, like all shamanic tools, is alive and has its own Spirit master. Sometimes, wooden amulets are sewn to the belt. Each metal belt is created in a unique style particular to its owner.

Commentary

Grandmother Nadia:

I remember asking Grandmother Ama about using Grandmother Tika's yampa after she died. I said to Grandmother Ama, "Everyone is using it when they dance at the elder gatherings. Is it permissible to do so?

Grandmother Ama replied, "Now when it comes to using a deceased shaman's yampa, you must take a few things into consideration. Before Grandmother Altaka died, she didn't want anyone to use her yampa after her death. That is why it was taken to her granddaughter's house for safekeeping. Altaka Olchi was a great and powerful shaman. She was a jakpachi shaman (a shaman who had the type of powerful spirits that could kill you). If you take and use anything from these types of shamans, then a tragedy may befall you. Don't take or use anything from these types of shamans, especially their shamanic tools and items. Now, Grandmother Tika was a great shaman but not a jakpa shaman. You can use Tika's yampa.

• • •

Magical Staff or Walking Stick

The walking stick is either employed by a shaman or used as a cure or protection for the common person. It is called a *kenapu*.

A shaman's staff is usually constructed from wood. On its upper portion is depicted the head of a shaman's main helping spirit on the road traveled by the shaman. This type of staff can also be the pre-scriptive cure given to the client by their shaman. The shaman will see what spirits to make and will instruct the client to procure the staff and its ritual elements from a specific type of tree. If the staff needs the images of spirit helpers carved onto it, then the shaman will send their client to a specific carver along with their instructions for the creation of the staff.

COMMENTARIES

GRANDMOTHER TIKA:

My husband's leg suffered from great pain, so into the taiga I traveled, and I carried away a branch of a larch tree. I had done a ponga (fortune telling) with my snake spirit made from stone. My husband was in the Great War (WWII), and his leg had been wounded by many bullets, and because of the war, his leg always suffered greatly. Slowly, his leg got better, and it was always fine when he walked with his new kenapu. Everything turned out well.

··

GRANDMOTHER NADIA:

In the past, my leg had great pain. Grandmother Tika said, "Go and help yourself. Go into the taiga and carry out a branch of larch. For women, you want to find a branch that looks like a Y, with these two small pieces extending from the main branch. Take it and carve different spirit helpers on the walking stick. Make a frog and a snake. Your leg will be fine if you take the kenapu and walk with it. It will quickly help the pain in your leg, and it will completely go away. Men never use a kenapu with two branches. They only use a single straight staff.

· · ·

WOODEN STREAMERS

Wooden streamers of willow, rowan, or bird cherry are made into caps or headdresses, arm and leg bands, and belts to be worn around the waist of the shaman during conjurings. They are called *gemsacha* or *sisakun*. The spirit of the particular wood flies into these streamers to provide strength and protection to those parts of the shaman's body during a healing session. They are also tied around the sacred spirit carvings used in bear rituals or funeral rites for shamans, twins, or the mother of twins.

These wooden streamers also serve other purposes. First, they can be employed in any ritual setting in sending prayers and good tidings into the spirit worlds. They can be used by any person who wishes to contact the Spirit of the Forest, Water, Heaven, and so forth. With the help of these streamers, people can create an open dialogue with the spirits. At the same time, the streamers act as nets to catch or repeal destructive forces. Harmful spirits get tangled up and confused if they enter them. They become trapped without an exit.

These wooden streamers are also used by powerful shamans to clean a patient during a session. They act like an antenna connecting the shaman to the patient. When these streamers are placed in the shaman's hands, the shaman will begin to stroke the patient from head to toe in a cleansing fashion. These streamers remove and retain all of the patient's illness. The name of this specific ritual is *Sisajaha* or *Sisayagi*.

COMMENTARIES

GRANDFATHER MISHA:

Without the wooden streamers, you cannot purify yourself or the sick person of harmful spirits.

•

Not a single conjuring over a sick person took place without the use of the gemsacha.

•

Gemsacha is made in the morning before a conjuring.

..

GRANDMOTHER TIKA SPEAKING TO GRANDMOTHER NADIA:

When the lower back is in pain, go and make some gemsacha. Divide the shavings into four piles. Braid each pile together, then take two braided piles and braid them together, then take the other two and braid them like the others. Then you will have two braided pieces. Tie them together around your waist. Make designs on them of a snake and tiger spirit. Wear it and wear it, and slowly you'll feel well.

..

GRANDMOTHER ALTAKA:

A shaman uses the wooden streamers to take the person's illness and transgressions away from them.

...

I have seen Grandmother Nadia use both the streamers and a *gespu* during a conjuring, and I inquired about the difference between using one or the other. She replied, "Grandmother Tika uses her gespu most of the time. Tika said to me once that if a client is not present and the conjuring is long distance, you have no physical body in front of you. To draw the negative energy out, use the gespu because it does the same good work." Grandmother Nadia also remarked that when employing the wooden streamers, a shaman can make a mistake if they don't use them correctly. Like antennas, they can transmit the offending illness from the client directly to the shaman because of their (the streamers) strength.

SPIRIT GATES

For the Ulchi, the most spiritually potent material in nature is wood. Each specific tree has its own magical virtues, but the species that are considered the most powerful and healing are the willow, larch, and rowan. The wooden streamers used to made spirit gates are usually made from one of these woods.

When conducting rituals to trees or the water element, a pair of wooden sticks approximately twelve to sixteen inches in height and one-quarter of an inch wide is taken from one of these trees. At the end of each stick, the wood is thinly sliced into curlicues that are not cut completely away but remain attached to the base of the stick. The two sticks, with the curled shavings on top, are placed in the ground about eight to ten inches apart, either parallel to each other or angled toward one another, creating a triangle with the earth. By placing these ritually carved sticks in either of these geometric positions, an opening to the spirit world naturally occurs.

When one is giving food or liquid offerings to the spirits outdoors, everything has to be delivered through this type of doorway. If a Water ritual is taking place, a little boat laden with offerings is launched through the opening. The wooden curled shavings provide protection from any harmful spirit that might endeavor to enter the human world through the open gate, as the offending spirit would become entangled in them.

SHAMAN'S HEADGEAR

Shamans will own many types of headgear or caps, depending on the type of magical work they conduct. These are called *dayligda* or *apu*. There is headgear for healing, for specific rituals and ceremonies, such as working with children's souls or leading the dead into the next world, and for special occasions. The material may be leather, metal, cotton, or wooden streamers. Different sets of spirits ride aboard each type of cap. The caps made from leather may be two leather straps

crossed over and sewn to a headband, or they may take the form of a skullcap or pillbox or a similar design. If the cap is made from fur, the material may come from the animal spirit that works with the shaman. The cotton cap is usually of a skullcap or pillbox design, and helping spirits made from cotton are sewn onto it. The headbands made from thin wooden strips, or streamers, come from either the rowan, willow, or bird cherry tree. These caps were important spirit helpers employed by Grandmother Tika during healing ceremonies.

Commentary

Grandmother Tika:

When you sing, and the wooden streamer cap falls off, then this is great. All of the illness has been cast off!

. . .

Shaman's Skirt

The skirt, like the headgear, is constructed either of fur, leather, or cotton material. All along the front and the back of the skirt, the designs of specific spirit helpers are drawn, painted, or sewn and embroidered.

The skirt's motifs may be divided into three sections signifying the powers and topography of the three worlds. Spirits of the Cosmos will be found at the top of the skirt, Middle World powers in the center, and Lower World creatures at the bottom, just above the hem of the skirt.

Shaman's Vest

As with the skirt, the material used to make the vest will vary in style and color. Grandmother Yetchka wore a traditional-style Ulchi dress that reached below the knees. She did not wear a specific vest. Grandmother Tika wore an older style of shaman's vest. This was made of white cotton with various spirit helpers embroidered on both the front and the back. Grandmother Nadia wears a very ancient style made from white deer skin with her spirit helpers painted on the front and back. Many bronze mirrors are sewn on both sides of her vest as an added protection against harmful or disruptive invisible beings.

All styles of the shaman's vest will include bird feathers sewn upon both shoulders. This enables the shaman to fly into the world of the cosmos. The vest is never buttoned or closed. It must remain open in front to allow the helpful personal spirits to come and go from inside the body of the shaman.

GRANDMOTHER NADIA WEARING HER SHAMAN'S COAT

The vest, like the skirt, bears the designs of spirits from the three worlds, and these are placed upon the vest in the same way. Upper World spirits reside at the top of the garment, Middle World spirits in the center, and Lower World spirits toward the bottom. Most of the time, the design of a particular shaman's vest would be revealed to the shaman by their spirits helpers in the dream state.

LEFT • ULCHI SHAMAN MASK
RIGHT • BULAVA DANCE ENSEMBLE GIVA, PERFORMING SHAMAN'S DANCE

Shaman's Mask

The mask is always carved in an anthropomorphic form, with images of birds, reptiles, frogs, and other spirit helpers carved on the forehead, cheek, eye, and chin sections. The mask is made from various woods, depending upon the instructions of the individual shaman. Various types of fur are often glued or sewn upon the mask to create the look of hair, eyebrows, or a beard. The use of the mask has been in decline since the late 1940s. Although modern practicing shamans no longer wear a mask, these masks are currently used in sacred dances by members of the Ulchi folk ensembles *Giva* and *Geero*.

Face/Eye Cover

The use of an eye covering is helpful to the shaman during a spirit journey. It helps the shaman to concentrate on the task and remain undisturbed by any movement or light that may be present in the environment. The eye covering is leather and consists of a headband with long fringe that covers the shaman's face. The fringe extends past the nose and ends just above the mouth. Other Ulchi shamans have been known to prefer the use of very dark sunglasses to serve the same purpose as the eye fringe.

Spirit Boots and Gloves

Special seal, elk, or other leather knee-high boots and gloves, decorated with spirit motifs, can be included in the shaman's attire. The spirits placed on these boots and gloves give strength, protection, and endurance to the shaman's legs and hands during a spirit journey.

Bronze Mirrors

The bronze mirror (*toli*) serves various purposes. It is used to deflect negative spirits, capture the wandering soul of a client, or fly to the Sun and converse with the solar inhabitants during a journey. For the shaman, the mirror is associated with the great Bird spirit *Koori*. When owned by a common person, the bronze mirror is used as a personal protective and healing amulet.

The mirror can be between two and twenty-four inches in diameter. These mirrors represent the Sun or Moon spirits. Some of these mirrors are plain, and others may have the intricate designs found among Chinese and other Asian groups. Usually, only one mirror is worn around the neck of the shaman, while many may be attached to the metal spirit belt or sewn onto the front and back of the shaman's ritual vest.

Commentaries

Grandmother Tima:

When I was young, in my childhood, I was always ill. When I got sick, my parents would call for Bogdan Oneka—Bogdan, a great shaman from the Goldi village of Naykhin—to come and help me. He was the grandfather of Vladimir Passar. It was

GRANDMOTHER YETCHKA DRUMMING, BULAVA VILLAGE

around 1928 when I was five years old. This is the first time he came to sing for me. After the healing, he gave me a bronze mirror. My mother had given birth to eleven children who all died except me. Before the conjuring, I saw in a dream a bronze mirror. When I would feel ill, my mother would always take that bronze mirror and put it under my pillow. Usually, this bronze mirror is kept safe in a chest, but when I take it out, I smudge it with the smoke of sankura and tobacco. Later, I feel good and happy.

Grandfather Bogdan was a very great Kasa shaman. He would travel to Bulava to sing. He would sing for me and sing for so many others in my village. I was very young when he first came to our village. I think I was a little child still in my baby cradle.

This toli (bronze mirror) has the design of two fishes and waves of water. These great shamans, from their mouths, made these bronze mirrors appear. As I sat and watched, I would see these shamans mouths move as if they were chewing food. Then slowly they would pull these mirrors out of their mouths. The bronze was very pliable as it came out of their mouths but soon became hard and firm when it came into contact with the air.

I remember Grandfather Bogdan when he sang for me. He would hit himself on the head with a stick. Maybe he had a very hard head. Also under my pillow, my mother would place a katana for my protection and strength. When I am ill, I always take out my bronze mirror and smudge it and make offerings to it, and I then feel better. After my death, I will give this to my nephew, Dimitri Dechuli.

··

Grandmother Nadia:

I remember hearing stories about Grandfather Bogdan from many elders in the village. They said he came to Bulava one time and gave many conjurings to many people on that visit. He gave each and every client a bronze mirror. Many people in Bulava village still have these bronze mirrors.

Shaman's Amulets

Spirit amulets (*savens*) are made of metal, wood, fur, cloth, or plant material such as grass. Shamans wear amulets representative of their spirit helpers. Special amulets made from silver are worn only by shamans, and these usually represent the shaman's main spirit helper. The type of silver spirit varies with each shaman. The spirit must be assigned and given to them by the Cosmos master (*Ba*) in the dream state, and the permission of *Ba* is required before a shaman can wear this silver amulet. It is usually the most important amulet that a shaman wears, and it is worn completely out of sight underneath their shirt. This spirit is worn at all times and is fed every time the shaman has any type of meal. When the shaman sits down to consume food, the first portion is given to this particular spirit. Silver is considered to be the most powerful and spiritual metal among the Ulchis, and amulets dedicated to the Upper World spirits are always constructed of silver. Amulets are the living receptacles of spirits, and those that belong to shamans need to be carefully taken care of after their death.

ALEXANDER KOTKIN'S
SHAMAN BREASTPLATE

COMMENTARIES

GRANDMOTHER TIKA:

I wear all my spirit amulets at the level of my lungs, along with the shaman's pouch with silver. You find your spirit amulets, made of silver, from the cosmos. My silver Ajaha spirit was given to me by Ba.

•

261

My silver hoop earrings I wear when I sing for people. The dragon, Ajaha, and the snake spirits all come from Ba. My father's spirits that were given to me are made of leather and skin. The bee spirit sits above me and flies about, and this spirit is a great help to me when I am working with illnesses of the stomach. With all the spirits, every spirit must be cleaned with smoke using tobacco and sankura, and then given water to drink.

.

When I give a conjuring, I take the spirits that I wear around my neck and bring them from under my clothing to the outside of my shaman's vest, where they can be seen. I make an offering for each spirit amulet. I have three main spirit helpers that I use during a journey. First is the silver amulet in the form of the spirit Ajaha. This is my main spirit. The next amulet is made from silver also and is a large shamanic front piece representing the three worlds. My third spirit amulet was made of deer fur with the images of snakes and heavenly dragons. I also have a group of other spirits made from such materials like leather, fish skin, and papers, which I keep in a bag and wear around my neck. These spirits are used primarily for the healing of women's diseases.

..

Grandmother Ama:

All of a shaman's amulets, spirit helpers, and yampa should be buried in the earth after a shaman dies. This should also be carried out for regular people as well. The reason is that the dead have traveled to the sky and no longer need it.

However, in the past, living people would continue to use the amulets and spirit helpers of deceased people to heal different illnesses and diseases. These amulets and spirit helpers could be dangerous because they might inflict harm on the living, including their families.

If you don't clean, feed, and respect them, they can harm you. If you respect them and keep them in your memory, then they will help you. Give them food, love them, make offerings to them, and then your life will be well.

In regards to the pongachi spirits: place them in the earth or pass them down to your children after your death. The spirits made of silver, like Ajaha, should never be buried but given to your children. Spirits made of silver need care their whole lives. Kenapus can also be passed down to your children.

.

If you have savens that are broken, you should place them in the earth. When my parents died, I put all of their savens into the earth and any of my broken savens.

. . .

FORTUNE-TELLING SAVENS

Shamans who tell fortunes use a special spirit carving called a *ponga saven*. These can be carved in any size, but are usually eight to twelve inches in height and width. They are images of owls, snakes, mountain spirits, tigers, and so forth. They are used like a pendulum and hang from a leather cord tied to their back. They can also be made of stone and can weigh up to six pounds.

The shaman will tell fortunes while sitting in front of the home's hearth or at a fire. Special rituals and offerings are made to these *ponga savens* before a fortune-telling session (*pongachi*) is initiated. The *ponga* is not just a divinatory tool but a living spirit endowed with unique and individual powers.

The ritual usually consists of first fumigating the *ponga saven* with tobacco. Then the shaman will speak to the spirit, asking it to speak truly of events and not to deceive or confuse anyone with the answers that are given. Questions need to be asked in such a way that any answer will end with a yes, no, or unknown. The movement of the *ponga saven* during the divination will convey the answer of the spirit. Usually, if the *ponga* moves backward and forward, the answer is affirmative, and if it moves side to side, the response is no. If it doesn't move or turns and twists in a circle, the answer is unknown. *Ponga savens* are unique among spirit helpers as their behavior can be capricious or deceiving when they are asked for help and clarification on any matter. This is why a shaman will beg and cajole the spirit to be helpful and true in all of its answers. As any spirit will have its own unique personality, some *pongas* will naturally be more helpful and/or deceptive than others.

Shamans who employ *ponga savens* will often hang them on the wall opposite the doorway to their home. This spirit will stand guard and observe all those who enter and leave the home. They will convey all the information they gather to the owner at a later date.

COMMENTARIES

GRANDFATHER MISHA:

My father would turn the face of his ponga saven toward the wall when he would go on any long journey away from home. We always knew what day my father was coming back, as the ponga saven would turn itself around and face back toward the door on the very same day that my father returned. Afterwards, my father could consult with his ponga saven to find out what was going on in our home when he was absent.

∙∙

GRANDMOTHER TIKA TO GRANDMOTHER NADIA:

Sometimes your feet or hands will experience great pain. This happens in the morning and then again in the evening. It is a powerful disease. The snake, in the early morning, goes out and returns again to rest in the evening. In the afternoon, the feet and hands will not hurt. Why do you feel this pain? It is because the snake spirit had touched your hands, and it wants a pongachi. When the snake travels out in the morning, your hand is painful, and when the snake returns home at night, you find even greater pain in your hand. Your hand is ill. The snake spirit has touched it. Now, quickly make a ponga saven of a snake spirit with four legs and a tail. When it is done, never give it araki. Burn sankura and tobacco and clean and clean it with the smoke and give a pongachi, and quickly you will find that your hand is alright. You have helped yourself.

•

When I pongachi, I always use the Tiger spirit. When I have finished my song, I put it away. When I have finished my song, it has told me many types of information and news. You should put it in a safe place, but sometimes it is fine to hang it up inside the house.

•

I learned to do my singing and pongachi when I was still young. Every day, the joints of my arms, legs, and shoulders hurt. I had a dream about how snakes with scales forced me to make idols from larch wood. I asked Grandfather Misha to help me, and he constructed and gave me seven snakes that were twenty inches in length, and after this, I began to heal myself and tell fortunes.

• •

GRANDMOTHER NADIA:

When conducting the ponga ritual, you can sing or not. This is contingent upon the work of the individual shaman.

•

Ponga specialists are a little like a shaman because any spirit that works through a ponga knows everything. Why did people become ponga shamans? Why is it this way? At first, the ponga spirit will touch you in some way. This spirit will cause headaches or pain in your arms, hands, legs, or feet. A shaman will ask that

265

person, "Where are you hurting? In what part of your body do you find pain? Maybe you are becoming s ponga shaman of some kind."

•

When a client is coming for a ponga session, you must beg the ponga to work for you. You smudge the ponga to clear out any other energy that might be stuck to it. Sometimes the ponga won't work for you. Either way, a client must bring a small payment (odi) to the ponga session."

• • •

Salcha / Effigy Savens

The word *salcha* means "to take or absorb" and is used to describe an effigy or object that is created to absorb an illness and/or a particular destructive spirit. This object is known as a *salcha saven*, and it can be constructed from either wood or various plant materials such as grasses. The use of these effigies can be found in the practices of the more powerful shamans.

For the everyday person, having dreams where hunting objects appear is considered a precursor to illness and possibly death of the dreamer and/or family members. Upon awakening from this particular type of dream, a person will construct an effigy of the particular object and then go outside and recite the dream to the bird, rock, and plant people (all of nature). Once the dream has been spoken aloud, it is believed, the spirit of this dream will become shameful or embarrassed at being revealed to the world and will quickly depart from the dreamer. The effigy will absorb the energy of the dream and then will be cast away in the direction of the setting sun (west). A person will then make offerings to nature in the form of various traditional foods, water, and/or some type of alcoholic beverage.

Any Ulchi person accidentally coming across one of these items in nature will not only recognize it as being a *salcha saven* but will move away from it or change the direction of their journey. People understand that if they come into any physical contact with the object, they too could fall victim to its terrible influence.

They are also made and employed by the shamans during healing rituals for their clients or in the great Kasa rituals for the dead. They are usually constructed from a straw-like grass into the form of an anthropomorphic human doll with legs and sometimes with arms as well. They can also be constructed to resemble the image of a pig. During a conjuring, the shaman will use the effigy as a receptacle into which they will cast the disease or the spirit causing difficulties. Once the specific energy or spirit is trapped within the effigy, it will sometimes try to escape by moving about the environment. Some such dolls have been known to travel around the room of their own volition. After the healing ceremony is completed, this spirit is taken out into nature and placed in a location far from people, where it will hopefully remain undisturbed so that it may slowly decay back into the earth.

The discussion of this object is very taboo among the shamans. One tale I was able to extract was a personal history from the great Ulchi shaman Alexander Kotkin, who was deceased at the writing of this book. He had served as a personal shaman to a family in the village of Bulava for many years. The family in question had a member who had committed suicide and whose spirit had continued to plague the family in all aspects of their daily lives. Because cultural taboos dictate that suicidal souls cannot move on to the village of the dead, they remain on Earth, creating havoc and causing illness and bad luck for their remaining family members.

Grandfather Kotkin employed a *salcha saven* and captured the offending spirit within its grass form. He wrapped the idol in wooden streamers and hung it up in the rafters of the house. He then made ritual offerings to it and spoke to it in a type of deceptive way, saying that it would be greatly honored by the family. Kotkin could only try to contain this spirit in a *salcha* to make sure that its negative and harmful behavior could be blunted and assuaged. Hopefully, through his capturing it and placing it a special location, it would cease to wander and disturb the family members in their daily activities of hunting, fishing, and gathering when away from home. After he lured the wandering soul into this grass effigy and instructed the family to make offerings to it on a monthly basis, its destructive actions toward living clan members would hopefully, in time, decrease. This spirit would remain on the earth forever, and remanding it to a specific location was the only option.

The other tale of a destructive *salcha saven* comes from the Goldi people. The details of why this idol was originally made are lost to time, but the results remain in oral history. The story tells of a Goldi shaman who, after a ritual, placed the *salcha* on a trading barge that was traveling downstream, carrying goods from one village to another. The idol was unloaded at a neighboring village along with other provisions, and within a few months, more than half of the villagers had died in tragic and strange deaths.

In my discussions with Grandmother Nadia throughout the years, she would never speak of these matters, but of course, I was curious or perhaps stupid, wanting to learn more. Once I asked her to draw me an image of what these *salcha savens* looked like, and she took a pen and drew a quick diagram and then spoke no more of these matters. Many years later, while preparing for this book, I thought that if I had an image, I might be able to provide a photograph for the reader. It was fall, and I was shopping at the local market in my neighborhood. They had many bales of straw as a display item for their Thanksgiving offerings. I took a large handful of straw from one of the bales and quickly conveyed it to my home during one of Grandmother Nadia's visits to the Pacific Northwest. I presented it to her with great pride, saying, "Look, I brought the correct material. Can you construct a *salcha saven* so that I can see all of its dimensions and make a photo of it for our book?" She looked at me with great shock and horror and exclaimed, "What! Are you crazy! This is taboo! You must be crazy to want to do something as dangerous as this, and besides only men are allowed to make things like this!" At that moment, I knew that I had made a great error and never again asked about the process, understanding that even creating one, whether it is used or not, can put a person's soul in great jeopardy.

CASTING OUT SPIRITS AND DISPOSAL OF FOULED SHAMANIC TOOLS

When removing negative spirits, one must be careful where to dispose of them. The wooden streamers used to cleanse people are considered fouled and must be taken out into nature and left to disintegrate and decay. *Salcha savens* are also sacrificed in natural surroundings. If a person comes upon these items while outside, they are not to touch them. They will instead walk away in another direction. If a person were to come into physical contact with any of these types of ritual items, that person could become contaminated with the illness trapped within the object.

COMMENTARY

GRANDMOTHER NADIA:

A shaman always uses the drum to drive an evil spirit into a salcha saven. If they don't drive it inside with a drum, they will hold the image of the offending spirit in their mind, sending and commanding it to take up residence into the grass doll.

• • •

SPECIAL AMULETS FOR CHILDREN: SOUL BUNDLES

Young children are the most susceptible to harmful spirits. For this reason, they are called by other names instead of their true ones. Some parents will call their child "pig face" or "ugly one" or something similarly unpleasant. This makes the child's young soul unpleasing to the harmful spirits. Grandmother Nadia spoke about the fact that many people in her village didn't know her proper name for many years. When people would see her, they would address her only as "daughter." Hiding one's true name or identity during childhood helps protect one's young life from the interest of destructive spirits.

During Grandmother Nadia's childhood, her father, Dumbin, had two wives, and between the two gave birth to twenty-eight children. Only five of this group survived into adulthood. Until the arrival of Western medicine, infant death was known to be as high as seventy-five percent among the people. In the past, the shamans who worked with the souls of children held an exceptional position among the Ulchi due to the mortality rate among the young. These shamans would prescribe and construct a soul bundle for a young person in their care after the child had survived past the age of one. (Before one year of age, a child's soul has not fully developed into a human soul. This young soul has the qualities of a bird's soul and belongs to the Upper realms of Heaven and not the Middle World of humans).

Bundles contain various items from nature and are unique for each child. Here are some of the contents of Grandmother Nadia's soul bundle from her childhood:

1. Willow wands

2. Pieces of larch wood

3. Rowan wands

4. Wooden streamers

5. Sable or mink tails

6. Seal fur

7. Eagle, owl, or crow feathers

8. Old arrowheads

These items are wrapped in a red cloth and tied up with red silk. This bundle becomes the keeper of the young person's soul. When working on a child, the children's shaman will take this bundle, open it up, and use pieces of it during the healing. Mothers who were given a soul bundle when they were young can use their own bundle on behalf of their children. These older bundles are taken out, and the pieces of wood or streamers are renewed with fresh ones. The shamans say that the ritual of taking out a soul bundle, fumigating it with Labrador tea, and placing it back in a safe place will drive away an illness very quickly.

Medicinal Plants and Sacred Herbs

Many healing plants are known among the Ulchi and neighboring peoples. Knowledge of these plants and their medicinal use is preserved and transmitted within families, and is not the protected domain of the shamans.

Labrador tea (Ledum Palustre), called *sankura*, is used to dispel stomach and digestive illness. It is brewed into a tea-like concoction using both the leaves and stems of the plant. Dry stems and leaves are placed into a cup, and boiling water is poured over them. This tea steeps for about ten to twenty minutes and is then served to the patient. The leaves of this plant are sacred because it is the only plant found in the Ulchis' natural environment that can cleanse and drive away harmful spirits. The leaves are gathered, dried, and placed on a small metal plate, where they are lit on fire. As the *sankura* smolders, the little plate is carried around, and the smoke is offered both to the environment and to people. Bathing in the smoke ritually purifies the people. The dried leaves are also placed in a cup of water that sits on the altar for every shamanic conjuring. The shaman will drink from this cup from time to time, which will strengthen them during a healing ceremony. The use of this plant is reserved for rituals inside the home. *Sankura* is never given in outdoor rituals.

Tobacco (*domki*) is the chief herb for offerings to spirits and is required for all rituals, whether inside or outside the home. Usually, the tobacco offering is given in a dry, whole leaf form. If whole leaf tobacco cannot be found, tobacco that has been cut and dried for pipes or cigarettes can be used. When given during an offering, tobacco can be placed dried among the food offerings, or it can be delivered to the spirits by smoking and blowing the smoke toward the tree (as in the case of a Taiga ritual) or toward the face of the house idol when inside the home. A person may also give the house idol an offering of dry tobacco. This is up to each individual. *Ponga savens* must be awakened before a conjuring by blowing tobacco smoke upon their faces. Offerings of tobacco to Water spirits are always given in a dry form; usually, a whole leaf, if possible.

Vaysi, an onion wild crafted in the taiga, holds a similar position to *sankura* but is never burned. It is dried and cut into little square pieces and must be given in all outdoor rituals. It is presented to the spirits along with the traditional offerings such as berries, fish, fruit, millet, and rice.

COMMENTARY

GRANDMOTHER NADIA:

Knowledge of healing plants does not belong to a shaman or a special doctor but is kept by each individual clan. Healing remedies are passed down from one generation to another, from mother to daughter, but we kept the knowledge of certain plants within the family. The elders say that it is wrong to boast of one's healing power or knowledge of sacred plants. If a person is healed, they will not speak of how the herbs were gathered, the ingredients, or how it was applied. If you speak of it, the illness may become angry. If you boast about how it was driven away, then it may possibly return to the person. A particular family may have knowledge about a certain plant, how to use it, and will help everyone in the village, but they will never speak of how they made the remedy. Everyone has basic knowledge about the healing plants in our territory, and people may share a little information with others. Knowledge of specific recipes is guarded with great humility.

. . .

CHAPTER 12

Shaman Wars, Weather Magic, Nature Encounters, and Prophecy

Many ancient stories told of the wars between shamans, and how these disputes could go on for years and years. These wars were often based on professional rivalries, as when a shaman detected another shaman trying to intervene during a conjuring. If they saw an offending shaman during one of their shamanic flights, they could drive the soul of the interloper into a grass *salcha saven* and later destroy the doll. The hostile shaman would then suddenly fall ill and die. Years ago, Grandmother Nadia's shaman grandfather from her mother's side took ill and suddenly died. He was a beneficent shaman, but it was said that he was attacked by a foreign shaman who was jealous or angry with him.

The warring shamans fought each other by transforming their souls into powerful animals and other beasts. Grandfather Kotkin told many stories of battling harmful shamans and their spirits by

ALTAKA OLCHI, BULAVA VILLAGE

transforming himself into a lion and either chopping them in half or tearing them up with his claws in the Dreamtime. During the shaman wars, the combatants could transform into birds. This type of flying creature was preferred by the shamans who fought against each other. Such was the case in the stories below, recounted by the shamans and elders, about the battles that took place on the mythical shaman tree. Here the disputes don't result in death; they are meant to degrade, rather than destroy. Although this topic was rarely discussed by the elders, one can conclude from these accounts that by defeating another shaman, the victorious shaman could lay claim to the vanquished shaman's spirits, thus gaining a larger and more powerful retinue of spirits for themselves.

Many questions have been asked as to whether shamans were colleagues or competitors of one another, and the answer is that it depended upon the nature of their spirit helpers. Shamans, as individuals, may have quiet and introspective personalities but may employ very powerful spirits who are argumentative, jealous, kind, courteous, beneficent, or who behave like hooligans. When shamans come into contact with one another, they are accompanied by their invisible helpers. If the spirits of both shamans are compatible, the shamans will feel very comfortable in each other's presence, and if not, they may feel agitated and angry, and thus become rivals. Between those shamans who felt collegial with one another, friendships would be forged. These alliances were necessary because if a shaman fell ill and could not cure themselves, they would seek help from a shamanic colleague. Shamans who felt competitive with one another would avoid social situations that would bring them into direct contact.

Grandmother Nadia would say that if a family invited a shaman from a neighboring village to come to their home to help the family, any of the local shamans who felt uncomfortable at that shaman's arrival would leave the village and return only after the visiting shaman had departed. The local shamans needed only to be in proximity of the visiting shaman to feel agitated by that shaman's spirits.

COMMENTARIES

GRANDFATHER MISHA:

Sometimes when shamans get together, they can fight and argue with each other. One will say to another, "I am great, I am the best, and I am the most powerful shaman!" Then, as the shamans are birds, they will fly to a tall tree, and the ones sitting on the highest branches will say, "I am the most powerful shaman!" and then they will defecate on the shamans who are perched on the lower branches below them. This is how it goes between shamans. They fight and fight, and this is how it is. Most times, shamans don't like each other.

••

GRANDMOTHER NADIA:

When I was little, Ponga Valdu, my first shaman, and Altaka Olchi told me this ancient history of the old shamans. They said that when a shaman arrived back home after a yiyee, they would transform themselves into a crow or another type of bird and rest in a tree branch. If there were any other shamans sitting on the lower branches, then they would defecate on them. This is how shamans can be with each other.

•

People in my village are usually quiet about letting other people know that they are having a shaman come to their home. Family matters should not be discussed outside to others. Every time that Grandmother Indyeka was planning a trip to our village, Grandmother Tika would feel this upcoming arrival in advance. I know that Tika's spirits must have informed her. Tika would leave a day or two in advance of Indyeka's arrival and return home a day after Indyeka has departed to her village. Although Grandmother Tika had no idea what days or times Indyeka would be here, Tika's spirits always knew and always kept her informed.

••

Grandmother Ama to Grandmother Nadia:

Your grandfather's name was Sukin Kui, and our grandmother's name is Pulmaka from the Dechuli clan. Sukin found Pulmaka, and she became his wife. They gave birth to a very strong son and named him Daga. Sukin was a medium or average shaman. After he completed a healing, he would fly to the shaman's tree. Some shamans sat high above on the top branches, and some shamans sat below on the lower branches. The shaman who was sitting above your grandfather defecated on him, and from that time on, these two shamans began to fight with one another. They made a spiritual war, and sometimes a shaman's spirits may leave them and travel to a different shaman.

••

Grandmother Chimaka Valdu:

Ulchi shamans have their own magic tree. Sometimes they would get into arguments while walking, and turn into birds and fly to the tree to sit and rest for a while. Some would sit on the top branches, and some would sit on the bottom branches. Sometimes the ones on the upper branches would move over to be above the ones sitting on the lower branches, to imply that they were stronger than their fellow shamans below.

. . .

Jakpa Shamans

In the Ulchi tradition, there are no evil shamans per se, but there are those healers who may be classified as "*jakpa*" shamans. An evil shaman, to the Ulchi, would be one who intentionally sets out to harm another person. *Jakpa* is a term used to define a shaman who is working with very powerful spirit helpers who can inadvertently cause harm to others. This is not because the shaman instructs or guides them to behave this way. Rather, because of their immense power, these spirits can lash out at people whom they feel have offended them. If a shaman's spirits harm another, without the shaman consciously sending their invisible helpers, the blame or mistake may be due to the victim of the attack behaving in a manner that is contradictory to the rules of propriety concerning social intercourse with a shaman. Grandmother Altaka was considered one of the most powerful shamans in Ulchi history, but she was also seen as a *jakpa* shaman. If her spirits were ever offended by someone, that person would suffer the consequences of their actions.

In rare cases, the term *jakpa* can also describe the conscious actions and deeds of foreign shamans who send forth their spirits to directly attack another person, as related in the various tales of the shaman wars. There is a story that Grandmother Nadia told me about being set upon by the hostile spirits of a powerful Goldi shaman. Grandmother was just beginning her new vocation and was traveling with a group of

Goldi villagers. Amongst this group was an elderly shaman. During their time together, this shaman had exhibited some jealousy toward Grandmother. Grandmother told me, "We had all been together for about two weeks. I don't know if this was a test against my own spirits, but afterward, I felt physically ill. I cleansed myself energetically and restored my own balance. Later that day, this shaman quietly said to me that I must have very powerful clan spirits. This is all she said, but I knew that she had intentionally sent her spirits to me to cause harm. After this event, the Goldi shaman was very respectful to me in all of our interactions."

Now, this was a conscious attack by the Goldi shaman as a test. It was a malicious act, to be sure, intended to examine how Grandmother and her spirits would respond to the challenge. Obviously, a shaman would need the skill and techniques to protect themselves if threatened or attacked by a hostile shaman. They might need to send their spirit helpers to destroy an offending shaman who wished to cause illness or death. Actions taken in self-defense are not considered "*jakpa* behavior." For the Ulchi, any conscious spirit attack by a shaman would be seen not only as an aberration but as a failing in one's character, as it rejects the moral and ethical behavior dictated by their cultural taboos and laws of Nature.

COMMENTARY

GRANDMOTHER NADIA:

Grandmother Tika and Grandfather Misha would sometimes say that Grandmother Altaka was a jakpa shaman, but then again I have heard many shaman elders talking among themselves, saying that Grandmother Altaka was a jakpa shaman. Sometimes I have heard shamans accuse other shamans of being jakpa shamans.

•

Kuma was Altaka's daughter. She wore the amulets of her mother. Kuma had become a medium (Isachula), but before her death, she lost all of her talents. Grandmother Kobi said that the other elders said that maybe Altaka's spirits killed her daughter Kuma.

.

When spirits are approached rudely and incorrectly, they may transform themselves into hostile spirits that harm the living.

• • •

Families that have strong shamanic clan affiliations also carry those special spirits around them. A family's clan spirits could seek revenge against an offending party without the conscious knowledge of any particular family member. The family might not have a living shaman amongst their clan, but the spirits of their shamanic ancestry are always present and watchful as to the deeds of their living relatives.

Commentary

Grandmother Nadia:

A few years back, a man from our village was living in the city of Khabarovsk with his wife and two children. He had gone to the store to buy food and was hit by a driver and left for dead in the street. His poor family did not know why he didn't return until the very next day when the local television station showed the intersection of the accident and the family recognized his shoe that was next to the curb. After he was struck by the car, some person came and stole his wallet and identification, so the officials at the hospital did not know who he was or how to contact his family.

That family, who rushed to the hospital to see him, was greeted very poorly by the medical staff. His wife told me that the doctors and nurses were very obviously prejudiced about indigenous people and they were treated like illiterate barbarians from the hinterlands. The family, being in shock at the life-threatening injuries to the husband, was offended by the treatment by the hospital staff and attending doctor.

After a week of attending their loved one, the doctor came to see that this was an educated and well-mannered family, and his attitude began to soften when they came to the facility. It took a long time before the man regained enough strength to leave the hospital, but he survived and returned home.

A year after the accident, the attending doctor was struck and killed by a hit-and-run driver in the same intersection. I think that he offended the clan spirits of both the husband and wife. Both sides of that family have many ancient shamans in their past.

. . .

GRANDFATHER MISHA DUVAN, BAINBRIDGE
ISLAND, WASHINGTON STATE, USA, 1995

Control of Weather and Natural Phenomena

The more powerful shamans are known to be able to control and direct the forces of nature. The most compelling stories are of those shamans who can call forth thunder and lightning, direct the winds, calm a sky, or create and manipulate other events in the atmosphere.

COMMENTARIES

GRANDFATHER MISHA:

My grandfather, a shaman, played with the Thunder. He could control it. Once a hard rain was falling, and he was sitting in a little boat. He lived in the middle of a lake on a little island surrounded by silver water. At his command, a tree could grow, and on that tree, he could rest or sing whatever he wished. He could sing for rain, wind, or good weather and it would come to pass.

·

When I was young, I remember my grandfather and I were outside watching the people harvesting the hay during the fall. The day was beautiful and calm. Many people in the village began to tease him, and suddenly he grew very quiet. Inside his soul, he had become angry, and it started to rain, and thunder and all of the hay stacks were turned over from the weather. Then the rain stopped as suddenly as it began.

··

GRANDMOTHER K.V. DUVAN:

I was born in 1921 and was a little younger than Grandfather Misha. One day, when I was a child, I traveled in a boat to the fishing grounds with Misha's father. All of a sudden, black clouds appeared in the sky followed by a large downpour of rain. He said to me, "Do not be afraid, and row this boat calmly." All around us was a torrential downpour, but we remained dry inside the boat. He could play the Thunder and control Nature. That's the way it was!

· · ·

As an assistant to Grandmother Nadia, I have experienced her calling in the wind spirits to assist in the healing of a client. With doors closed and windows locked, it is not uncommon for her to enlist the aid of the North Wind, followed either by the door blowing open, right on cue, or a wind appearing in the healing room through an unknown aperture in space. When I queried her about the latter, she reminded me that the spirit of the North Wind needs no door or window to enter the world. This spirit just makes itself known by traveling through the invisible worlds through the fabric of the universe wherever it chooses.

During Grandfather Misha's first visit to the Pacific Northwest, a walk upon the shores of Lake Washington was how we began each day together. Grandfather would always bring tobacco and small portions of food to make an offering to the Water spirit of this area. This was his way of introducing himself to the spirits of North America. It was a way of building a relationship with the invisible inhabitants of this foreign land in which he had just arrived. If he was going to make his conjurings in this place, he had to first gain permission from the Land and Water spirits; otherwise, they would feel offended or angry or perhaps punish him for his transgression. Once the word got out, and these daily rituals became common knowledge, other friends joined our walks to watch, listen, and learn from this remarkable and unique man.

One day, we started out late in the afternoon. The sky was clear and cloudless with a slight breeze blowing in from the east. We walked behind Grandfather as he made his way to the shore. Like a gaggle of goslings, we quietly accompanied him to the ritual spot that he had chosen many weeks earlier when he first set foot on the shores of this lake. Crouching down on the pebbly and sandy beach, he began talking to the spirit of the Water. He then began his shaman's song while he tossed the tobacco out across the tops of the small waves lapping upon the shore.

All of a sudden, four mallard ducks arrived from the right and just floated in position, and from the left, two more showed up. Like guardian sentinels ever vigilant, they watched over the proceedings. Here was Grandfather, singing to the Water spirit, while a company of ducks was flanking him on both sides of the ritual landing. This little retinue of ducks was quietly bobbing up and down in the waves, just watching and listening to Grandfather as he cast his offerings across the water.

Of course, all of us who were witnessing this event turned to one another, whispering, "Do you see this? Do you see that?" as we pointed to the ducks, amazed at how they gave their undivided attention to the whole matter. A few moments later, a small school of fish came jumping out of the water in the center of the lake, while the ducks maintained their formation on either side. Our whispering gave way to elbowing one another and pointing at the little fish. Grandfather Misha just continued singing, completely undisturbed or unimpressed by the show of nature taking place in front of him.

A minute or two passed, and then, from a cloudless sky, a rainbow appeared in the distance, reaching down to the hills directly across the wide expanse of water. By this time, our eyes were as wide as saucers, as we stood there looking at those buoyant birds and the tiny fish propelling themselves straight up and down from the center of the lake. Once the rainbow appeared, all of us fell completely silent. As Grandfather's song began to wind down, the rainbow over the hills slowly dissipated, the fish ended their gymnastic routine, and the ducks slowly turned and paddled off in opposite directions. In stunned silence, we had just witnessed an event that left us completely gobsmacked.

This was not the only event in nature that I observed while in the company of Grandfather Misha or Grandmother Nadia that left me in wonder and amazement. Once, when we were taking our daily constitutional through a wild forest on Whidbey Island, a pair of deer sauntered out of the trees and made their way into the clearing where Grandfather, Grandmother, and I were standing. They came within three feet of us, stood and observed us for a while, and then slowly turned away and disappeared back into the woods and out of sight. Many times during a walk in nature, birds would arrive and hop beside us, matching our stride. Chirping, chattering, or whistling a song, these birds would accompany us for two or three minutes, then abruptly fly away back into the canopied landscape. When the birds would appear, Grandfather and Grandmother would speak to them, saying, "Hello. How are you? How are your families? Do you have any news for us?"

It wasn't merely that wild creatures in nature were unafraid to approach us; they actually seemed to have been interested in these Ulchi visitors. Later on, these types of events became so commonplace that my surprise transformed into a mild curiosity, which arose every time we embarked into an outdoor setting. By then, I would only wonder about the next encounter and who we might meet when traveling through the forest, walking by the ocean, or taking a hike in the mountainous regions of Washington State.

GRANDFATHER MISHA DUVAN

Prophecy

A shaman's vision is intensely personal, and it can cause them a great danger to share the experience with others. Because of this, a shaman may intimate about a vision but rarely, if ever, shares the deeper meaning of the prophecy. Although prophetic visions may come to many of the shamans, only Grandfather Misha was willing to share one of his more powerful visions, recounted below. Grandmother Nadia said she heard him tell it many times to her, and although the story was the same each time, he added a few more details in one or another version of the telling.

Grandfather Misha:

I saw an old woman who said to me; soon everything will turn upside down. The dead will become the living, and the living, dead. The earth will turn into oceans, and the oceans will become land. The people will turn into dogs and the dogs into people. There will be a terrible apocalypse in the world. Perhaps you will not live long enough to see this, but it will be a terrible time.

• • •

Commentary

Grandmother Nadia:

Even with this, he does not tell the whole story. There are mysteries to the vision that he never spoke about.

CHAPTER 13

• • •

Shaman's Procession, Village Healing, & the Shaman Purges

Researchers from various disciplines have called a shamanic journey by many names: conjuring, séance, healing, and so forth. The Ulchis call this journey a *yiyee* or singing. The preparation for a journey is dependent upon the type of healing or ritual that is being performed, and whether it is for the entire village, a family, or a single individual. However, it usually includes an *ungi*, or shaman's procession, which enables the shaman to gather strength and energy before the conjuring.

A group of homes to be visited during the procession will have been chosen in advance by the shaman or sometimes by the shaman's primary assistant, who is known as the *lavji*. These homes are most often the houses of the shaman's clients who live in the village. The number of houses is important. The odd numbers are considered the most potent and sacred, and the Ulchi people value the numbers three, seven, and nine. In the early morning hours, the *lavji* will travel to each of the specified houses to announce to the home's owners that the

GRANDMOTHER INDYEKA DJAKSUL IN FRONT OF HER HOME, SOPHISK VILLAGE

shaman plans to conduct an *ungi* through their home that day. This allows time for each family to begin the special preparations necessary when welcoming a shaman into their abode.

The procession may start in the morning or afternoon. The procession is led by the main assistant, who is followed by secondary assistants and then the shaman. Using a curved knife, the *lavji* cuts their way through the air, using a back and forth circular motion. The procession travels through the streets of the village in a serpentine fashion.

As they arrive at the first home, the members of the *ungi* are greeted by the inhabitants. This family will have prepared special food and drinks for the occasion. The shaman will walk into the various rooms of the home, gathering energy along the way. The inhabitants present the shaman with ribbons of many colors, which are sewn loosely onto the shaman's robe. The status of a shaman can be judged by the number of ribbons upon their clothing.

When sewing the ribbon onto the garment, it is forbidden to tie it in a knot, as this might allow a harmful spirit to be attached to the shaman's robe. The spirit could become entangled in the knot and remain with the shaman permanently. Instead, the ribbons are allowed to hang freely upon the garment. Because they are not completely secured, a ribbon will drop off from time to time, and any person may pick up it and keep it for themselves. These fallen ribbons are considered sacred objects, and those who gather them take them back home as a type of powerful amulet for protection.

Once the visit to the first house is complete, the inhabitants join the *ungi* as it makes it way to the next dwelling. The procession moves from the outside of the village into a home and then back outside, picking up participants along the way. This process is repeated until all of the assigned homes have been visited. This procession will either arrive back at the shaman's home if the conjuring is being given to an individual and or their family members or a predestinated place if the conjuring is being given for the whole village. This snake dance through the streets may take hours to complete. The shaman will have chosen homes of people who are considered spiritually rich. In this way, they can draw upon favorable forces before the evening conjuring. Most conjurings take place in the evening after the sun goes down. The day is the time of the living, while the night is the domain of spirits and the dead.

This procession is conducted not only to give strength to the shaman before a conjuring but to bring joy and happiness to the shaman's spirit helpers. It is important to create an atmosphere of merriment for the spirits prior to the work.

Before Grandfather Misha would conduct a healing in the Pacific Northwest, he would usually request a long walk in nature or have us take him to Lake Washington to walk along the shore. It was in these natural environments that he would gather his strength for an upcoming conjuring. Grandmother Nadia was very different, as she usually had me take her to University Village, near my home, to make her *ungi*.

She said that this outdoor shopping mall is a great place to gather strength because all of the people walking about, shopping, laughing, or meeting with friends, produce a joyous environment. Whether the procession takes place in a traditional village environment or an urban setting, its importance should not be minimized, as it is the time for the shaman to energize themselves, talk to their spirits about the upcoming healing ceremony, and create a happy experience for their spirit helpers.

COMMENTARIES

GRANDMOTHER NADIA:

I remember that just before Tika's death, she came over to my house and said, "Let's go to Marinsk village and make an ungi together." My home became the only house for this in the village. The shamans would arrive, stay awhile, and eat and drink, then travel back to their residences. Grandmother Tika and Grandfather Misha would come over, feeling very tired, and we would dine together and talk and talk and talk. We would have a very long visit together. They would find their strength. Our talks were delightful because they both would speak of their memories, legends, tales, and the latest events in the village. These were such joyful occasions for me.

•

I remember the ungi that Grandmother Altaka would make through the village. I was a little girl, but my mother was always a part of the shamanic procession. The ungi always started from the south to the north, and since our home was in the most southern part of the village, the ungi always began at my home.

My mother was one of the first assistants to Grandmother Altaka in the ungi and walked very close to her throughout the entire ceremony. The ungi traveled from here to there, in and out of many homes and gathering people along the way. We usually finished at my best friend Rosa's house. When the ungi traveled into each home, food, water, and vodka/araki were given to the shaman. The people would also clean the body of the shaman with the Labrador tea/sankura smoke. After the smudging, the shaman would feel helped and well.

• • •

A Village Conjuring

A traditional village conjuring could be called for a number of reasons:

1. Personal healing

2. General offering

3. Misfortune that had befallen a clan or village

4. Prophesy

5. Introduction of legends

6. Shaman's individual journey

People would travel from far -away places to attend such an event, and it would take days to get there, due to the large geographical distances between one village and another. Grandmother Ama told Grandmother Nadia that Nadia's mother, Goga, was always excited to hear of an upcoming conjuring: "Your mother, as long as I can remember, would always travel to hear a shaman whenever they would be giving a *yiyee*. Sometimes she would travel to Ukta or Dudi village. Your father, Dumbin, was never very happy about this. He would always grumble and complain." Grandmother Nadia reminded me that her mother was sixteen years younger than her father and that her mother loved to socialize and attend all types of parties, whereas her father was a very serious, quiet, and contemplative man.

When people would gather in preparation for the conjuring, everyone would take up the drums, dance sticks, rattles, and sacred streamers. They would bring their instruments and show off their rhythms. The people would sing and dance and imitate the actions of a shaman. This was a humorous or farcical interlude before the evening's event would take place. The people, having attended many of these gatherings, would perform imitations of particular shamans, duplicating how they moved, sang, and danced in their own unique styles.

GRANDFATHER MISHA (RIGHT) AND ELDERS DURING VILLAGE SHAMANIC CEREMONY

The participants would howl with laughter because they could identify the particular shaman being "spoofed" or emulated. This was intended to relieve the dramatic tension and heighten the emotional impact of the ceremony employing contrast with the shaman's upcoming journey to the beautiful and frightening lands of the spirits.

I remember Grandfather Misha, during one of his visits to the Pacific Northwest, preparing for an evening seminar. He was in a rather jocular mood and began to perform the dances and movements of the shamans whom he observed growing up. He would say, "Now this is Grandmother so-and-so from Bulava village." He would dance her dance, drum her rhythms, and exaggerate her facial movements in an uproarious comedic performance. Then he would move on to his next imitation of a different shaman. With these slapstick performances, Grandfather Misha demonstrated his artistic genius when it came to physical comedy.

The skill to reproduce a shamanic performance also had another underlying meaning and purpose. When a new shaman was just beginning their individual practice, they would model their rhythms, melodies, and movements after those of the shamans they had observed, until they were able to develop their style as prescribed to them by their spirit helpers. These group performances were also a type of "testing ground" for possible upcoming shamans in the culture. The elders would sit and watch all of those who were participating. They would watch to see how a person might dance, drum, sing, or enter into an ecstatic state of consciousness. The elders would then point out particular people and say to one another, "Look how so-and-so dances or sings. Look how they have truly found their ecstasy. Perhaps, someday, they might receive the shamanic call. Yes, they have shamans in their clan blood, and they have powerful spirits. We will surely keep an eye on this person's growth."

This communal prelude to a conjuring was all about creating a proper environmental setting prior to the actual shamanic event. The atmosphere had to be charged with the energy of the participants, as this would insure a powerful place in which the shaman would begin their song. Drumming, dancing, laughter, and an overall sense of camaraderie were the emotional underpinnings necessary for such an event.

COMMENTARIES

GRANDMOTHER NADIA:

These events were our entertainment. They were like going to the disco. People would arrive from throughout the territories and share food, gossip, and enjoy each other's company. It was a great social time! People would dance, clean their bodies with the wooden streamers and fir branches, drum, and sing. Everyone would celebrate before the shaman's healing. The old and young people loved these gatherings. I remember my mother was a beautiful dancer and drummer. In the past, all the old people were skilled drummers and dancers.

If there were no shamans at the event, people would still come together and celebrate in these ways, and the people, the people who played at being shamans, had such beautiful voices.

.

I remember Grandfather Misha telling me that when he was young, he would go to all of these gatherings and imitate the shaman and that is how he learned to perform the shaman's dance.

.

When the shaman's song was complete, everyone will get up and dance with the shaman. People will drum and dance, moving their arms, legs, and hips, thus freeing themselves from illness and harmful spirits. Through this dance, we rid ourselves of ill health or negative energy. Each person would dance their specific dance expressing their unique improvised style. They would sing in the voice of the raven or voices of the other animal people in the taiga, but within this, each would be moving and improvising within the rhythm of the shaman's drumming. This happens at the end because you are in the process of ridding and freeing yourself from unclean spirits and things.

.

After the conjuring, the people would give the shaman refreshments. They would sew scraps of material onto the shaman's robe. They didn't give big gifts because that was taboo. This was done so that the shaman wouldn't get sick after a conjuring.

• • •

THE SHAMAN PURGES OF THE 1930S

These village conjurings had been held for as long as anyone could remember, so I queried Grandmother Nadia about the shaman purges by Stalin in the mid-1930s in the Ulchi region. Stalin's "Reign of Terror" had executed or imprisoned numerous shamans from other Siberian tribes, and this policy also took a heavy toll on the Goldi (Nanai) shamans in the southern territories of the Amur. I was curious about any length of time during which these village conjurings had not been conducted and the status of shamanism during this period in history.

She said, "Now, our village had a collaborator who lived among us, and he was a Goldi man [Grandmother Nadia asked that we not reveal his name so as not to inflict harm or embarrassment upon his living relatives]. Since everyone knew what he was up to, he was never given important information by anyone. Shamanism never disappeared from our culture. We never stopped practicing it, although it was outlawed for a time. The elders would gather secretly in someone's home, especially those homes that were at the edge of the villages or in the taiga, as not to attract any attention. The shamans and elders would gather to discuss our traditions and legends, and then shamanic conjurings would take place. I know this because my house was one of the homes set aside for these meetings where people gathered. It was in the time of Khrushchev, in the sixties, that things began to turn around. It was once again permissible to speak of these things. Like a breath of fresh air, we were able to openly display our traditions."

The Ulchi shamans were miraculously spared from the "Reign of Terror," but other types of false imprisonment did take place in the region during that period. Saida Rosugbu had a younger brother named Bokta. Bokta Rosugbu was arrested in October 1937 in Auri village. Dumbin Duvan, Sergei Angin, Grandfather Kai, and Grandmother Pushina were also arrested and charged with being spies for the Japanese. They were falsely accused, detained, and then carted off to the gulag in Nikolayevsk-on-the-Amur, which is situated in the Nivkhi territories north of the Ulchi region. None of them spoke the Russian language, and their Russian captors knew nothing of Ulchi. They were imprisoned for many months and finally released and forced to walk back, a distance of many hundreds of miles. It took them over a month to return home in the dead of winter. Dumbin, Grandfather Kai, Grandmother Pushina, and Bokta were the only ones set free and returned half frozen and in poor health, suffering from malnutrition. Sergei Angin never returned and was either executed or died of starvation.

Grandmother Nadia said, "I wasn't born at that time. My older sister Shura told me this story, but our family never talked about our father's imprisonment. It was a sad and tragic period in my family's history, so we didn't discuss it much with one another. I only remember hearing my sister speak of it twice. We figured that they spared my father and the others due to their age. They were all older people who probably had nothing to do with spying for the Emperor of Japan."

The Soviet officials in the Ulchi region seemed to be more concerned with Japanese espionage rather than hunting down, imprisoning, or executing the local shamans.

CHAPTER 14

Shamanic Healing and the Soul

When a person asks for a shamanic healing, they must first attend an interview. Shamans may not agree to work with every person who seeks them out for a healing. They will first sit with the prospective client and ask them what is occurring in their life that has caused them to seek external help.

The client will then discuss their physical or psychological symptoms with the shaman, who will ask specific questions based on the client's situation, in hopes of gaining a deeper understanding about possible conditions that may have led to their weakened soul. If the client is a newcomer, the shaman may ask about the family. Questions of marriage, children, and profession may be discussed.

Behind the scenes, while the interview is taking place, the spirits gather inside the conscious mind of the shaman. As the client speaks, the spirits also speak within the shaman's consciousness. The shaman must focus on both conversations simultaneously, as the spirits provide new insights concerning the distress of the petitioner.

Most shamans are specialists in some way. Some are skilled at healing specific types of illness and incapable of healing others. When conducting an interview, a shaman might say, "Oh, I am very sorry, but I cannot help you. I would recommend that you go to Grandmother Tika. She has had great success with this type of problem." If a shaman is unable to take on a particular case, they will usually refer the client to another shaman.

GRANDFATHER MISHA'S SHAMANIC DANCE IN BULAVA VILLAGE GATHERING

The interview process can take between ten to thirty minutes, with the longer sessions usually reserved for newcomers. Shamans may also work with specific families or clans for many years in an ongoing therapeutic relationship.

When the shaman is called to perform a healing, they may spend the day at either their home or the client's home, working on each individual member of the family group. The shaman could be a resident of the same village as the client or could come from a different territorial region. If the shaman has to travel to a different village, they will be the honored guest in the family's dwelling for the duration of the healing work.

Grandmother Indyeka had several families that she would work with who were from Bulava, and she would travel there from her home in Sophisk village from time to time. She could end up in Bulava for over a week, working with all of her clients.

Family members could also travel to a different village to see a specific shaman. If the need were immediate, a family would make the arduous trek, which could take many days and nights, to arrive at the shaman's dwelling.

The shaman never believes that they are responsible for the successes or failures of the healing work. They say that the spirits are the ones who should be praised. Shamans see themselves purely as conduits for the healing process. They are happy and surprised when the spirits come, and the eventual outcome of the conjuring is a great success. They can petition help from their spirits, but this does not guarantee that the spirits will agree to their requests. The spirits may not want to heal a particular person, or they may be in a bad mood or acting capriciously.

When a shaman attempts a healing, they will always say to the client, "If I am successful, do not praise me, and if I fail, do not blame me. Do I have your permission to try?" The shaman asks permission of the client prior to beginning their work, and can only hope that, if they (shamans) live a good life and keep ritually pure, the spirits will be inclined to offer them their assistance.

Most complex healings take at least three sessions to complete. These sessions are conducted either once per month for three months, once every six months, or at the discretion of the particular shaman's spirits. It is common that the first session takes place in the shaman's home. The next sessions may or may not be held in the home of the client. Conducting the healing in the family's abode allows the shaman to make a connection to the client's household and clan spirits, thus providing possible new information concerning the illness.

Once a shaman begins a healing, the periods of time between the sessions are spent listening to the spirits' messages concerning the client. Grandfather Misha said that between the healings, he was thinking about his client each and every day. He was listening to his spirits concerning the case. The information from the spirits may be the prescription or cure—which could require a series of specific rituals to be performed or a particular spirit amulet to be constructed and worn—or it may be advice about the client's everyday life. New information including remedies may also be obtained during a shaman's dream states.

When there is a difficult illness, it is rare for the client to feel completely healed at the end of one session. If the shaman feels that the healing was a success, they will inform the client that a complete recovery will take many months but that, each day, almost imperceptibly, they will feel a little better and eventually find relief.

In these more difficult cases, during the first session, the client will feel a specific somatic tingling sensation, called a *siljuni*, starting from the top of the head and extending down to the chest cavity. The second session will produce the same result, except the physical sensation may extend to the knees. The healing process is considered complete when this tingling or "electrical" impulse is felt starting at the top of the head and traveling down the entire body and through the soles of the feet. Although this outcome usually takes three sessions, the full effect has been known to occur in only two conjurings.

Commentaries

Grandmother Nadia:

When it comes to a particular disease, a shaman's ranking is not important. Some small shamans can be specialists with powerful diseases, so it just depends on the illness.

··

Grandmother Tika:

Then my tiger children come and sit to either side of me. When I close the top of my clients' heads (sukpungi), they feel the electricity move down through their bodies, starting at the top of the head to the bottom of their feet. When they feel this, then all will be well. If they don't feel this electricity (siljuni), then my work will not help them. It may take two, three, four, or five sessions before they may be helped. It is good to wait a little time between these sessions, perhaps three days, a week, or a month. This waiting time is to take a rest from the work. The singing wants the rest because in this way it is helped.

· · ·

If a shaman cannot help you, then go and find another shaman. Perhaps a different shaman can help you with your illness. What type of illness that a person suffers from—one will need to find a shaman who works with that specific disease, a shaman whose talents are developed to work with the offending pain. That is why sometimes a great shaman will not be able to help. They may not be a specialist in helping a certain illness, and yet a small shaman may be able to help a person with a specific illness. Because there are so many types of illness, a person must find the correct shaman who has the experience of working with a specific disease.

Long-Distance Healings

Shamanic healings are also performed for people who cannot travel due to distance or health. In these cases, the shaman will ask for clean garments that the client has worn close to the body. The type of clothing that is most effective is the undershirt or another undergarment because it lays closest to the skin. The cognitive beliefs, emotional affect states, and intrinsic nature of the individual live within their clothing and personal objects. The shaman can diagnose the problem of the client just by having a piece of material that was worn close to the skin. Through direct contact with the cloth, a shaman will understand the nature of an illness and attempt to heal it. Clothing carries the psychospiritual organic patterns of the owner/wearer, and the shaman will use the clothing as a bridge to interface with the client. The clothing serves not only as the energetic substitute for the person but also as a spiritual portal that allows the shaman to directly interfuse with the soul of the client in the invisible worlds. As any used material contained the life force of the owner, people would exchange and recreate new clothing from older garments to combine their own life force with that of the former wearer.

Commentaries

Grandmother Nadia:

In the past, my mother would always take materials from other people to make clothing for her children. You never threw away any material! When my daughter Vita was born, my mother went to a certain family and took material from them to make Vita some clothes. My mother said that this material was from a good and healthy family and it would help Vita to grow strong. I think after my first child, a son, died quickly, then when Vita was born, my mother decided that Vita, my second child, should have special protection for her life.

That family had nine children who all survived and grew up well. I didn't know that this was what she was doing until she brought me the material. She said that this was our tradition and said that Vita would find strength. The females in that family are all still alive and strong and healthy.

•

When visiting the United States, I have seen so many shops that sell used clothing from other people. I cannot walk into those kinds of stores anymore. When I walk in, I feel so many different kinds of energy from all of the previous owners. Much of the energy is very harmful, and it gives me a headache. I cannot believe that people in the West buy and sell clothing from people

GRANDMOTHER TIKA VALDU ANGA

they do not know. Clothing will contain the energy and karma of the first owner, and Westerners are so ignorant or oblivious to the energetic patterns radiating from the material. If you know a person who has a good life and they pass something down to you, then this is great luck to wear and use it. People should be very careful when it comes to wearing another's clothes.

• • •

Healing Oneself

All shamans will sing for themselves. These journeys are necessary as they serve to strengthen, inform, and increase the skill set of the shaman while traveling and interacting in the spirit worlds. When a shaman seeks their own self-healing, they may or may not be successful, depending upon the severity of their illness.

Commentary

Grandmother Tika:

If a sick shaman woman conjures over herself, she prays that somehow her own spirit helpers will come to her aid and help to heal her. If they won't heal her, then she goes to another shaman.

•

When I was twenty years old, I had a dream where I was in the Upper and Lower Worlds. In the Lower World, there was a blue sea with seven mountains, and at the top of every mountain was a light. Here they took my soul and tied it to a tree, and above my head, I see a tiger.

•

For a time, I grew ill, so I enlisted the help of another shaman who did a conjuring for me. This shaman found my soul tied to a tree in the Lower World. In my dreams, I also saw my soul tied to a tree with a tiger hanging over a branch. This old shaman

woman was able to free me from these bindings and return my
soul to my physical body. My health began to improve, and later
I became stronger and more vital.

• • •

Concepts of Multiple Souls

According to their beliefs, a person's soul is given to them by their first ancestors. It is immortal and defined as a thread that is passed down from generation to generation. If a person violates any of the taboos or laws, this thread can break, causing the person to become a harmful spirit without any hope for future lives through reincarnation. As in many indigenous cultures, the Ulchis believe in multiple souls. They say that every adult person has three distinct souls that are independent and interdependent with one another.

The original birth soul also has a developmental stage of growth. For the first year of life, it is considered a heavenly soul, or *ome*, whose inherent properties assign it to the world of the Cosmos or land of the Celestial birds. This soul grows out of the earth maintaining its Upper World qualities. For this reason, many taboos exist until a child reaches one year of age. If a child younger than this becomes ill, a shaman is powerless. They are forbidden to intervene. If a child dies before reaching their first anniversary, special funeral rites are held. The body is wrapped in wooden streamers and white cloth and taken out into the forest, where it is hung in the branches of the tallest tree in hopes that the *ome* will quickly return to Heaven and reincarnate back upon the Earth. If the child survives, the *ome* slowly grows into a mortal, or human soul called an *urga*. The *urga* develops for eighteen to twenty-four years until it reaches maturity. After this time, a person is finally considered to have developed their adult soul.

This adult soul is comprised of three distinctive parts. The soul that resides in the heart is called the *doe* or *doe meva*. This heart/mind is considered the seat of consciousness similar to the xin in Chinese or kokoro in Japanese philosophy. The second soul, or dream soul, is the *juli*. The *juli* travels during sleep to the realms of spirits, deities, and to variable unseen worlds. The *juli* can also be referred to as the wind soul. Because a shaman is taught by the spirits, this dream soul must be skillfully trained, as dream recall is an absolute necessity for shamanic training. The third soul, called the *panya*, is similar to a doppelganger. It is a complete physical representation of the person. When people view their own shadow, they are looking at their *panya*. The *panya* lives its own life as a type of etheric double. The *juli* comes and goes from the human body at will. It is in a state of constant movement. When it strays from the physical self for long periods of time, it can become vulnerable to attacks by harmful spirits, causing its human host to increasingly become physically ill or psychologically disturbed in various ways. This is the soul that the shaman seeks when performing a conjuring. The nuances and attributes of the three souls and their inherent qualities are interpreted by shamans in various ways.

Commentary

Grandmother Tika:

When you do a conjuring, you travel through seven layers looking for the soul. The soul can be located in any of the three worlds. Your spirit helpers are the ones who search for the wandering soul and the illness. Once in a while, the spirit helpers can be disobedient. When they are capricious, I will punish them and then beg them for help. Keep your spirits close at hand and feed them often.

•

I learned to give fortunes when I was still young. I do this by singing. Every day, the joints of my arms, hands, legs, and shoulders were in great pain. I had a dream that snakes with scales forced me to make a spirit totem from larch. When I die, my spirit totems must not be fouled by other people. I want them to go to a museum where they can be kept in safety.

• • •

Classical shamans never "retrieved the souls" of their clients to place them back into the body. Why is this so? The *juli*, or wind soul, is responsible for the psychological and physical health and well-being of the individual. This soul is traveling to and from the human body all the time. It is never inside the body but envelopes this physical form from the outside. This soul is analogous to a person's " dream body" while in a REM state of sleep.

The wind soul has its distinct personality and proclivities within the framework of its existence. From a psychological perspective, this soul has been described as a type of adolescent personality who can behave stubborn and defiant. Its home exists in both the visible and invisible worlds. Although it travels to and from its physical host, maintaining health and balance in both visible and invisible reality, it can get into trouble if behaving in a disobedient manner.

The wind soul forms a partnership with the physical body while maintaining a separate life. When they are in balance, both biological and psychological homeostasis occurs. However, this soul may refuse to interact with the physical body due to a chronic or acute state of illness, cognitive dissonance, or some type of traumatic event. In such cases, the wind soul will refuse to properly engage with its physical counterpart, due to the psychological or physical pathology attached to its material form. This soul will then view the body as a type of "haunted house" and make a choice not to return to or live in such an environment. When this soul refuses to return to the body, the original psychological or physical illness is compounded, resulting in a deepening of the specific physical illness or psychological pathology.

When the wind soul does not return to its physical counterpart, it becomes even more vulnerable to all types of attacks in the invisible worlds in which it lives. Harmful spirits may capture and torment it, dragging it away to secret places in the invisible worlds. Even if it tries to escape the clutches of these beings, it may not have the strength because as the physical body weakens, so does the wind soul within this complex symbiotic relationship. When this soul gets into these dangerous predicaments, its pain, fear, and trepidation are transferred to the physical body. It becomes an orphan without a home. The wind soul and the physical body must work together as wholly integrated partners to avoid imbalance that affects them both.

COMMENTARIES

GRANDMOTHER NADIA:

You can literally see from a person's face if they are experiencing soul loss. You can look into their eyes, and they will have that glazed look as if nobody is home. They can seem disinterested in everything going on in their life or appear spacey in some way. When a person worries a great deal, then the soul will fly away. Too much thinking can cause this also.

.

At the top of the head, in the center, is where a person connects to the other worlds. It is the path that the soul takes when entering and exiting the body.

• • •

The work of a shaman is not about a healing process per se. The shaman often will need to fight the offending spirits who have laid siege and captured it. If victorious, the shaman will escort the errant soul to a place of rest and safety, and only then will the client naturally recover their health.

Commentary

Grandmother Nadia:

The shaman's job is to make the patient safe, and when the shaman has the soul in a safe place, and then there is a balance in the organism. Souls wander, and it could be at this moment that your soul is wandering. If I were to look at you very attentively, I could tell if your soul is wandering. For example, when you look at a person, they may have a lost look in their eyes. It can be seen in one's eyes if things are all right or not. There can be disturbances, or there can be worries or odd conditions of the soul. In such incidences, your soul needs to be returned because it is wandering without a master, without a home. This needs to be rectified and calmed. Our conjurings are done to get the soul to a safe place. Every month, when the soul is in a safe place, an offering must be made to maintain the balance. When a soul is wandering, you may have just a lost feeling or unease. This is all expressed on the face of the person. Grandmother Tika looks at the area between the eyebrows on a person's face or in the region of the heart to see if the soul is not home. She knows what's happened in the past, what is happening now and in the future. She's very specific.

• • •

The Personal Shaman and the Storage of Souls

Simply using the services of a specific shaman does not make them your "personal shaman." You must ask a specific shaman to attend to your soul in an ongoing relationship. This is a large request to make of a shaman, who will either agree or decline to meet your needs. When you are a child, your parents may ask the "children's shaman" to be your personal shaman. As an adult, you would ask a shaman on your own behalf.

If the shaman accepts such a request, a special ritual is performed three times, once each month for three months. During the first ritual, the shaman conjures about the life of the petitioner and returns with information about which spirits are helping them along their path. In the second and third month, the shaman journeys to seek out the client's soul. The shaman conveys the soul to a special hiding place in the other worlds.

All shamans have various places in which they will store souls. Grandmother Ponga Valdu, an old blind shaman in Bulava village who worked with children, had a secret place in the Pole Star where she stored the souls of youngsters. Grandfather Misha would fly away to a sacred mountain (*djasu*) where he would deliver the souls in his care. There are two or three entrances in this sacred mountain, and Grandfather Misha separated men and women's souls into these different caves. This mountain has powerful protectors who stand guard over the souls that have been placed there for special protection. The spirit protectors of the sacred mountains appear in the form of a woman or a man accompanied by a powerful dog.

When a shaman travels to one of these sacred mountains, a conversation between the shaman and the Mountain spirits occurs. The shaman will ask of the Mountain spirits that the soul they are conveying be placed inside one of the inner caverns for safekeeping. Since all shamans place souls in some protective location in the invisible worlds, we can assume that the shaman has a more intimate connection with the particular spirits who guard these powerful places of safety, located either in the mountains of the Middle World or the stars of the Upper World.

A shaman who commits being a personal shaman to others must travel, from time to time, to the realms where the souls are placed. There, they make offerings to the spirits who guard the souls, as the shaman cultivates a strong relationship with these protectors. Most of the time, the souls placed there will stay in the area, but from time to time, a soul will escape. I once asked Grandfather if, during a journey, he ever flew to one of his secret places to take an inventory of the souls under his care. How would he know if a soul that was being guarded had escaped? He said two things to me concerning this matter. First, souls do like to wander, and from time to time they'll escape the special places they were taken to by a shaman. If this happens, it is incumbent upon the shaman to find a different or stronger place in which to keep the soul. Second, as far as doing an inventory of souls under his care, he said he never goes to check those stony safe caverns. If one of the souls escapes, usually the Master spirit of that place will come to him in the Dreamtime and inform him that so-and-so's soul has gone missing. When he awakens, he will perform a conjuring to take it back to a cavern of safekeeping.

Having your soul guarded in a secret place will make it harder for destructive spirits to find, attack, and harm you. This can also ensure great health, happiness, and luck in your life. If your personal shaman dies, they will continue to be your protector from the other side. They may come to visit you in your dreams. Whether or not they are living, it is important to give offerings to your personal shaman from time to time, because they remain an intimate part of your life forever.

Commentaries

Grandmother Nadia:

When you are away from home and traveling, your personal shaman may fly to you as an animal in nature or appear to you in the dream state to make sure you are protected and safe. The shaman will see and hear everything you are doing, and later they'll be able to describe all of the places that you have visited in exacting details. Usually, they come in the form of birds, and they'll sit in trees.

•

I remember my sister Shura telling me a story that when she was feeling illness in her foot, our mother, Goga, had arranged to bring her to a shaman upriver to the Goldi village of Naykhin. My sister was much older than I, and this happened in her youth before I was born. On their journey, my mother spoke of a dream she had that the shamans had already placed Shura's soul into a small house. In that dream, my mother saw her happily playing in that house as children play. Shura said that from that time on, she never had any more pain in her foot. The shaman had healed her before she arrived in the village.

•

Although during my youth, my primary children's shamans were Grandmother Ponga and Grandmother Altaka, I remember a time where my father, mother, and I traveled in a boat to another village to see a different shaman. I just remember how the boat was laden with gifts for that shaman. My father was always very generous to the shamans for their help.

•

As an adult, I would always travel to Sophisk village to see Grandmother Indyeka. I would see her once or twice a year in the springtime or autumn. When I would arrive, I could find myself alone for a session or find myself in a company of her other clients that had also arrived for a healing. Everyone would gather for the nightly sessions. Sometimes I knew the other people, and sometimes they were new to me. So here we all were in Grandmother Indyeka's home. We would eat and share refreshments before Grandmother Indyeka began her work. Some people would come by themselves but would want Grandmother to also investigate the health of their other family members who were not present in her home. Others would come for a general healing or other personal reasons. If there were others, then you would just have to wait your turn. If Grandmother couldn't get around to all the healings that night, then you would need to return the next evening. I remember once in Bulava village when Grandmother arrived to see the families she had been working with for years. There were about twelve people waiting for her. She started her work around nine o'clock at night and wasn't done until three or four the next morning. I was always amazed how long she could work and how many people she could help at one time.

•

All powerful mountains will have a place of safekeeping for souls. In our territory, our djasus are located in Bulava, Bogorodsk, and Kadi. Different mountains, special mountains in the territory of Nizhniy Khalbu and Nizhniy Gavin, also have these places. When I do my conjuring in Seattle, I take the souls to Mount Rainier. There is a powerful djasu in that territory.

• • •

Causes of Disease

According to the Ulchi shamans, all disease is due to an imbalance in the holistic relationship of the mind, body, and spirit of an individual. When any piece of this tri-part organism is out of balance, disease will result. The disease may be caused by a prolonged absence of the wind soul, whose behavior may be causing trouble in the invisible worlds or who may be reluctant to energize and reconnect with its human host.

Breaking taboos, offending spirits, experiencing unresolved physical or psychological trauma, or living a life without balance can also open a doorway to illness. All types of diseases have their own unique inborn consciousness and will arrive in the form of a hostile force from the invisible realms. When the organism is weakened, it becomes even more susceptible to the ever-present negative forces surrounding all living beings.

To maintain health, the Ulchis teach a type of "mindfulness" that revolves around one's cognitive/behavioral processes. Positive thoughts, actions, and deeds attract positive outcomes and helpful spirits while negative thoughts, actions, and deeds attract the opposite. The adage "You reap what you sow" and "What goes around comes around" is a principle embedded within their ontological foundation. They stress that the body needs to be maintained through proper exercise and nutrition and that right relationship to Nature and her spirits must be ongoing. Dysphoric states such as stress, anxiety, fear, and depression must be healed, eliminated and transformed. What one exposes oneself to in daily life must be controlled and regulated. Choosing to associate with unethical or vampiric people, focusing excessively on reading or listening to negative news, watching violent movies, or speaking judgmentally about people or situations can weaken the psyche and attract harmful spirits into one's life.

The environments in which one interacts must also be taken into consideration, as specific places in nature are unhealthy or spiritually dangerous. Self-regulation, awareness, and control of one's psychological states are imperative and must be cultivated not only by the individual but by family members as well. Actions and deeds performed by one family member will have consequences for the entire family group.

However, the behavior and actions of each person's wind soul are another matter entirely. A person may follow the dictates of Nature and the societal laws, endeavoring to live a strong and ethical life, but may find, from time to time, that they experience an unusual or strange illness.

Ancestors or a recently deceased family member may also contribute to an illness of any kind. This may be due to a failure of the family to follow the complex dictates and societal rules governing the dead, which can result in the deceased person's soul bothering or harming the living. Beneficent spirits may also send illness and misfortune to one who hunts, fishes, or wild crafts in various regions in the environment, due to improper actions or requests on that individual's part. Self-correction can usually ease the situation and is often part of the cure prescribed by a shaman after a healing, but in more complex situations, the shaman may need to intercede with the offending spirits on the person's or family's behalf.

CHAPTER 15

Elements of the Shamanic Journey

In the most accurate terms, the organic process of a shamanic journey can be described as a self-induced hypnagogic state in which the shaman remains fully aware as they enter into a psycholog-ical/ physiological state commonly known as threshold consciousness. This transition is accompanied by a wide variety of sensory experiences such as tactile sensations, sounds, geometric patterns, and figurative images of spirits that occupy Heaven and Earth. There are also the picturesque landscapes of the alternative universes that are explained by the shamans as layers betwixt and between the three worlds. Most of the hypnagogic images contain an auditory component.

These experiences, within the context of the healing event, can last for minutes or change within the blink of an eye, propelling the shaman onto a new visionary landscape. Physiological sensations of flying, floating, fighting, walking, running, climbing, or resting accompanies the hypnagogic state, as do powerful emotional responses to fear or euphoria. Rather than classifying the classical shamanic experience as a schizophrenic episode or disorder, an alternative assessment of the evidence could suggest a self-controlled loosening of ego boundaries, resulting in visions, premonitions, and discourse with the inhabitants of the invisible worlds.

The shaman's body or a specific body part can be possessed by a spirit or ancestor, resulting in involuntary movement. If possessed by a deceased shaman, the practitioner may imitate the individual sounds, drum rhythms, or physical expressions of their former colleague, explaining later that they had no conscious control over their physical actions. This type of possession is considered a great gift of strength from the ancestors.

The shaman's interoceptive senses serve as a diagnostic tool, mimicking and replicating the client's illness within their own body. These internal experiences are either confirmed or denied by the client within the context of the healing session. The shaman will query the patient at different intervals during the session, asking if certain pains or discomfort are present within the musculoskeletal structure or the internal organs. If the disease is life-threatening, a residual effect can be transferred to the healer, resulting in temporary illness or lack of vitality for the shaman and/or their family members. Because of this, a shaman is always cautious when taking on a case that involves a critical illness. The need for foresight or discretion will also accompany any cases where general bad fortune, suicides, tragedies, or chronic displays of mental or behavioral disorders such as anxiety or depression are involved.

Preparation for the Shamanic Journey – Setting the Environment

The journey can be roughly divided into three distinct parts: calling the spirits and traveling into the invisible worlds, arriving and capturing the soul, and returning and saving the self. Commencement begins only after the requisite offerings have been made.

Once the client has finished preparing the offerings for the upcoming ceremony, the shaman's assistant turns out most of the lights in the room, leaving only the dim glow of a candle or the embers in the hearth. The shaman stands up from their seat and walks over to the main altar in the room, upon which sit the spirits of the home, as well as the offering dish containing all of the proper ceremonial foodstuffs. The shaman then takes the cup containing vodka or water into their left hand. They place the middle finger of their right hand into the cup and perform the ceremonial *chicturi*. The liquid is splashed and sprinkled first to four corners of the home, then upwards to Heaven and downwards toward the Earth. Then the feeding of the family spirits begins.

The House spirit is the first to be given offerings, as the shaman says prayers and gives thanks to the spirits of the environment in which the healing will be conducted. They also ask forgiveness from the House spirits for the noise and ruckus that they are about to make. Then the shaman feeds all the spirits of the home by placing alcohol or water to the mouths of the wooden idols. After the ritual feeding of the house spirits has taken place, the shaman feeds their own personal spirits, who help them travel to the other realms. These include the spirit of the drum, drumstick, metal spirit belt, cap, and any special amulets that they are wearing. To feed their drum, the shaman places alcohol or water on the inner part of the rim or on the four leather straps inside the drum that represent the shaman's roads. Then the spirits of the drumstick are fed, followed by those of the metal spirit belt, or *yampa*. Prayers for strength, protection, and a good journey are requested.

Once the offerings (*chuvachi*) have been made, the shaman can proceed. Their chair or place is set next to the altar. Each shaman will begin their journey in their own way. Some begin by standing, while most will start from a sitting position. There is also a small table placed close to the shaman. On this table are put three small cups. One cup contains water, the next contains vodka, and the last holds a concoction of water and *sankura* leaves. At various times during a conjuring, a shaman may stop and imbibe either the vodka or the *sankura* and water elixir. This not only serves to strengthen them but this act is how offerings are made to their spirit helpers. Grandmother Nadia explains that ingesting food or drink, or smoking tobacco is another way to feed the spirits. What a shaman eats or drinks during a ritual is transported from their body into the spirit realm.

The table also serves as a secondary altar, as the shaman may place any of their magical paraphernalia upon it for the evening's work. This can include but is not limited to the wooden healing streamers, an amulet to be given to a client, or clothing belonging to a client if it is a long distance healing. In the case of an amulet, they will perform a specific ceremony during the healing to awaken it and bring it to life. The particular healing spirit will be asked to take up residence within the amulet before it is presented to the client. They will place the spirit into the amulet by pressing down on top of the amulet with the end of the drumstick. During the conjuring, the shaman will continue to feed their own helping spirits, such as the drum, drum-stick, personal amulets, and *yampa*, from the cup of vodka or water at various intervals.

COMMENTARY

GRANDMOTHER TIKA:

You must always feed and give water to your spirit idols before conjuring. Sometimes you often begin your conjuring without the requests of your clients. Why is this? It is because the spirits want to be fed and nourished and the spirits will compel you to give them an offering.

• • •

CALLING THE SPIRITS

The journey starts with a call to the shaman's helping spirits. As the shaman begins, they cover or hide their face behind their drum. This placement of the drum also serves as a protection from negative or hostile energies that may wish to intrude during the shamanic flight.

The shaman's song to their spirits is unique, and through it, they call, beg, and request the presence of their helping spirits. When they call to the spirits, they must wait and see who arrives. Sometimes all of the spirits arrive, sometimes only a few, and at times no spirits will make their presence known. In the latter case, the conjuring must not proceed. The shaman will inform the client(s) that no spirit has arrived to help them. The client(s) are then instructed to come back in a few days and allow the shaman to try again. Sometimes the spirit of the drum can be unco-

GRANDMOTHER INDYEKA DJAKSUL GIVING A YIYEE FOR CLIENTS THAT TRAVELED TO HER HOME, SOPHISK VILLAGE

operative. If its timbre does not sound correct to the shaman, the conjuring must wait for another day. Even though the absence of spirits or the failure of the drum's proper resonance does not happen frequently, it can occur from time to time.

A shaman will never begin a journey without being accompanied by their spirits. At the first strike of the drum, the spirits awaken and begin to pay attention to the shaman's song. As the shaman calls to them, they may respond by flying to the drum and resting upon the rim or sitting on their shoulders—or they may decide that they are too busy with their own lives and ignore the call. The drumbeats start out slowly and quietly, and this measured, somber rhythm can continue for a long time. The personal vocabulary of the drum is made up of specific rhythms for each spirit helper. When a particular spirit appears to the shaman, the drumbeat will change momentarily to mark that spirit's arrival. For an Ulchi who has previously participated in a particular shaman's conjuring, the arrival of specific spirits is recognized through these changes in rhythm.

The shaman sits in the dark, eyes closed, and focuses their attention on the area of the heart and between their eyebrows, inside their head. They also turn their attention to their somatic experiences as a primary way of diagnosing illness and discord. These elements open the portals to the other worlds. As the spirits arrive, one by one, the rhythms may speed up. The shaman then sings their thanks and gratitude for the arrival.

The format of a shaman's journey or conjuring is unique to that individual. The first section will always be very similar in form and structure. The shaman uses, in essence, the same format to call their spirits every time, no matter the circumstances. The ending, or return from the invisible worlds, will also be similar each time, as it is based loosely on a similar theme. It is the segments of travel in the other worlds and the capture of the soul that are always distinctive, unpredictable, spontaneous, and unrehearsed.

Once the shaman has performed the preliminary offerings and invoked their spirit helpers, the actual conjuring begins. The shaman must travel upon their road to the other worlds, aided by their spirit helpers. The road of each shaman varies greatly, and each has their own personal which is intricately bound to either the Upper World or Middle World. When we speak about an Upper or Middle World shaman, we are referring to a primary path of that particular practitioner. Their road or path is analogous to the entire lifetime of their soul, starting at birth, encompassing their early years and middle age, and ending with death. This is why a shaman is taught to consciously travel halfway down a personal road. Traveling to the end would cause immediate illness or even death. The concept of the road is associated not only with shamans, but also with other living people, rocks, rivers, mountains, grasses, and spirits. Everything in existence has a soul; therefore, everything has a road.

COMMENTARY

GRANDMOTHER NADIA:

Small shamans can only walk one road. They usually travel to the same place. It is only the more powerful shamans that can travel here and there to the Upper, Middle, and or Lower Worlds. They can even travel to the nine worlds beyond the Cosmos. Children shamans just travel to the Pole Star. Now, remember that children shamans sometimes can be as powerful as the Kasa shamans because children and babies cannot communicate to the shaman, telling them where they hurt or what is going on in their lives. So the shamans must travel to the Sky.

.

When first you call your spirits and find something appearing to you that is frightening, then you must drive it away with the sound of the drum. Only then proceed with calling in your spirits.

• • •

SHAMANIC DRUMMING RHYTHMS

The structure of shamanic drumming varies, with changes in pitch and timbre as well as complex rhythmic patterns. The conceptual framework is best understood as various tonal/rhythmic frequencies associated with all types of spirits. To invoke a specific spirit helper, one must first learn the correct rhythmic pattern. If the rhythm is not produced properly, the specific spirit will not arrive. All types of spirits have their unique frequencies/organic patterning in nature. They can be the helping spirits of the shamans, the animal or plant spirits of Nature, or the protective spirits of their ancient clansmen.

When Grandfather Misha and Grandmother Nadia would teach these various spirit patterns to Western audiences, Grandmother would explain, "These are our classics, like your Mozart. You must learn our classics before you can move on to the more complex and hidden rhythms of the universe."

Although there is a set of "spirit classics" that every Ulchi learns from childhood, the rhythmic patterns of each individual shaman vary depending upon their personal spirit helpers. As each shaman discovers a new helping spirit in the world of the beyond, they will also be introduced to a new rhythmic pattern or vibratory frequency associated with that specific spirit.

When a shaman enacts a group healing ceremony in a village setting, the audience joins in the journey as both witness and participant. Each person not only understands the shaman's narrative but knows what specific spirits may be arriving, due to the changing rhythmic patterns within the song. The person or people who are present during the conjuring are thus able to follow along with the adventure. They hear where the shaman is, what they are doing, and who they are encountering. The people are captivated by the story and the unfolding drama of the narrative. They vicariously experience the journey feeling that they too are being swept away by the circumstances of the conjuring.

This "joining" is not just the visual replication of events through imagination but more of a symbiotic mutualism benefiting both shaman and their audience. These patterns are always in flux, whether a shaman is working with a group or an individual. The rhythms vary every time because no two journeys, along with their accompanying spirit visitations, are ever alike.

Once, when Grandfather Misha and Grandmother Nadia were teaching a group of neo-shamanic enthusiasts in the United States, they were introduced to a Western interpretation of shamanic drumming. These workshop members performed a steady, monotonous beat that had no tone variance and ended abruptly. At its conclusion, Grandfather Misha and Grandmother Nadia were left perplexed, shocked, and dismayed. Later on in the seminar, when the participants asked about drumming techniques, Grandmother addressed the group.

COMMENTARY

GRANDMOTHER NADIA:

The rhythms are played by the shamans in response to what the spirits are telling the shaman to do. During a shamanic singing journey (yiyee), a shaman may stop very suddenly and begin a completely new rhythm. It may depend on what the shaman's spirit helpers are demanding the shaman to do. A shaman may work with the voice of the swan and all of a sudden the tiger appears, and momentarily, at that moment, the rhythm is changed, and a new rhythm begins. It's always an improvisation.

Now, please excuse me for what I am about to say, as I may insult you in some way, but when you first showed me your drumming, I did not understand. It may be that your culture is like this, but you all had the same one rhythm, and that was all. There was no improvisation. No singing. There was nothing to show me what you were meeting along your road. There were no hindrances; there was only the one rhythm. I do not want to offend you in any way, but it was something that I did not recognize or understand. When our shamans travel, it is so interesting. The shaman starts out slowly and then, all of a sudden, there is a quick change, and it becomes a completely different rhythm, or else the shaman stops drumming all together and just sings or just works with a rhythm. It's such choreography, from the point of view of a choreographer. That is why I have studied the shamans and I, myself, am pulled unnoticeably into the path. I started out studying folklore of my peoples and was pulled deeply into shamanism, and now I am considered the carrier of shamanism for my peoples. When a drum is played with a monotone, well, it may be magic or a trance. When a shaman travels, they may be momentarily in three different places and fighting. At this time, other spirits may come flying in. If you look at the way a shaman works in their culture, they will even cuss!

When Grandfather Misha was working in Paris with Giva, our indigenous folk group who traveled and performed throughout Europe in the late eighties, we agreed just to do a show. Grandfather was just going to sing for ten minutes. When he began to beat his drum, all of the spirits arrived. He said, "No! Fuck you! You have to get out of here! I'm driving you away!" Now our group on the stage, who understand the Ulchi language, began to laugh. The French people didn't understand what was going on, but they laughed also. Now you understand a little bit about where we are coming from. It was difficult for Grandfather because he is not a show-business shaman. It is very difficult for him to just put on a show. It is very difficult for him to turn off. He got carried away by his spirits.

That is why when you go into a trance; it starts out slowly and gradually. Your paths will be different, and your spirits will be different. There are fights in all of these shamanic journeys. The shaman's road is not straight! Even in our life in the Middle World, there is no straight path, no matter how rich you are. There are always unexpected hindrances, and the same is true for the road of a shaman. The shaman should find and fight and calm and put everything in its place in the invisible worlds and then return to the earthly realm. It is a huge tragedy if a shaman's journey (yiyee) is stopped in some way [referring to the abrupt and artificial ending to the seminar members' drum performance].

· · ·

The one-tone monotonous rhythm indicated, in the language of Classical shamanism, that each member of the group was on the exact same journey, meeting the same spirits, in the same otherworld landscapes, and that this journey concluded for each participant at the exact moment in time. In Classical shamanism, the rhythm of a journey starts out slowly and quietly, as the variations of the drum's tone and rhythms result in progressive and deepening states of trance. Once a journey is complete, the shaman returns slowly and gently into the world of the living. Grandfather and Grandmother said that the method of sudden and disjointed reentry back into this Middle World was dangerous and would cause soul illness. Whether a person is engaged in a trance state or asleep, one must realize that their soul is wandering. This is the soul's most natural state. It is a great taboo to quickly awaken a person from a natural sleep state or to jump out from a hidden location to give someone a fright. Any sudden shocks or trauma to a person's psyche can result in soul loss.

GRANDMOTHER NADIA IN THE SAKHA REGION, SIBERIA, CA. 1997

QUALITIES OF TRANCE WITHIN A SHAMANIC JOURNEY

The type of trance work that is accomplished by the shamans has been described in Western literature as a flow state or controlled trance, as opposed to the absorptive possession models found among other indigenous peoples of the world. The baseline to the practice begins with motion, movement, singing, and drumming. The key to this process is to maintain conscious awareness while simultaneously entering an altered state of consciousness without a complete surrender of a self-aware state. There is a quality of "mindfulness" during

331

the experience, in which the shaman is both participant and observer simultaneously. Grandmother Nadia always speaks about the need to "control" and "allow" the journey to unfold naturally. Of course, the "intention" always remains the same: seeking out illness, enlisting the aid of helpful spirits, learning the conditions of the illness, finding the soul, fighting any blocks or hindrances that may interfere with the desired outcome (to find and procure the soul), escorting the soul to a secure environment, performing decontamination processes for the shaman in both the invisible and visible worlds, understanding what prescriptions should be given to patient after the healing, and completing the final cleansing of the patient's body. The balance in such a trance state is achieved when the shaman can be completely immersed in the ever-changing landscapes and events in the invisible worlds. They must allow the spirits to work through all of their senses while they retain self-awareness to achieve their desired goal.

Shamanic Flight

During the shamanic journey, after the spirit helpers have arrived, the shaman must make their way to the other worlds. This is accomplished in different ways and by various means. When Grandmother Tika, a Sky shaman, was ready to begin a healing, her winged tiger spirits took her onto their backs and ascended into the heavens. Grandfather Misha would climb to the top of a sacred mountain and then turn into a bird or other animal and begin his ascent into the sky. Sometimes he would launch himself into the Heavens by climbing to the top of his shaman tree, and from there begin his journey into the Upper

World. Grandmother Nadia ascends into the Heavens from the top of her shaman's pillar. The departure into the invisible worlds is usually a fixed element in most journeys, although the details of the expedition may vary. These particulars can include the type of weather the shaman must travel through, the ease or difficulty of the terrain, and their encounters with spirits, helpful or harmful, along the way.

No matter the amount of time a shaman spends in these other worlds; they are still considered an "outsider" or visitor there. The invisible worlds are domains of the spirits, who guide, teach, reveal wondrous things, and keep us out of trouble. A shaman always listens to the advice of their spirits and is completely obedient to their commands and requirements.

During their flights to the other worlds, a shaman must always maintain some connection with the mortal realm. This can be accomplished in various ways, most often through the use of a *suna*, or shaman rope. This rope may be physically tied around the shaman's waist or may take the form of an invisible cord, which is tied around their waist through imaginative visualizations by either their personal assistant or elder members of the community who are present during the conjuring.

COMMENTARIES

GRANDMOTHER NADIA:

Different shamans, when traveling to the other worlds, tear themselves away from the earth in different ways. Some go up the Tree of Life. Grandfather Misha tears himself from the top of a sacred mountain. He always asks permission to fly from his grandfather (father) and grandmother (mother), as well as his ancestors. Then he asks his spirit helpers to come and join him in his flight, asking them to help him find the soul of the client upon this road. As he ascends, he'll rest on different colored clouds. Each cloud has its own landscape, mountains, villages, animals, and inhabitants. After this, he'll travel to the stars. He likes to rest on the Pole Star. Sometimes he'll travel beyond the stars.

··

GRANDFATHER MISHA:

I traveled beyond the stars to a clear, transparent land. It was clear like glass. I saw a frog there, and I thought why is there a frog in the clear, transparent heaven? This is the frog that controls and gives rain to the earth.

· · ·

SECRET LANGUAGE OF THE SHAMAN

Shamans can also sing in special languages that are given to them by their spirits. Grandfather Misha had a spirit language that came from an unknown source but also included words from the Yakut tongue. Only a shaman's assistant who has been working with a particular shaman for an extended period of time may be able to understand the meaning of the languages that a shaman speaks.

COMMENTARY

VERA DUVAN:

The language of the shamans is very expressive and very individual, and that is why it is difficult to translate the songs into any other language. They use such words and expressions which no one else speaks.

· · ·

SHAPESHIFTING

The art of shapeshifting involves a metamorphosis into an animal, insect, reptilian creature, or element of nature and is a necessity at various times during the journey. It may occur in the beginning stages of shamanic flight or during the shaman's travels in the invisible worlds. It may also be used to confuse hostile spirits during the return to the world of the living. This transformation has at times been observed by clients, who witness physical changes in the shaman. Depending on what the shaman is changing into, they will feel different parts of their body will grow, stretch, shrink, or expand, resulting in a dynamic somatic experience.

I queried Grandmother Nadia about the actual technique of shapeshifting. She commented that the spirits would teach you. Then I asked whether, when a person shapeshifts, their consciousness is alone within the form of a specific creature or whether they share a dual consciousness with the other being. She replied that both exist at the same time in a shared reality of conscious awareness.

VERA DUVAN PLAYING
UDJAJU (LOG DRUM)

Shamans can travel in different forms to various regions of any territory to inspect or gather information about people, places, or events. Grandmother Tika would transform herself into a mosquito or bee from time to time during a healing. This allowed her to be a rather inconspicuous creature as she gathered new information about a region in the other worlds.

Ancestors and deceased shamans may also employ shapeshifting to return to the land of the living. Grandmother Tika would speak of

her father visiting her in the body of a bluebird, and Grandmother
Nadia spoke of feeling Grandfather Misha's energetic presence in a
bird that visited her home a few years after his death.

COMMENTARIES

GRANDMOTHER TIKA:

*You must make a spirit, and during the search, you are transformed
into the form of an animal, like a bird.*

•

*When I give a healing song, my body is transformed into the skin
of a tiger. I feel my body sprouting fur from the pores of my body
and completely enveloping me. This is true!*

••

GRANDFATHER MISHA:

On each stage of the journey, I change my form.

••

GRANDMOTHER NADIA:

*I remember, before I first came to the United States, Grandmothers
Tika and Indyeka told me that they would travel with me to
make sure that my road was safe and protected. During my time
in the Pacific Northwest, when I was outside in nature, I would
observe these two specific birds in tree limbs, just sitting and
watching me. No matter where I traveled in these territories,
I kept seeing these same two birds. Once I returned home to
Bulava, I asked the grandmothers about this. They said, "Of
course, we were watching you, and we saw everything that went
on for you." The grandmothers began to talk about everything
that they had seen, the houses, people, plants, and animals. They*

described everything in detail although they had never traveled outside the Ulchi territories!

•

This happened in winter. The hunters were coming home from the hunt and were riding on two sleds. The dogs were suffering from hunger and were barely able to drag the loaded sleds. When the hunters stopped at a neighboring camp, they found there the great shaman Bogdon Oneko, who was staying there with his granddaughter. Grandfather Bogdon decided that he wanted to ride with the hunters to the next camp. Out of respect and obedience to the shaman, the hunters agreed, but found themselves at a loss; how would they carry him on tired dogs with loaded-down sleds? The shaman soothed them, saying, "We'll get there before the sun goes down.

The hunters looked at each other with confusion, because even with fresh dogs, they wouldn't arrive until night. Grandfather called out, "Go on ahead and I'll catch up with you." The hunters again were amazed and replied, "Do you have a sled?" They began asking him, thinking that the shaman would come after them on a dogsled. Grandfather ordered them to go on their journey.

When the hunters had traveled a little way from the camp, the dogs suddenly pricked up their ears, sniffed the air, and immediately took off headlong ahead. Feeling that something was wrong, the hunters turned back and saw a tiger leaping towards them. The entire way, the tiger chased after them, and indeed, they came to the camp before sunset, jumped from their sleds, and rushed into the hut, where they told what happened.

They were again amazed when they saw Grandfather Oneko saunter into the hut a few minutes after their arrival. They all hurried to the door and looked out to see what he had ridden to the encampment.

They followed his tracks and saw that beyond the barn, the human tracks stopped, and they could see that some kind of animal had been lying there, and beyond that were the tracks of the tiger.

They could all see that the shaman had turned into a tiger and had run after the hunters the entire way. Everyone knew that Grandfather was a powerful shaman who deserved great respect."

"In the recent past, some shamans would wear an entire skin of a deer, bear, or another animal. In their conjurings, you would see them transform into the creature. It was frightening and wondrous.

..

GRANDMOTHER TATIANA:

I remember in the past watching many shamans sing, and sometimes fire would come forth from their mouths. Everyone would see these things. I believe in shamans. Sometimes they tell the truth.

• • •

ARRIVING IN THE OTHER WORLDS

Only after a shaman is securely on their road may they seek the client's wandering soul. Many times, during a healing, a shaman will see various paths that stretch out before them. The shaman may become confused and ask their spirits which one to take, as a shaman is always consulting their spirit guides while they travel. They will ask questions such as "Do I go here or there? What should I do now? Is this okay?"

Other difficulties may also arise when they are seeking out the wandering soul. Sometimes the soul is found in the roots of trees, locked in an underwater cavern, or held hostage by the wicked spirits. The shaman must rely on the help of their spirits to guide them to the correct location, and at the same time, the circumstances of the soul loss must be ascertained if they are to succeed in retrieving and protecting it in a safe place (*djasu*).

While a shaman conjures, they sing the entire experience, describing the details of the geography and topography of the spiritual worlds, the spirits that they are meeting, the offerings that are being made, and so forth.

At times, a shaman will interrupt their singing, and the narrative will transform into a dialogue with a spirit encountered along the way. They will hold a discourse in which the client(s) are only privileged to hear one part of the conversation, similar to eavesdropping on someone else's telephone call.

The client(s) may hear the shaman saying, "Who are you? Okay, what do you think? Is this so? Should I do this? Okay, thank you." The shaman's responses are followed by brief moments of silence as the spirits reply directly to the shaman. The client hears only the questions, requests, or answers from the shaman, and remains unaware as to the actual contents of the discourse.

While singing, the shaman describes the situation, the inhabitants they encounter, and the occurrences taking place. They relay their own feelings, fears, expectations, and discoveries as they travel back and forth in time. They may be talking to a spirit in the Upper World when suddenly they find themselves underwater in the Middle World, swimming with the fish. They can be literally thrown through time and space in the blink of an eye. For the shaman, this is very disconcerting and sometimes bewildering.

For the shamans known as *kulamukachi* shamans, the episode unfolds so quickly that they cannot describe the journey through any type of narrative. Their vocalizations sound like they are singing "in tongues" or in some unintelligible language. It is only with the *kulamukachi* that the participants hear the exploits of the shaman's journey after the conjuring is complete. Grandmother Yetchka was this unique type of shaman and only gave certain details of her journey after the fact to her clients.

The shaman undertakes their journey for a specified reason, whether to find a lost soul or to personally investigate the land of the spirits. When this "jumping around" in time and space occurs, it can make it more difficult to carry out and achieve this goal.

All journeys are difficult and tiring, some more so than others. Shamans will have familiar locations in the other worlds, where they will rest from time to time during a journey. These may be

ULCHI KULAMUKACHI SHAMAN, RELATIVE OF THE DUVAN CLAN, 1907

clouds, places near the water, mountaintops, or cool, luxuriant valleys. Depending upon the degree of difficulty of a conjuring, a shaman may choose to visit one of their special places for a while to rest and gather their strength.

COMMENTARIES

GRANDFATHER MISHA:

I do nothing; it is the spirits who work through me. They completely help me.

..

GRANDMOTHER NADIA:

When I begin my journey, I am aware that I need to control myself. If something arrives to frighten or disturb me as I begin, I make a wall between myself and this unwanted spirit. Never touch a shaman when they are doing their work!

.

Why do I eat copious amounts of food after a healing? It is because I find harmful spirits in my throat. Western doctors don't absorb their clients' pain, but shamans do! Sometimes my head will throb or spin when I am working with a client. All shamans feel the corresponding pain of their client in their (the shaman's) own body. When I work with a client, I will see holes in the body of the person. I will see these holes in the head, throat, or stomach. Epilepsy has special holes. The North Star spirit will help you with throat problems, and the Big Dipper spirit will assist you in problems of the head and stomach. Before I work, I make sure to have a good dinner, but after the healing, I will eat much food because my spirits want food and vodka. During my healings, my head spins and flies about, and the food helps to clean me out.

.

I always interview people before I do my healings. I ask them about why they have come to see me and what I can do to help. Afterwards, I ask them to give me their permission to begin the healing. I sometimes eat raw eggs to help clear my throat. Grandmother Tika and Grandfather Misha ate raw eggs also. When I complete a healing, all of the illness of my client will stick to me, so I will wash my face and comb my hair after the healing, then I will eat. When you hear me clear my throat in my healing, it is because I am driving out and expelling harmful spirits.

.

It is permissible to do the magic making while your client sleeps. When I was a child and Grandmother Altaka gave me a conjuring, I would sometimes be sleeping. Grandmother Indyeka helped people with epilepsy. When I did a healing with a man who had the same illness, I did my conjuring in a quiet way as not to invoke the seizure spirit. It is important to remember that as a shaman, one must control the force and power of the healing.

•

Shaman's spirits have different faces, different types, and different levels of strength. They have their own special qualities and special powers. They may want you to give them water. They will come to you in your dreams. The spirits will come to you and speak. The great shamans will give them a song and take them to their drum and, as they arrive, mark the rhythm of the drum with a loud beat. They will teach you how to sing and drum. The novice shamans may not know how to sing or play the drum rhythms. The novice will begin by talking up the drum and drumstick and just begin, as the spirits will teach everything.

•

For myself, it is wondrous, as I am very surprised what words, melodies, and rhythms issue forth from me as I do the work. The spirits work through my body. You must really need to believe that it is through the spirits that your work is accomplished, and through your contact with them, you will gain all knowledge. You cannot do this yourself; it is only the result of the spirits.

•

I remember that in the past before I took the road, everyone would hear all the great shamans say these things, and most people thought that perhaps they were lying or telling stories of spirits. No one quite believed them that it was through the spirits that they did the work. I would listen and talk to all of the old shamans and ask them questions, and they would all say the same thing about their helping spirits. I would listen to their songs and stories, and it was always the same. It was only when I began the shaman's road and found my own spirits and had my own experiences that then I believed completely in everything that they said.

•

When the shaman sings, they see different spirits. Dependent upon the client's specific illness, the shaman will see different spirits who arrive to help them. The faces of the spirits appear, and sometimes they will help you slowly or sometimes quickly.

• • •

SPIRIT POSSESSION

The shaman's spirits are always coming and going from the host body. They stand behind the shaman or to the side. They sit upon the shaman's shoulders, or they enter the shaman's physical body for periods of time. Protective spirits, such as former shamans, deceased family members, and ancestors, are also known to take up temporary residence in the shaman's body.

Both the helping and protective spirits may lodge themselves in the shaman's consciousness, as well as in their body. When a spirit is residing in the shaman's consciousness, the personality of the shaman is not displaced. For these periods of time, the shaman shares a symbiotic relationship with the spirit. Both "minds" exist together and remain separate. There is no complete merging, as the shaman is acutely aware of both their own and the spirit's personalities.

The spirit may also choose to occupy a particular body part for a short period of time. This can occur when a shaman, during a conjuring, finds that a deceased shaman has appeared to help them with the work. Suddenly, the drum hand of the shaman becomes possessed by this shaman spirit. The drumbeats change, as they begin to play the rhythms of this former shaman. The current shaman cannot control their arm or hand and must allow this process to complete on its own.

Animal spirits may enter the shaman's body and become the animating force behind the dance, and it is a common occurrence for people to observe the shaman shapeshift into a tiger, deer, bear, or other creature. Whether it involves a drum rhythm, a particular dance, or a way of working with various shamanic tools, spirits have the ability to control the actions of the shaman's physical body.

Addressing the Spirits

When a shaman is speaking or in contact with a spirit, there is always great trepidation. As a temporary visitor to the invisible worlds, the shaman is keenly aware that their presence and actions in these worlds do not go unnoticed by the local inhabitants (the spirits). In their narratives, a shaman will repeat various phrases such as: Forgive me, listen to me, I beg of you, don't harm me, I am just playing here, I am only a student, I am not a shaman. If the shaman were to address the spirits in an aggressive or boastful way, dire consequences would result, and the spirits would lead them down the wrong path or to the land of the dead, which would result in instant death. Spirits must be addressed with great humility, caution, respect, and fear, as they can take their revenge at any time.

I remember when Grandfather Misha was conducting various teachings throughout the Pacific Northwest. At one morning lecture, he arrived and said that he could not continue discussing the tradition until he had resolved an issue he was having with a powerful Tiger spirit from his homeland.

Tiger Spirit of Lake Kadi

Grandfather Misha:

There is a great mountain that rises above Lake Kadi. That guardian spirit of that lake has been watching what I have been doing and saying to everyone. He is very upset and agitated. I did a ritual this morning to ask that he forgive me and step away from me. I have told him that I have come to this country to teach people our ways and not to do harm.

I said; don't be so angry with me. Don't be so tempestuous with me. I am not thinking badly of you. I am just here to teach people. Kadi spirit remained very agitated with me and created havoc for me, and now I am ill. What can you do? Let it be that way. If he puts pressure on me, then it will be that way. If he puts pressure on me, then I will die where I fall. I will be very cautious now in my relationship with him. I am very worried about what will happen. If I make a small mistake and he does not know what I am doing, he will act abruptly. If he does not understand what I am trying to do here with the people, then he can take me instantly. I just kept telling him that I came here to teach people, but he's getting angry with me, saying to me, "You go on home soon, old man." Kadi spirit is a very terrible, terrible spirit. I kept saying to him that I wasn't doing anything here, but I was just showing people what to do and that I said nothing offensive about him nor did I speak anything ill about him. Last week, when I taught and did my conjuring at Jan's home, he was content, but this week he is very agitated with me. The rituals at Jan's home were proper and happened so naturally. All of the offerings to the fire and water spirits were correct, and he did not bother me.

COMMENTARY

GRANDMOTHER NADIA:

All people, especially shamans, are naturally apprehensive, afraid, and a little panicky when it comes to offending spirits. They are fearful of the revenge that a spirit could take on them.

• • •

Questioning the Client

During the journey, the shaman will pause to ask specific questions of the client. They may take forms such as these:

1. Do you have pain in a specified location of the body (arm, head, stomach, kidneys, etc.)?

2. Are there problems concerning your mother, father, or other family members?

3. Have you forgotten to feed the spirits of your home?

4. Has your work been going poorly?

The client is instructed to only answer "yes" or "no" to each question, and not go into any detail or offer any explanation. The spirits do not like long and drawn out answers, and if a client wishes to explain the circumstances, the shaman will become agitated and angry.

While this is taking place, the shaman is feeling the illness of the client in their own body. Whether the illness is new or old, the shaman will experience the identical pains in the same area of their body as their client, and this will help determine the questions asked. I have observed many healings by Grandmother Nadia in which she has asked such questions. After a client's answer, I have heard Grandmother Nadia thank the specific spirit who gave her the information. The spirits are also always informing the shaman as to other ailments that may be affecting the client's soul illness. Between the spirit dialogue and their empathic feelings of the client's illness, the shaman can pinpoint the areas of distress that will need to be examined and addressed if the person is to make a full recovery.

When Grandfather Misha was conducting a healing session for Grandmother Nadia, he discovered that part of her soul loss was due to a very old injury she had experienced as an adolescent. He discerned the particulars of how, what, and where the injury had occurred. He described to her the geographical location, time of year, and other details concerning the event.

Sometimes a shaman will discover during the journey that the client's illness or bad luck may be due to past-life problems. This is rare but happens on occasion. This is because there are other roads, running parallel to a person's path, which is the complete experience of former lives. In the village of Bulava, Grandfather Misha had been conducting a healing for a man who was experiencing ill health. While speaking, Grandfather Misha began to refer to the man as "her." Grandfather Misha talked to him about a life in which he had been a woman and had a couple of children. Suddenly the shaman's song changed, and Grandfather Misha began to speak to this man about his current incarnation and advised him to go and give offerings to his mother's sacred tree. The Tree spirit was unhappy and was causing a part of the problem. Later, the man performed all of the Tree spirit's requests, and his life and health took a dramatic turn for the better.

WOMEN PLAYING ON UDJAJU (LOG DRUM), 1934

It is very important to pay attention to the details of any shamanic narrative, as they may travel back and forth in time concerning the cause of an illness present in a client. The shaman may sing, "I am young, my body is strong," and then the next moment speak of old age and infirmity. This is an indication that the shaman has been on a segment of their road that conformed to an earlier period of their life and then found themselves momentarily twenty years into their own future. These jumps in time can also pertain to fragments of the client's former incarnations.

Offerings along the Way

As the journey continues, a shaman will stop at various places, meet spirits, and make offerings. The offering given is usually of the same types of food and drink customarily given by people in the natural world. There are times when a certain Spirit master will request a very specific offering. This obligation must be met by the shaman.

The actual "offering process" can occur in many ways. Sometimes, offerings are given invisibly by the shaman. At other times, the shaman will go to the altar and eat or drink the food that was laid out before the beginning of the conjuring. When the shaman takes the food into their own body, the spirits —including the spirit helpers who live inside and outside of the shaman's body—are sated. What is eaten by the shaman finds its way to the land of the spirits.

Specific offerings can also be given a day or so after the ceremony. If a shaman has promised a certain offering to a particular spirit, they will go to a sacred place in nature and make a small offering ceremony to fulfill their promise.

Safeguarding the Shaman

In rare occurrences, a shaman may die during a conjuring, so various precautions are taken along the way to safeguard the traveler. Death can occur from a powerful attack by hostile spirits or loss of control by the shaman during a journey. A shaman's ecstatic state is called *yuyun* by the Ulchi. The experience of the journey can impart to a traveler such an exhilarating state of euphoria that the subjective sense of self may disappear. If the shaman loses themselves within their own ecstatic state, they will be tempted to remain in the spirit world, which would result in immediate death of the physical body.

I observed this danger once when Grandfather Misha was conducting a seminar in Portland, Oregon. He had been journeying and was led by his spirit helpers to the Thunder road of his shaman father. He was excited about taking the road to see where it would lead him. His behavior during the journey had changed from showing care and cautiousness to exhibiting an exuberant, almost reckless sense of exploration. Grandmother Nadia was in a panic and called to him in the Ulchi language to return home (come back to his body) and forego the journey down the Thunder road, as this could have resulted in his death.

This is one of the main reasons that a shaman will always have a personal assistant or elders around who understand that, as one listens to the shaman's song, special attention must be paid not only to what spirits are being encountered but to the emotional and cognitive state of the shaman during the journey. A shaman must avoid any temptation to lose oneself completely within the ecstatic state.

CAPTURING AND RECOVERING THE SOUL

After a shaman has located a client's wandering soul, they will seek to capture it by various means, always with the help of their personal spirits. If the soul is held hostage by harmful spirits, the shaman may choose to fight, ask for the soul's return, offer a payment, or steal the soul back quickly and quietly. The shaman Grandfather Alexander Kotkin had an iron net that he used to capture and subdue wicked spirits as he took back the wandering soul. The Master spirit of the iron net was powerful and effective. Other shamans will have various magical objects that physically exist only in the invisible worlds.

Depending on the strength and power of the harmful spirits, the recovery of the soul may be quick or difficult and long.

When the wandering soul has been located and secured, the shaman endeavors to make a hasty retreat from the spirit worlds. They may carry the soul or place it in a special pouch called a *puta*, which they wear on their body. Each method is unique to the particular shaman, and they will never divulge their special techniques.

Taking the soul out of the spirit worlds is possibly the most dangerous task of the journey. Here the ability to shapeshift into a small animal, bird, insect, or larger mammal can come into play. The shaman must return down a crooked path, zigzagging here and there to avoid and confuse any harmful spirits who might be attempting to track them down and prevent them from retrieving the soul.

While on their journey back to the world of the living, the shaman will stop and ritually cleanse themselves in a sacred lake or ocean setting. This is similar to a decontamination process. They must wash off any negative or harmful energy that has accrued while traveling in the other worlds.

Cleansing the Body and the Healing Song

There are various means by which a body can be cleansed and de-contaminated. The most common ones involve the use of either the shaman's drumstick or the *gemsacha*. The entrance to the wind soul is located at the top of the head, and so the shaman will press down on the client's head using the drumstick to close the soul opening in the physical body. The use of the *gemsacha* is a trickier matter. A pair of these wooden streamers is held in the hands of the shaman, who strokes the client with them to removing harmful and negative forces from around the body. This stroking can also be accomplished with the drumstick. The *gemsacha* also serve as a connector to the client's karma, and thus new information about the client and their ancestors can be gathered during this procedure. Some shamans chose not to employ the wooden streamers for this reason. They say that when healing a person, it is wise not to explore too deeply the events that led up to the imbalance. Some of its causes may pertain to past family actions that follow the individual, and revealing them would be closely akin to opening a "Pandora's box." As in the drumstick ritual, the ends of the *gemsacha* are placed on top of the head and pressed down upon the skull, thus closing the entrance of the wandering soul. All the while, the shaman's spirit helpers are talking to the shaman and providing information about the client.

Another type of "fixing or closing" is called a *sukpungi*. This is performed after the soul has been conveyed to the protective "*djasu*". The shaman will bite down on the top of the client's head, insuring that the soul opening has been closed completely. The *sukpungi* is only performed by powerful and experienced shamans, as other shamans may be fearful of the possible consequences that could occur if they carried out the technique. I remember when I had this experience during a personal healing given to me by Grandfather Misha. It was most frightening and unexpected but left me feeling relaxed and energized simultaneously.

Each shaman will have been given a specific healing song by their spirits. This song is used when fixing, healing, or cleaning a soul. The healing song invokes the major spirits and asks that the soul is healed and the illness be driven away.

COMMENTARIES

GRANDMOTHER LINZA:

You should never sukpungi other people! During a healing, if you make a sukpungi, you can absorb all of the illness from your client. You can just sisaji (using the wooden streamers) to clean your clients and cast off all of their diseases. Only great Kasa shamans can sukpungi. After these shamans make a sukpungi, they will become ill for a short amount of time.

••

Grandmother Nadia, speaking about Grandmother
Linza's comment:

*Although Grandfather Misha did the sukpungi from time to
time, I did hear the same information from all of the older Ulchi
shamans.*

••

Grandmother Tika:

*Before my father's death, I saw him in a dream. He insisted that
I sukpungi the top of his head, but I wouldn't do it! My father
said that if I didn't do it, I would become sick and suffer terrible
tortures.*

•••

Self-Preservation and Return

This section of the conjuring is known as "Saving Oneself" and
constitutes the final part of the journey. The shaman has traveled to
various worlds, with the spirits' assistance, and has had a specific goal
to achieve (capturing a wandering soul, foretelling future events, or
contacting a specific Spirit master).
Now it is time to return to the world
of living people. This return trip
uses the second most important
musical tool of the shaman, the
yampa, or metal-coned spirit belt.

When beginning a conjuring, the
shaman may be sitting or standing
with the *yampa* already secured
around their waist. However, some
shamans prefer to wait until this last
section of the journey to place the
belt upon their body. Either way,
the shaman, wearing the *yampa*, will   VERA DUVAN

dance themselves back from the other worlds and return to everyday reality. Although the shaman has already gone through the process of decontamination from the spirit world, the *yampa* will cast off and drive away any last energetic elements that still may be attached as they exit the spirit world and return to the land of the living.

GRANDMOTHER NADIA DUVAN AND J. VAN YSSLESTYNE IN OCEAN HUT (HOGDU)
THEY BUILT ON EBEY'S LANDING, WHIDBEY ISLAND, WASHINGTON STATE, USA

FINAL RITUAL TO THE HOME

Once the shaman has returned to the world of the living, they begin a song of gratitude. They dance to the altar, singing their thanks and praise, and asking forgiveness of the house spirits for making such a noise in the home environment. Then they begin their songs to the spirits of the corners of the room. Each house and each corner is guarded and protected by a specific spirit, and these corner spirits have a hierarchy. The shaman will sense the personality of each of these spirits; discover which is the most powerful, and present a different dance to each one, depending on their nature and what they demand. The dance is given as a type of offering.

The corner spirits are the protectors of the home and the keepers of information about the home and the actions of the family who reside there. While a shaman is dancing to a corner, they are also discussing information with this spirit. This spirit may be forthcoming with information that could be useful in a healing, and may also demand that a special offering is given to it. The shaman informs the family of the request, and it is the family's responsibility to insure that the request is fulfilled.

After the dances to the corners have been completed, the dances to the four directions begin. Starting in the south, the shaman typically moves clockwise to each of the remaining directions. Although the direction of movement may vary, depending on the individual shaman, the clockwise direction is preferred in Ulchi tradition.

Then the time arrives when the shaman must send their spirit helpers back to their respective places. They give thanks and praise and bid them fly away home.

When the dances to the altar, corners, and four directions are complete, the shaman must lock down the door to their own soul. Taking up their drum, they dance and drum to the center of the home. There, they beat a quick and steady rhythm as they spin in a clockwise direction while making the long vocalization "*hey.*" This whirling action must be performed three, seven, or nine times (odd numbers are sacred in the Ulchi tradition) and end with a final drumbeat. This last beat is struck while the drum is positioned above the shaman's head like an umbrella. This serves to close the top of the head, the doorway of the soul, through which the soul travels in and out of the human body. The shaman's soul leaves from the top of their head during a conjuring and returns through this same opening. As this last strike occurs, a loud "*pay*" is called out. The word *pay* in the Ulchi language means "to cast out or to throw away." The shaman calls their wind soul back to their body only at the conclusion of the journey.

THE SHAMAN'S PAYMENT

Once the conjuring is complete, the participant(s) share food and drink with the shaman. It is at this time that the second part of the shaman's payment, known as an *odi*, is presented by the client.

The *odi* will vary, but it is always given to the shaman in two parts. The first part is presented before the conjuring begins. Money, both silver, and paper are placed in a small white bag, which is hung around the shaman's neck. The amount will depend upon the wealth of the client, with a rich person giving more and a poor person less. This payment is seen as a type of protection for the shaman. Some shamans may ask for other types of payments. The spirits will decide upon a payment and inform the shaman of their needs. No matter the request, a shaman will not proceed without the proper *odi*. The client who has requested the healing must comply.

Traditionally, the second part of the payment is usually a small porcelain bowl and a piece of cloth around five feet in length, although other items may be requested such as meat and fish, fishing nets, tools, and other types of various household items. The cloth will be used to make new clothing for the shaman, and the bowl will be added to their personal household crockery.

COMMENTARIES

GRANDMOTHER TIKA:

An odi must have a cup or a bowl, material, and silver in a bag. Why give silver? Silver gives strength to the shaman. Always a shaman will want these types of presents.

••

GRANDMOTHER NADIA:

An odi is a sacred gift, and it is given quietly without a big show, so to speak, to the shaman. It is not so much a payment as it should be looked upon as a sacred gift or as a cooperative effort on the part of the shaman and the client. It is given to ensure the shaman and client's health and well-being.

•

Remember that shamans do not want to sing. They never want an odi. It is the clients who want the singing, and it is their responsibility to bring the gifts. My father had such great respect for the shamans. He did not want to offend them and always lavished them with many great gifts for their work. My father would always give deer and elk meat, fish, fishing nets, silver coins, furs, plates, and cups. This is why I believe that I survived my childhood illness and found a strong road in life. Because of my father and mother's great respect for the shamans, they prepared my road. Always give great respect to the shamans!

·

It will appease the spirit helpers as it is a type of "wish" on the part of the client that the shaman lives well after the healing ceremony. If the odi rite is not carried out properly, the shaman, client, or both could/would become ill.

·

It is different here in the United States to expect people to give the proper offerings. I just can't imagine Westerners arriving with plates, cups, material, fishing nets, etc., for my odi. Money, well, money is enough, and maybe little presents. With money, I can return home to my village and buy the proper provisions for my odi.

··

Grandmother Ama:

Never ask for a pig odi to be given as a shaman's payment. It is very bad! Why is it bad? Living blood will call in destructive spirits and send death to you or your relatives. Living blood can send illness to your family.

·

Some Ulchi may ask for a chicken man (rooster). They make a tudja and a small ritual house. They will kill the chicken man; make the chicturi (sprinkling of the vodka or water), Kasi Guliyi (prayers of happiness) to the spirits. Very, very few Ulchi have done this rite. Cholo was a male shaman. We didn't know his clan name. Cholo asked for this type of shaman's payment for a conjuring for my husband, but my husband didn't want to follow Cholo's directions, and we refused to do any work with this shaman. The Goldi follow these types of directions for sacrifice, just killing animals, but we Ulchi people don't follow these rules.

● ● ●

Prescription and Further Instructions for the Client

After the conjuring, a shaman will prescribe secondary procedures to augment the healing. These can include the following:

1. Creation of a wooden amulet that will be worn by the client. These amulets are either worn around the neck or sewn into clothing. The specific type of amulet will vary, depending on what instructions the spirits have given to the shaman, who will usually direct the client to a woodcarver to create the specific design. The face of the amulet could be a carved with the face of a bear or a specific anthropomorphic spirit. The image of a snake, lizard, frog, or an aquatic being could also be recommended. The amulet might also be constructed to include an image of the diseased body part, such as the leg, arm, stomach, or shoulders.

2. Rituals to the Sun, Moon, Stars, or other major heavenly spirits.

3. Rituals to the spirits of the home and Middle World.

4. Rituals to the client's family and clan.

5. A combination of various ceremonies.

6. The inclusion of specific foods or herbs in the diet.

7. A psychological assessment of the client's behavior and affect states which may be exacerbating the presenting problem. In these cases, the shaman may remind the client that a balanced approach to their daily life will help to restore equilibrium to their psyche.

COMMENTARIES

GRANDMOTHER TIKA:

When you conjure, you already see what kind of spirit to make that will cure the sickness. After this, when you make the spirit amulet, you must be sure to smudge it with Labrador tea and give it vodka.

While doing this, bring in the sacrificial offerings and pronounce the prayer request that the sickness leaves the client and that the client is cured. You would instruct the client to take the spirit amulet, make offerings, and place it on their body in times of sickness.

..

GRANDMOTHER NADIA:

Do you remember that Russian woman who came to me for a healing? Her soul had completely flown away! She went to this doctor, and he prescribed medicine, but nothing worked. Of course not! Doctors don't understand how to help with soul loss. When I finished with her, she felt completely different and told me that she believed in shamans. That was why her soul ran away. It was so afraid. Only a shaman can find a frightened soul. A doctor has no skill with this.

•

Always call my clients when I am gone and ask them how they are feeling. If my spirits have helped them correctly, then they will feel much more at ease, and their pains will be gone.

If you find you have an illness similar to another person's illness, then you can share a specific spirit amulet that was made to help that particular illness.

•

When you feel good, you can take the amulet and hang it up, or when you are feeling bad, you quickly wear it once again.

•

If you cannot procure an amulet, then it is permissible to find an old one, made for a specific illness, and borrow it for a while.

• • •

THE SHAMAN'S RECOVERY PERIOD

Shamans may respond in varying ways after the work is complete. They may find themselves ravenous and may spend many hours eating copious amounts of foods. They may physically feel energized or completely depleted, needing to sleep for the next ten to twelve hours. Depending upon the work with the client and the difficulty of the conjuring, the shaman will either choose to socialize or excuse themselves for a well-needed slumber. They have taken the illness of the client onto themselves, and long periods of rest may be necessary to restore them to their own good health. If a specific illness is of a serious nature, the shaman can become sorely afflicted and need to spend a much longer period in self-recovery.

COMMENTARIES

GRANDMOTHER TIKA:

There are still many things that Western medicine cannot heal. Many people who have been let down turn to a shaman for healing and many of those have found cures where a doctor or hospital could not help them. A Russian woman came to me with a very grave illness of the reproductive system. The Western doctors could do no more to try to help her, as they had exhausted all of their treatments. She had been treated for a very long time, and the doctors said they could do no more for her. I worked with her and did a conjuring that lasted three nights in a row. They were very long sessions. We would begin after sunset and continued into the next day's sunrise. At the end of those three nights, I myself became gravely ill because it was very hard work. At the beginning of my healing, I was caring and looking after this woman, but by the end of three days, she was looking and caring after me. She was healed, and we still stay in touch and meet with one another from time to time.

..

Grandmother Nadia:

Sometimes, after a healing, my head is spinning. It feels like I am being walked on by other people. When you work with a client, they kind of leave an energetic stamp on you which can be debilitating.

...

After a completed conjuring, it is taboo to ask the shaman any questions about their journey. If a shaman were to discuss any details, their spirits would become offended and either punish the shaman with illness or abandon their connection to them.

For the shaman's assistant, a few questions for clarification may be permissible, but even then a shaman may only give a few more details. As an assistant for Grandmother Nadia, I have often asked her about specifics in her healing work after the completion of a journey. She will only answer a few of my questions and then tell me to stop asking, as her spirits are becoming agitated and angry. She said to me, "A shaman must never speak of the events of a healing ceremony, or harmful spirits will go after those with a loose tongue! A little talking is okay, but one should never reveal the details."

THE SHAMAN'S ASSISTANT

The shaman's assistant, known as a *lavji*, is a helper, slave, friend, confidant, and nanny to a shaman. They are responsible for all the many details of a ceremony. In their role as a buffer between the shaman and the people, the assistant acts as a liaison, telling the people where to meet, the type of *odi* to be given, the time of the event, and the preparations they need to make prior to the shaman's arrival. In their nanny role, they make sure that the shaman rests, eats, and remains undisturbed by outside events or people before the ceremony.

GRANDMOTHER NADIA DUVAN AND J. VAN YSSLESTYNE AT UNIVERSITY VILLAGE FOR UNGI PRIOR TO AN EVENING CONJURING

A shaman, prior to an evening's conjuring, will prepare in different ways. Some shamans prefer to go out and mix with people to raise their own energetic levels and may require that their *lavji* prepare an *ungi* procession through the homes of their personal clients. Others prefer to remain quiet, and rest and sleep before a ceremony, always listening to the voices of their spirits while in this state of solitude.

The duties of the assistant are as follows:

1. Arrive at the location of the conjuring before the event.

2. If the shaman wishes for an *ungi* procession, contact the people beforehand and ask them to prepare for the shaman's arrival at their homes. If a procession takes place, the assistant is required to lead the party of people.

3. Bring the herb *sankura* (Labrador tea) that will be used for the cleansing of the shaman and participants prior to the ritual.

4. Make sure that a chair for the shaman is set near the altar.

5. Check to make sure that the proper ritual foods are set out on the altar.

6. Place and prepare the three ritual glasses on the altar.

7. Prepare the shaman's costume and special caps that they may wear.

8. Help to dress the shaman, remembering any other amulets or special pieces that they might require.

9. Prepare the *yampa* and assist the shaman in tying on this belt.

10. Place the cotton *odi* around the shaman's neck.

11. Make sure that the drum(s) are in tune.

12. Call the people to the event.

13. Call the shaman to the event when all is ready.

14. Turn the lights on and off at the proper moments in the conjuring.

15. Drum for the shaman when the soul-fixing or general healing takes place.

16. Answer questions from the people about the shaman's work if so directed by the shaman.

17. Prepare special food and drink for the shaman before and after the event.

18. Repair any piece of the equipment, costume, or other items when necessary.

19. An assistant must anticipate the needs and requests of the shaman. Some shamans do not have personal assistants but instead rely on elder members of the community who understand these specific duties and the requirements of the ceremony.

The assistant must also listen and follow along with the shaman as they journey. When the shaman ventures out into the other worlds, an invisible rope (*suna*) is connected to them by the assistant. If the shaman runs into trouble or gets caught up in their state of ecstasy, it is incumbent upon the assistant to help them escape from this perilous circumstance.

CHAPTER 16

Shamanic Landscapes and Dream Portals

PERSONAL LANDSCAPES

Each specific shaman will have their personal landscapes that they travel to for various reasons. The landscapes of a particular shaman may exist in the invisible worlds or be located on the earth.

These locations are usually not talked about to anyone unless the shaman specifically wishes to divulge the information. I was very fortunate that Grandfather Misha spoke to me about one of his personal landscapes, which he traveled to during conjurings from time to time. In Grandfather's autobiographical story "Journey to Kadali," he traveled with some of his family members back to their original clan territories to visit their relatives. On this journey, they took refuge in ancient cave/rock houses that once belonged to the race of *Kuljamu*, who used to inhabit the area. This was one of his most important places to return to during his shamanic flights, for it was in this place that he could access an ancient stone book that contained all of the information about every human life, from beginning to end, that ever existed in the world.

Grandfather also talked about a sacred grove of trees, near the village of Bulava, which held power and protection for him. When Grandfather fell ill, due to his personal *tudja* being accidentally cut down, he traveled deep into the taiga for his own personal healing. He wandered into a grove of trees and, exhausted from his travels, fell asleep. That night, the tree spirits paid him a visit in his dreams, telling him he would find health and protection with them. Upon waking, he made ritual offerings to his new *tudjas*. This grove became his primary place of self-healing and power, to which he could return either by taking a physical journey or by one of his shamanic flights.

When I traveled with Grandfather Misha and Grandmother Nadia to seminars in Oregon and California, I observed Grandfather finding new sacred locations in the natural world. While in Oregon, Grandfather and Grandmother taught a weekend seminar at a private site whose acreage included a grove of old-growth trees. These were probably the biggest trees in girth that Grandfather had seen in his lifetime. He was smitten with this grove and would talk to these trees all day long. Then he would say, "Look at their branches! Can you see how for hundreds of years they have been home to generations of bird people, mice and squirrel people and many more peoples?" During his visits to the Pacific Northwest, before his death, I don't remember another time when I observed him so full of joy and happiness. This old-growth grove became a new sacred location for him to return to once he traveled home to Bulava village.

While in California, Grandfather Misha would draw invisible designs in the palm of his hand over and over again. I asked Grandmother Nadia what he was doing, and she explained to me, "He is making a map of the exact location of what he sees. When he is dreaming or in shamanic flight, he'll be able to navigate back to this place by remembering how he diagrammed everything with his finger on the palm of his hand."

GRANDMOTHER NADIA DUVAN

Commentary

Grandmother Nadia:

Each shaman travels to an intensely personal landscape. They don't have a corresponding place in the Middle World unless you hear them going to or naming a certain geographical place.

• • •

Collective Landscapes

The Lake of Souls and the Ancestral village of *Alme* are but two of the realms that shamans discuss among each another. Other collective locations include Pleistocene landscapes including their corresponding flora and fauna, nomadic encampments, Sacred Seas and Oceans, Cities in the clouds, etc. For this publication, we are only permitted to discuss the following. However, deeper and more specific information about these invisible landscapes is a closely guarded secret that a shaman will carry to their grave.

LAKE OF SOULS

Lake Ome is a sacred location in the invisible worlds where ancestral shamans reside. It is also the originating location where the soul of a shaman comes into existence before entering life upon the Earth. The ancient shamans who live here mark these newborn souls in a special way, so that they will grow into shamans on the Earth.

COMMENTARY

GRANDMOTHER NADIA:

I remember traveling to this place in my dreams, and I found myself sitting by the lake with nine shaman women all dressed in white. We were just sitting there together, and I felt like I was being tested in some way. These women felt as if they knew me and were happy to see me, and the whole experience was quite peaceful.

• • •

ALME VILLAGE

Another location in which ancient shamans reside is Alme village. They take the form of animated skeletons, walking, talking, and going about their lives. A living shaman who travels to this location must always be careful not to interfere with the activities of village life and should remain outside the community's ongoing events as an observing witness.

Commentaries

Grandmother Indyeka:

When I always sing, I never go and sit in Alme village! I will fly to the top of a tree, and from there I watch, from there I sit.

I can watch the sunrise, and when the Sun rose, I would just sit there and rest. As I sat at the top of the tree, I would look down and see all the ancient shamans sitting in the village. It is very frightening to be in Alme village. It is forbidden to be there with them.

..

Grandmother Nadia:

The most ancient shamans are skeletons walking about that place, and that is why Grandmother Indyeka never sat with them in the village. I remember asking Grandmother Tika and Grandfather Misha about Alme, and they said the very same things about this village.

...

Dream World or Land of the Spirits

The dream world is the primary portal that gives an individual direct access to the spirit world. Each person must be skilled in navigating this reality through a type of lucid awareness within the dream state. A piece of the tri-part soul travels to and from these worlds during the night to receive direction, education, and information from a variety of spirits. These spirit encounters may be harmful or helpful, depending upon the nature of the spirits encountered.

Deceased relatives who make contact in the Dreamtime do so to "visit" and/or impart information to the living family member. People who reconnect with their deceased clan relatives in dreams are required by tradition to give a food offering the following morning. This ritual is done at the family's *tudja* before the Sun has reached her highest point in the sky. Making the food offering is not dissimilar to feeding a living guest who arrives for a visit to one's home, as deceased family members who visit in the Dreamtime are also seen as hungry spirits who must be sated with a ritual offering.

Other spiritual visitors can include helpful or harmful sky, land, or water beings who may contact the dreamer for various reasons, depending upon the context of the encounter. Also, at times, one may find one's dream soul traveling through various geographical regions within the three worlds without direct contact or interaction with any specific being. If one has a happy encounter with the spirits, the information and experience will be preserved in memory. One might then go to a shaman or elder and discuss the dream and ask for clarification or an interpretation that would deepen the meaning of the experience. These fortuitous dreams, in which there is contact with the spirits, must be analyzed, pondered, and incorporated within one's consciousness awareness.

Nightmares may indicate that one's soul is under attack by hostile spirits, and one must take action on awakening. Dreaming of various everyday objects, such as hunting or fishing equipment, may indicate that spirits of the land or sea are unhappy or angry with the dreamer.

COMMENTARIES

GRANDFATHER MISHA:

If you see a knife in a dream, then this is a bad sign. You must make a salcha ritual. Early in the morning, go outside and fashion a knife out of wood. Then quickly, very quickly, speak to the birds, the dogs, and trees about everything that you saw in those unpleasant dreams. Then throw this false wooden knife away from you in the direction of where the sun sets.

•

If you see a bow and arrows in your dreams, then this is also unlucky. This is an Amba (predatory spirit)! Do the same with the bow and arrows. Don't be shy about doing these things." [Nadia added that seeing any objects that are associated with hunting in one's dream portends danger to you or your family].

··

Grandmother Ama:

If you see a young child, children, or twins in a dream, it means that Ajaha is the owner of your soul, and your path in life will be very good.

··

Grandmother Nadia:

Ba sends you messages through your dreams. All of the time, you must keep well the spirits of the Sky and the Earth in your heart.

·

I remember, a couple of months after Grandfather Misha died, I had a dream that he had found his wife in Buni village. Around the corner and down the street from my house is an old tree that had fallen a long time ago. Old people, from time to time, come and sit and rest there and carry on conversations with each other. In my dream, I saw Grandfather Misha and his wife sitting on this tree and talking and talking. Then they got up from the tree and walked together down the road. When I woke up, I thought that it was interesting that Grandfather had found his wife in the underworld. I was very happy for him.

· · ·

The harmful Ebaha sky spirits can also wreak havoc during sleep, attacking the dream soul of the sleeper. Grandfather Misha recalls one of these dreams.

COMMENTARIES

GRANDFATHER MISHA:

One night, I had a dream and saw a beautiful woman. She wore a rich and very expensive set of clothes. She came toward me. She began playing this game of hide and seek with me, by holding her hands together in front of her face. She moved her head from side to side, peeking out at me, then hiding again behind her hands.

She stole my shaman's clothes and my spirit amulets and quickly ran away. I was so startled that I immediately woke up from my sleep. I picked up a small twig of larch wood, which was close by my bed, and I quickly threw it across the room in the direction of that young woman. My wife shouted at me, "What! Are you crazy? You wake up from a dead sleep and throw this wood across the room!"

I told her my dream and my wife said, "Oh, my poor husband. You suffer greatly. That beautiful young woman stole your shaman's clothing and has taken it to a very dark territory. My poor husband, who will sing for you? Who can search and take back and return your soul to your body?" That's all.

..

GRANDMOTHER YAYUKA:

I remember seeing an Ebaha in a dream. In my dream was a table in the middle of the water and above the table were beautiful Ebahas flying above me. They wanted to take me along with them, but I protested and said no. I will travel by myself on a boat down the river. You know, the Ebahas can anticipate the drowning of a particular person. That's all.

...

In Grandmother Yayuka's dream, we find information concerning the nature of an *Ebaha* visitation during Dreamtime, as they appear to be carrion-like, having the ability to predict the impending premature death of an individual.

What Western psychology might classify as an "anxiety dream" would be called a "liar dream" by the Ulchi. This liar dream, which is considered an animated conscious being, is thought to become embarrassed and shameful at its retelling and will recede and run away from the dreamer's mind.

COMMENTARIES

GRANDFATHER MISHA:

If you have a bad dream or see bad things in your dream, when you wake up in the morning, go quickly outside and speak your entire dream to the birds, grasses, dogs, tress, and the earth. Now, why do I say to do this thing? It is because the harmful images will not stick to you or cover you.

..

GRANDMOTHER NADIA:

When you have a bad dream, and you don't go out and tell Nature about the contents, it tends to stay stuck in your mind all day. You will find yourself thinking about it at various intervals, and the energy will be relived over and over again. If you go out early in the morning and quickly talk to those beings in Nature, you will find yourself forgetting the dream very quickly. The liar dream will have run far from you, and it takes its energy along with it.

• • •

MAXIME KYALUNZIGA PLAYING
A METAL MOUTH HARP

THE DREAM WORLD OF THE SHAMAN

In the territory of night, ancestral clan spirits, deceased shamans, and major Nature spirits will arrive and instruct a new shaman in the vocation. These spirits will slowly present the beginning shaman with their ritual clothing, tools, drums, and/or other paraphernalia. When this occurs, it is incumbent upon the dreamer to remember the specific designs of the items and to have them constructed for themselves in the waking world. The presentation of specific ritual items takes place over many years, but this is not a hard and fast rule, as some shamans may receive their shamanic clothing in shorter periods of time. The spirits will also teach the novice shaman their healing song, as well as the drum rhythms that will accompany a healing/singing. All details concerning the shamanic vocation are imparted in the dream state, as this is the starting point of the shaman's road.

COMMENTARIES

GRANDFATHER MISHA (SHAMANIC DREAM):

I journey along the road of my father. This road leads to a very frightening territory. I remember a dream I had in the fall. I saw my father, and he came into my house.

Next to my house was a spirit saven. Later, my father instructed me to make offerings every month to this saven. "You will never be a shaman," he said. "Never sing for men or women. Ill people will have to live with their illnesses; otherwise, Ba will give you an unhappy life."

I said to my father, "I am not a shaman! I am not a shaman!"

My father said, "Maybe you will be a shaman in the future. You want to become a shaman, and you want to take this road. You will travel down this road but not completely. If you go, then only go halfway and then return home."

"A little time passed, maybe a few days, and then I had another dream. I saw my mother in this dream. Her name was Chainya. My mother said, "My poor son, I see how badly you live. I see that all of your bones are crushed and broken. I know everything."

My mother was not a shaman. I said to my mother "I called to myself the beginning of my shaman's path."

"No, no," said my mother. "It is forbidden! Here and there, from time to time, make an offering to all of the people; otherwise, you will have a very bad life. Please, if you must take the shaman's road, then only walk half way and not completely."

My mother continued to speak, saying, "I know you have become a little crazy. The three females Ebahas from the Heavens stole your soul. That is why you have felt so ill."

I said to my mother, "Yes, I saw those three Ebahas when I was fishing in my younger days. I have heard them in my dreams. I hear the sounds of the Ebahas flying, and quickly they fly over the mountains."

"Not long ago, I had a dream. I was sitting with my son and daughter. We traveled together over the Yellow Sea, the Red Sea, and the Blue Sea to the place where my father's soul is kept. My

*children said to me, "Come with us! Don't be afraid! It's not
frightening! Your father's path is straight and true." I looked
down the road, and I could see a terrible fire approaching me.
"Don't be afraid!" My children said. "Grandfather [Misha's
father] will extinguish the flame with his rain!" The fire came
closer and closer, and it burned us with such a great heat, but just
as it grew closer, a pouring and drowning rain appeared, and the
fire was extinguished. My children called to me, saying, "Come,
oh come further down this road, and we'll travel across the Red
Sea, across the Blue Sea, across the Yellow Sea to the house of your
father. Don't be afraid!"*

*When we reached the sea, we saw an enormous storm, a terrible
storm, and all the water was boiling like oil around us. In the
middle of this red ocean was a house made of stone, and next to
it stood a great large stone pillar. On the top of this shaman's
pillar were the sacred wooden streamers. "Don't be afraid," said
my children. "Don't cry. We'll stop by this house and see if your
father is inside. We will see if he is at home." We went inside
this house, and in the center of the room was a great stone table.
I looked at the top of the table and saw three images carved into
the stone. They were the faces of my father, my sister, and myself!
I saw my own image. We had not brought food offerings, so
we offered our own words of thanks. We offered a prayer, with
our own words, asking for forgiveness, asking for happiness, and
giving our heartfelt gratitude.*

*We left the house and traveled farther, and after some time, we
arrived at the edge of the great Blue Sea. The water was also
boiling like oil at the edge of the Blue Sea. There at the shoreline
stood an ancient old woman. As she caught sight of us, she called
out, "Why have you come here?" I called back to her, saying, "I've
come here, but please don't be offended by my presence. I have
come here because my children have led me here. I am frightened,
and it is not my fault. They [the children] asked me to come with
them." It was in this place that I saw this old woman holding*

a great stone book, a great Chinese stone book. She said, "Yes. I know all about you. Everything about you is written in this book. I know all about you and your sister and your father. You are fine, so don't be afraid. I will protect you. I will be with you until you reach a great old age. I will keep you safe."

Then this ancient woman stretched out her hand toward me, saying, "Take with you this gold medallion with these images carved upon it." I took it and looked at it and saw my father, sister, and my own image carved upon it. It was like a photograph. I looked down and saw myself wearing this gold medallion with all three images upon it. The old woman said, "Don't be afraid. The medallion is very light and weighs almost nothing at all. You'll never notice the weight that it bears upon your body." Then this ancient woman looked intensely at me and said, "Soon everything will be upside down. The dead will become the living, and the living will become the dead. There will be a terrible upheaval in the world. Perhaps you will not live long enough to see this, but it will be a disastrous time!" Then the old woman said, "There are three yellow stone books. I want you to go and find them, and then gather them together. You will not become a Kasa shaman. Your duty on this earth is to make the rituals of happiness. Make these rituals to the sky, for the waters, and for the land and the taiga!"

You see, this is what I do.

··

Grandmother Tika:

To become a shaman, you must have unusual dreams during various periods of your life. A voice will come in the dream and dictates and insists that you do special things. The voice commanded me to eat any kind of meat, even human, but I refused sharply and asked my grandmother to help me. I was still obliged to drink human blood.

Several times, I had dreams of walking where there were obstacles, or dreams of where I flew if on wings. I had dreams of hiding in different places in the Upper, Middle, and Lower Worlds. It is especially frightening in the Lower World, but in the Upper and Middle Worlds, there are dangers also.

In my dreams, my father taught me how to play the drum and how to sing to the spirits. Every shaman has their road and must remember to walk only halfway down the path. If they journey straight down their road all at once, then their life will be short.

.

When I was twenty years of age, I had a dream. I saw myself rise into the sky. I was walking through the clouds when I came across an opening in the Heavens. My spirits dragged me everywhere, and I suffered very much. If you obey the will of the spirits, then you will become a shaman. I didn't want to be a shaman, but because of the constant visions in my dreams, the voice forcing me and dictating what I should do both day and night, I had no choice. There was no peace, and I was afflicted with constant pain. I had to become a shaman.

.

I had a dream, and in this dream, I found a pair of heavy shamanic boots. These boots had the design of a dragon embroidered upon them. A shaman's equipment includes a drum, drumstick, voice, and your personal song, a shaman's boots and jacket. All of these things you will find in your dreams. You will find them slowly, but from time to time, some people find them quickly, and it comes to them very clearly. A shaman's cap they will also find in their dreams. The shaman's road is a very frightening road. When you grow into a shaman, you are visited by illness after illness, and this lasts for a very long time.

.

What if you become a shaman and there is no one to sing for? Then sing for the living elders and shamans. If there is no one to sing for, you will not learn the shaman's road well. What kind of shaman's road will you travel upon? How will you learn everything? Who knows, maybe you will discover an old shaman's talent. Who can you sing for if all of the shamans are dead? Okay, it will be okay. The spirits, the elders' spirits, the shamans' spirits, and your clan spirits. Sing for them. This is the truth that in the dream world you will find everything. Don't be afraid.

If you find meat in your dreams, never eat it. If the spirits give a shaman meat to eat, then never eat it. Why? It is forbidden. If a shaman eats that meat that the spirits are giving them, then they will become a jakpa shaman.

··

GRANDMOTHER NADIA:

Grandfather Misha and Grandmother Tika told me that there were struggles between shamans. Who knows? Shamans could battle in their dreams. Remember that all shamans must respect their spirits, or their spirits will leave and travel to another shaman. Always remember to make offerings to your spirits.

·

It is up to each shaman to both sleep and dream prior to the arrival of a patient. It is during this sleeping time a shaman's spirit will come and talk to the shaman about the patient who they will be seeing later that night.

·

In 1989, I had my first shaman dream, where I was given a silver Ajaha spirit, and in 1990, I found the Masi and Kolinga dream. In 1992, I was given a shamanic staff (kenapu) and I came into contact with the elder Golden Grandfather of the Cosmos. In 1994, I had this amazing dream where I was in the heavens, and I saw this one huge eye looking at me. In this same year, I found a huge snake. In 1997, after Grandfather Misha died, I was given a drum, drumstick, my song, and my voice, and in 1998, the spirits tested my voice and my drumming and my soul just opened! My lungs had great pain, and there was such discomfort in my throat, but when I began my song, all the illness in my lungs and throat were cast off. All the elders said to me, "Go ahead and try to sing!" In the year 2003, Grandmother Altaka Olchi came to me in a dream and presented me with a shaman's jacket. I asked her in the dream, "Why are you giving this to me?" She didn't say a word but remained quiet. In 2000, I also had a dream where my mother and two other women gave me a shaman's dayligda (shaman's headband made of wooden streamers). I was so surprised. Since Grandmother Tika had died, I went to Grandmother Indyeka. Who could I ask? I talked to Grandmother Ama and told her my dream, and I said to her, "Why did these two women and my mother give me this dayligda? Who are these three old women?" Grandmother Ama said to me, "If your head has had pain, then maybe they came to help you with this gemsacha headband, so quickly go and have this made for yourself. Those old women are your grandmothers, your mother, Goga's mother, and your father Dumbin's mother. They brought you your shaman's cap, and maybe this means that they want you to become a shaman. The mother of your father, your grandmother, was a Manchurian shaman. Her older brother was very rich and had a store in Auri village." Then she said nothing more. I asked Grandmother Indyeka about the dream, and she said, "Those old grandmother shamans have come to sing for you and help you, and Grandmother Ama is correct. Go and order a dayligda to be made for you right away!"

I remember how Grandfather Misha used to make the gemsacha headbands for my ensemble Giva. Willow wood was used because there was no bird cherry wood. I wore this and made use of it.

.

Variation

I remember my first shamanic dream was about Ajaha. It was so beautiful. I went to Grandmother Tika and Ama about the dream because my mother had died just a few years ago. I said to them, "Why did I have this dream and what should I do?" Grandmother Tika said, "Go quickly and have a silver Ajaha made for yourself! Ba has given you this spirit!" Later, I saw a Masi spirit made from larch wood, and this was for my own protection. In this dream, my family clan had given this Masi to me. Grandfather Misha and the other elders said to quickly have this made, so my husband, Maxine, carved one for me. They said to remember to sometimes give the Masi offerings, feed with butter, berries, and other types of food—the same as my Ajaha spirit. Later, I saw the eye in the Cosmos, and there was such an overall feeling of goodness and happiness. Later, I had a dream where this gigantic long snake came and wrapped herself around my body and then traveled on. I wasn't afraid. I could feel her warmth around my body. The evening that Grandfather Misha died, I had a dream where an old man came and gave me a drum, drumstick, a song, and drum rhythms. Then I had a dream about my mother, Goga, and two other grandmothers who came and gave me a shaman's dayligda made of gemsacha. They placed it on my head. The old grandmothers were my father's mother, a Manchu shaman, and the other was an old Ainu woman from my mother's clan.

Later, in February of 2003, Grandmother Altaka Olchi came to me in a very regal ceremony and presented me with a white shaman's jacket. It had frogs, lizards, and snakes on it, with the head of a bear along with many other spirits. Grandmother Altaka then began to dance. It was very much like a ballet. It was like she was flying and she was turning round and round. It was a most beautiful dance. After the dance was done, we sat down together on the earth, and she took me inside of a house.

Who can I speak to about this? All of the elders have died. A year before Grandmother Indyeka's death, I traveled to her home in the autumn by boat. I had Grandmother Indyeka sing for my Masi and Ajaha road. She gave me a yiyee, one time for my Masi road and twice for my Ajaha road. Three times total. Then later, Grandmother Indyeka said, "Why do you travel so far to see me? Everything is complete now, and everything is good. You are finished, and your road is opened and well. I have sung everything for you. The old ancient shaman people all sit with you."

Later, I had a dream about the ancient shaman women. They were all sitting around wearing white shaman clothes, and I was sitting among them. They were giving me some type of test or examination. I wasn't afraid. They were old grandmothers, and we were sitting by a lake. Later, I asked Grandmother Indyeka about this visionary dream. It was one of those times I had traveled to see her for a yiyee I think, or perhaps it was a time that I just went to visit. Grandmother Indyeka said to me, "You are fine. Don't worry, because all the old grandmother shamans are there for you."

I remember, before Grandmother Tika died, when I had this type of dream, I would go and quickly ask Grandmother Tika, "Why I am seeing these things and why I am feeling the way I do?" Grandmother Tika said, "Oh dear, maybe you have found your shaman's road. Poor dear, when I die, and the other elder shamans already being dead, who will sing for you?" I said to Grandmother Tika, "I don't want this! Why have I found this type of road? I don't want this! Why do I have to be taught such things through dreams, because I don't want this!" Grandmother Tika said to me, "It's okay. Don't be afraid because you will find everything in your dreams. The ancient ones will come to you and teach you all that you need to know about the road. They will give you everything. Just remember to respect them and keep the ancient ones in your memory and soul."

Grandfather Misha said the same things to me. He would say about himself, "I play at being a shaman. I just like to play and play and play at it." He would never say that he was a shaman. He would never say, "Perhaps I (Misha) will be a shaman one day." Grandfather Misha or Grandmothers Tika and Ama would never say to me, "This is amazing Nadia that you are a shaman." They would only say to me, "You will learn everything in your dreams. You will find what you need to know from your spirits and the ancient ones. They will teach you in your dreams." They never said anything more about these matters.

I was always surprised at what they said to me. There was no pretense about them. They never said, "You are not a shaman, and don't go down that shaman's road because it is forbidden to do so!" They never said such things. Instead, they showed me great respect in regards to what they said to me and would listen quietly to all that I told them. Later, they would say, "Who knows, the shaman's road is a very strong and hard road. You will find your shaman's road from your dreams." I had so many questions for them, but they would only answer with this one statement: "You will find everything in your dreams." They would never say, "Oh, you are a new shaman," as if they were going to award me a diploma! Now those people in the Altai and Tuva give diplomas. [Nadia laughs]. I remember so many people in Western countries asking me if the old shamans of my culture hand out diplomas, and I would always answer, "What! Are you crazy! Never! Only the Great Sky Spirit can give you a diploma!" [Nadia laughs throughout this statement].

•

First, I had dreams all the time where I was flying above the canyons in another country. The earth below was as red as the sunset. When I was about forty-five years of age, these dreams came to an end. Later, I had a dream that the Cosmos Master (Ba) came and presented me with a silver Ajaha spirit. The Cosmos Master came over and, in a very regal fashion, hung the spirit of Ajaha around my neck. Later, in my dreams, came the

Masi spirit. I saw that this spirit was made of larch wood. The Cosmos Master gave this to me also. Then I had another dream where I was flying. I flew into the Cosmos and saw this one large eye in the heavens looking directly at me. This territory in the sky was a clear and transparent beautiful silver color.

Later, in my dreams, I went flying higher and higher into space where I came to an opening in the universe. I looked inside this small opening. It was as dark as dark could be, and it was so very cold. In between the darkness of this place was a very ancient old man who was about nine stories tall and he was completely golden in color. His face was an Ulchi face with a long white beard and long flowing robes. His skin, his hair, and his clothes were all golden.

I remember that when I had my spirit dreams of Ajaha and Masi that my hands would experience great pain. I quickly ran to Grandmother Tika, Ama, and Grandfather Misha and asked for their help and advice. "Why, why," I asked, "Why do my hands hurt so much?" The shamans said to me, "At what time does it hurt? Evening? Morning? Afternoon?" I said to them, "I have pain in the morning and the evening." Grandmother Tika said to me, "Go quickly and make a snake ponga saven. Work with this spirit daily for yourself and your family. Slowly the pain from your hand will run away, and you will feel better in time. You will have helped yourself! Also, make a kenapu with the designs of lizards and snakes carved upon it, and this will help you also." Tika explained that because my pain was felt in the morning and evening, then it was the snake spirit who was in charge because the snakes go out early in the morning from their lairs to hunt and only return home at evening to rest. Maybe in the early 1990s, I had great pain in my hands and legs, and that is why the old shaman people told me to quickly make a kenapu and ponga saven, and this is why I continued to collect all of this information from them.

•

I remember talking to Grandmother Indyeka about my many dreams, and she said, "Don't be afraid to try the shamanic ways because if you do not try, you will become ill. Everything will be revealed to you in your dreams and during your singing. Your spirits are very strong and will defend and guard you!

..

GRANDMOTHER LINZA:

A long time ago, I had a very interesting dream. At that time in my life, I had no children. I saw in the dream my husband's penis, which weighed about eighteen pounds, and every night he wanted to have sex with me. The reality of my life was that I had blood in my womb. In the dream, I was so angry at my husband that I picked him up and carried him on my shoulders and brought him up to the top of a mountain. When I reached the very top, I threw him off. His body exploded into thousands of small pieces and scattered everywhere. Afterwards, the pieces of his body became better, and he did not want to have sex all of the time. His body pieces became benevolent and kind, and in reality, the problem I had with my womb stopped and was healed. Because of this dream, the pieces and bones of my husband's body became my good helping spirits.

• • •

FUTURE OF ULCHI CLASSICAL SHAMANISM

As Grandmother Nadia was the last practicing shaman of the Ulchi, the continuation of this Classical style rests precariously on the verge of extinction. Part of the problem lies in the loss of the language by younger generations who now converse only in Russian. Another issue is that they have moved away from their native territories for economic reasons to procure work in the larger cities. The loss of language, as well as their cultural identity, has cast them adrift in their own personal sea of uncertainty and doubt concerning the spiritual underpinnings of their ancient heritage. The teachings come from the spirits in the dream world, and only those who can understand their native tongue will be able to comprehend the secret oral instructions.

Commentaries

Grandmother Nadia:

Grandmother Dalika's granddaughter, Rosa, lives in Khabarovsk, and she has found the shaman's talent. Her grandparents were powerful shamans. She said to me, "At night, I have these dreams where the old ones come, and they talk and talk and talk to me. I don't understand what they are saying because I do not understand the Ulchi language." Here are the spirits trying to instruct her, but she has lost the language, which is a problem of our youth. She works as a chiropractor and helps people in the city, so maybe this is a new type of shaman talent but not our ancient tradition.

.

Later, I feel that all of the Ulchi people will want to know their traditions, the doro, and their shamanic heritage. I think they will want to understand this deeply but especially how to make the proper ritual offerings. All the clans had great shamans; therefore all the Ulchi have shamanic talents, but when I am gone, who will teach them?

• • •

GRANDMOTHER NADIA DUVAN

CHAPTER 17

Shamanic Narrative Songs

In this chapter, I have chosen to include many examples of shamanic narratives from a variety of genres. This is only permissible because the shamans who created these narratives have died. I have provided the dates and locations of the journeys where possible, as well as the types of journeys conducted. The shamanic narrative is a pure poetic song that is created spontaneously and is unrehearsed. It deals directly with the environmental conditions of the time and space in which the journey is being conducted. No shaman's song is ever the same twice, although one will find similar themes pertaining to the topographical regions that a particular shaman travels in their personal journeys.

Shamans who travel in the heavens will have their own special relationships with clouds, stars, and other cosmological locations, and those who travel in the Middle World will visit sacred lakes and mountains, forest locations, meadows, and oceans. Some shamans will primarily travel through specific regions, while more powerful shamans may travel through both the Upper and Middle Worlds. All of these conditions are based upon the individual shaman's abilities and powers.

No matter the complexity of the narrative, a shaman never sings everything that is going on for them in the journey. Even during the most detailed accounts, the people present probably hear about thirty percent of the journey. Much of what occurs with the shaman and their spirit helpers in the other worlds during a conjuring remains secret their entire life. To speak in great detail would incur anger from the spirits, who would become furious and offended. They would leave forever, never to return as helpers, and would punish the shaman and their family members for the indiscretion.

Children's Journey, How to Make Sick Children Well

Grandmother Naichika Udy

Ulchi territory
Date unknown

> *Mother and Father*
> *Father and Mother of the living children*
> *While my Moon is growing*
> *While my Sun still shines*
> *I will try to teach you*
> *Mother*
> *Until the boy can shoot with his bow and arrow*
> *The fish that jumps from the water*

Until the day he outwits her

Until the day he stuns her

Until then I will teach

Until then I will raise him

Beyond and besides this is the little girl

Until she gets married

I will raise her somehow

Mother and Father

Mother

Don't let them go outside

You must guard your children well inside the house

Don't let the days grow tiresome

Let them have fun!

Don't let them grow bored

The shaman's toys will grow

Set out a silver dish on the plank bed

And with a clang toss a golden dish to the right

With a clang toss a golden dish to the left

And try to amuse them

A young boy must have his fun

Taking a small child on my knees

Somehow I will tie on him a bib the size of a little bag

To my breasts the size of bags I will hold him

Nurtured with breast milk let the pale

   child, the thin child grow plump

Let him grow pink

Living children are like growing twigs

Evenly and well proportioned

Like my growing moon
I will nurture them
Until the time, until the end
Father, Mother, this is the way I raise growing children
This is how I nurture them
Old mothers and ancient grandmothers
Like fish skin on a cutting board thinly stretches to that size
This is how I will raise and nurture them
Let children grow and stretch out as far as
 the thread cut from fish skin reaches
Old people
Your craftsmen uncles
Your craftsmen fathers have made an
 arrowhead, shaking their heads
They have carved a fire bird
A shining feather cut so straight
They stuck the arrow into the earth
At the base of the arrow, nine coals smoke
And the smoke rises in a column
When children were born, we set out a dish of refreshments
We set it out straight and never crooked so
 that nothing would splash or wobble
We made a lining and evened it out
The boy
May he learn to shoot with his bow
May he kill birds and ducks in abundance
Until then I will teach him
The little girl

May she learn to use the needle

To hold a knife for cutting

When she carries water using the yoke

May she be strong enough to carry two buckets

Until then I will teach her

Father and Mother

Mother!

I took the small child

And in the shaman's vessel made of clay

With the saliva of many lizards and frogs

I will wash him somehow

Afterwards, when he cries

I will dress him in shaman's clothing

And he will grow into it

Cut as it is from a frog skin somehow

Made as it is from black lizard skin somehow

Stretched as it is from lizard skin somehow

I will turn him to the right, I will turn him to the left

Somehow I will dress him

Then I will put him down to sleep in the shaman's cradle

With many rattles shaped like lizards

I will tie them to the cradle

Tied somehow with the skin of a good boa

I lay him right down, right in the cradle

This way and that way I rock him

With the sound of those many lizard trinkets

I entertain him, and somehow I amuse him

Then I drag you out against your will

Holding you to your shaman mother's breast

Taking the breast, first the right, then the left

I let you suck

This is how I bring you up

This is how I nurture you

Here must you cast off the tortures of sickness

Here must you lose them

Father, Mother

Mother!

Sometimes you must compel them

Steam is rising from the shaman's food

Ready and warm

If the child cannot eat with a spoon

You must teach him

If he cannot eat with chopsticks

You must teach him

If he cannot eat, you must feed him

If his color is pale and body thin

Somehow he will grow plump

Somehow he will grow pink

Until now and until the end

Shaman's vodka

Red vodka

Yellow vodka

Somehow you must force him to drink

Six glasses of this vodka

To make the paleness go away and the red cheeks to return

Somehow you must convince him to drink

On the plank bed inside there is a pretty girl

On her knees, you must place the child

The premature child

Not yet become a man

He must be made a man

Not yet become a woman

She must be made a woman

Raise them in this way

Nurture them in this way

The boy so he can walk over the plains

And cross the mountains

The girl until she grows into a person who

 can catch a jumping fish by the tail

Until she learns to dress a fish

To cut it in half

You must raise her like this

You must teach her like this

Afterward, at the end of this

Sitting one day with faces turned toward the forest

I will teach the girl

I will show this girl how to cut with a knife

 many delicate things on the cutting board

Afterwards, at the end of this

When someone takes her for himself

When she goes to the hearth of another

Until then I must teach her

Afterwards, at the end of this

The boy

When the old people are in their places of quiet
In places of battle
Having passed through the hole of the thorny ring
Tomorrow and today it is he who must
  decide the fates of those people
And afterward, at the end of this
When he passes through the thorny
  ring and is on the other side
May the sun's light from the boy's chest be reflected
Let him stand up firm and straight

Personal Journey for the Shaman and Group

Grandfather Misha

Whidbey Island, Washington
1995

I make a great noise here
I make a great sound
Those in the heavens turn in their places
I've come to sing here
Don't be offended
I'm a small person
I am small, and my body has become blue
High above the city grows a tall tree
Please don't be offended
We've traveled a long way across the sea to be with you
It is very important
Please accept us
Please accept us well
I am not a shaman, and I have not
*   come here to be a shaman*
Don't be offended by my presence
We have come here only to sing for you
I have come to this land where the sun sets
I come here to sing my song
Don't be offended by me

Addressing the homeland of his mother and father:

Gurenba

I've come here to sing my song

Don't be afraid

Don't be surprised

Don't judge me

I sing my song

I'm not asking you for your help,

guarding Spirit of the Taiga

I appeal to you come to my aid

Think of me

Don't leave me here

Don't strand me here

I appeal to you, Mother, Father, Sister

Lead me well from this place when my journey is done

I begin my journey here on the edge of this mountain

Guide me straight, guide me true

I beg of you crying

I'm very tired now

Help me so that I can break my tie with the earth

Help me here

The earth is turning

Stomping and pounding on the earth

Help me break this connection

Turning, rising I will follow

I search for the path of the ancient ones

I seek the path of my father

I can't see the path; I can't find it

I turn and tumble

Is it a dream?

My head is turning

I can't tell

I can't find it

Help me find my path

Don't let me get lost in my own words or my path

Spirit of my mother

Help me

I sing to you in the voice of the cuckoo

Help me find my voice

Help me to find my place

An ancient spirit appears to him.

I'm living at this time, but I don't know the legend

Help me

I appeal to you

I beg of you

I won't ask anything of you

My father, my brother, the ancient ones lived

What legends they lived by, what histories I do not know

Many snakes, many lizards

Snakes with three heads

A three-headed dragon

The snakes, the lizards, the three-headed dragons

It seems that this history is a long one

The ancient people, they came across the ocean

  by making themselves a boat from wood

Fearing those creatures

Those spirits

They crossed the great ocean and came to this land

I don't know, and no one knows now
  who it is that made this history
Who it was, who took that first step

Another ancient spirit with large eyes appears.

Here in great fear and surprise I sing my song

Sister, as the sun sets I sing my song

Has the moon appeared?

I do not know, but forgive me here as I
  sing my song and dance my dance

Here I stand on the edge where the ocean begins

Here I stand on the edge where the sun falls

Here I begin my journey

Here on the edge where my father's path begins

There where the sun falls

Rolling and tumbling and traveling with the yellow cloud

Traveling with the blue cloud

Catching up with the red cloud, I begin my journey

My relatives were great shamans

Great shamans

Great tiger spirits

Black nature spirits

That is where its home begins

Taking me along with it

Iron Grandmother, Iron Father

Help me

I will survive this road as I can

You see my heart is at fault here

You have wounded me

Hey! I begin now
With all my heart and all my soul, I beg
*   you to give me strength and life*
The strength to live and sing
To all among these places
To this mixed-up and turned upside-down world
I've come here
I've traveled a long way
I see all
Protect me
Help me here
I soon shall return home
I think that in my dreams I will find again
*   that you will lead me home*
What should I do?
How should I do this thing?

Grandfather asks for advice from the spirits.

Here there are three tall mountain peaks
Help me
Can I break free from them here?
Mother, Father, Sister
I am searching
I don't know myself what will come next
Help me, I beg of you
The Blue Star
Nine stars sparkling
I travel among them
Father, tell me where is my path?

Show me this path

Can I take this path?

Is this path possible for me?

Can I break free?

I beg of you

I beg for your assistance

Don't touch those who are sitting here

My relatives were of the Yako people

My wife told me that the ancient ones
  were sometimes offended by me

They flew far, far away from me

Through the blue cloud

Through the yellow cloud

I travel now

I create such a noise

I make a great sound

Forgive me

Well, what can I do?

At this point, I must break free

I'm not wandering anymore

Take me from this spot

I can't breathe in this place

Let me break free!

I wait and sit in the bow of this boat

Mother

I will go on

I will begin

I will go on

What else can I do?

Here I break free into the yellow cloud

Here I can fly upwards

Hurry, hurry

I am tired of all of this

I cannot see the earth

Ajaha, guardian spirit of the sky

Take me by the hand

I'm already very high, flying high into the heavens

Flying through the transparent world, don't let me fall!

The blue cloud turns bluer

The yellow cloud deepens in its intensity

Who will take me through?

Mother, tell me

Altar, guardian spirit of my home

Guardian spirit, what is this?

You don't want to protect me?

You don't want to keep me and lead me through?

My wife knows

My wife sees

Thank you

Where should I look?

Where should I go?

I will fly to the earth together with you on
*   the very edge of the mountain*

Here, I keep and guard the souls of my children

For three years now, I have not had any news
*   from them or where they are located*

I have no news

Here Grandmother and Grandfather are chastising me

Here, I am simply coming to be

Don't chastise me, Grandmother!

Here, on the table, I'll lay the thick book

I will sing here on my birthday.

In the voice of the cuckoo, I will sing

Forgive me and take pity on me

Help me well

Here at the opening of your door

The illuminated door

I see the edges of the great stone book on the stone table

Why have you written my name on the stone table?

I am saving myself

I am protecting myself

I'm tired

At this time, Grandfather Misha stands up and begins to dance.

The blue grasses

The blue ancient man

I sit on these three stone stools

I sit down

I am trying very hard

I sing in the voice of the snake

In the voice of the birds

Do not harm me

Here and there are streams, rivers, and lakes

It is so beautiful here

Do not touch anything here
It is forbidden
It is taboo
Here I simply sing
The soles of my feet are iron
It is here that I will break free
Here I simply bow down
Do not chastise me
Quietly, quietly from here I will break free
Forgive me
It is from here that I will fly free
The places here are not our places.
Don't be offended by me, brother
Don't grumble so loudly
I am afraid that you will soon begin to play the great storm
The great, great storm
I pray
From here I will try to break free to travel
To return to my home
To tell in my homeland the legends
I will bow here before the earth of my ancestors
Blue Star
Don't be offended by what I do
I am just going to save myself here
Help me break free
Help me find the way home
Will I fly or not?
By the Blue Star, by the Yellow Star spinning

Will I break through?

By my father's road, I will try to go through

I beg you

I beg you to please bestow on me the strength to
break through and find my way home

I do not even see the light of the earth

I will travel by the edge of the earth

By the edge of the rivers and lakes

I will sing

I try to sing in the cuckoo's voice

The bird's voice

I travel

Crawling, crying, begging to you

I beg for your assistance

To fly and fly away together with you

I try to return home to Bulava

I beg of you

Help me!

With my drum, I sing

Keep me from making a mistake on the path

Father, Mother, help me well

Help me and assist me

Here the faces of his father and mother appear to Grandfather Misha.

I don't understand the mind of my father

Don't play with me, don't chastise me!

Why?

Give me your hands and show me the way home

Spinning above my body
Spinning above the mountains and finding the path
The corner of this house
This is a strange house with different laws
Forgive me
Don't be offended by me
I am a stranger here
It has befallen me here to sing my song
To petition you here
I am not a Busawu or Ebaha
I am simply singing
Father
My father's road is a dangerous one
Why?
Because he has played the thunder
It is a dangerous path
Protect me
Show me the path that I seek
I speak in the voice of the beasts
I speak in the voice of the guardian spirit
I turn about myself
Protect me here
Thundering voices
Keep me from making a mistake on my path
Guide me well
I do not know where I am
Everything has turned inside out
There is no flesh on my bones

My bones have turned within

My internal organs have all become mixed together

Twisting and mixing

I turn nine times around myself

Don't be offended

Forgive me, please

He sees an ancient stone man.

Blue Star

I will remain on the Blue Star

Yellow Star

I will remain on the Yellow Star

Red Star

I will remain on the Red Star

Now I think everything will be fine

Three claps of thunder and I glow

Let us not meet on the path

I pray that we never come together on this path

Fly away

Break free

Fly away my spirit helpers to your homes

Thank you very much

It is well

Personal Healing for the Shaman and Group

Grandfather Misha

Whidbey Island, Washington
1995

My brothers, my fathers, have not come this way before

My brothers, my fathers, have not come this way before

I'm here as the first in the place of the big city

I've come here the first of my people

I've come here to this very beautiful place

Taiga, the woods

Forgive me

I've come here to sing

Forgive me, woods

I've come here to sing

To sing my song

Help me in this mission

Spirits of this place

Don't be offended

I appeal to you

I pray to you

Help me, assist me

Nine mountains

Nine seas

I flew over to where the sun is falling

I flew past the Blue Star

I rested here in the blue cloud, in the yellow cloud

I waited by the yellow cloud because up to my knees

Suddenly he sees a spirit and stops and is surprised someone has appeared.

Mama

Wait for me

Don't be offended

I've come to this path not to become a
  shaman but simply to sing

Forgive me, Father

Take pity on me

I have come this way to sing my song

Protect me well

Don't let me lose my way here

I'm not singing just to sing

I'm singing to share my song so that
  these people can hear me sing

Forgive me

I'm walking now to the taiga

I will go through the taiga to the woods

Suddenly, another spirit is bothering him and Grandfather stops and says:

Well, all right! If that's the way it ought
  to be, then let it be that!

Appealing to the spirits, Grandfather says:

I've come across the seven seas

I've come across the nine seas

I've come across the nine mountains

Pity me

Help me in my task, Mother

Think of me, pity me

Here I can hear the hissing of many snakes

Give me here

Hear me now!

Give me your permission, your word of approval

   to sing my song and to play a little while here

Here close by

Entirely close by this little island is a great body of water

I don't know why, but here I see far off in a distance

   atop a great mountain there sits an old, old man

He laughs at me

Why are you laughing here?

So Great Spirit

Don't be offended by me

My intestines, my organs, my bones,

   everything has turned inside

Everything has come apart and changed

I've broken my tie with the earth

Don't be offended by me, help me

Assist me in my task, Great Spirit

Soon I will break my tie with the earth

This is repeated twice.

Can I do this thing?

Will I break this tie?

Will I make this journey?

Great Spirit

Mother

Father

Take pity on me

I came across the nine mountains

The nine oceans

They've (referring to the people participating
in the yiyee) made an offering to me

They've placed silver about my neck

They've shown me this honor

Think of me

Pity me

Assist me in my journey

I came here with great effort

With great journey

Here Grandfather's own spirits were very agitated.

I've crossed the nine mountains to the
land where the sun sets

I've crossed the nine mountains, and
here the trees are different

I cross over the trees

I sing to the trees

An expression of surprise—unknown spirits have appeared
again to Grandfather. He sees them and drives them away.

Hey! Go away! I'm not making a real yiyee here

I'm singing my song

I'm not calling you, great spirits

I don't know anything

Continues to speak to the spirits with clever words.

Hey! My bones aren't protected here; my bones
* are naked without meat before you*
Don't attack me, I beg of you
Take pity on me
All right
Alright, if that's the way it's going to be
Around my belt, I have my snakes
The lizards
The dragons
I will sit here on the blue cloud
I will sing my song
Is it possible?
I am not trying to fool you
To the stars and sun, I ask of you
I have flown over the nine mountains
I have flown over the nine seas.
These nine mountains help me
Help me
I stand before you
I ask for your assistance
Don't be offended by me
I appeal to you now
I'm singing my song
I walk along the stones
Father! I rest here on three stones
Mother and Father, help me
Help me when it is very heavy and very dark on my soul
And now dance a little faster on these three stone stools

We will rest

I will turn and turn above them

I will sit here high and on top of the mountain

May I?

Here, here, here I am!

Help me my relatives, my sister

In these years past you have helped me

Come and help me now

The leaves on the trees

The snakes

The spirits

The lizards

Help me now!

Another spirit has entered.

Oh! Go away from here

Don't bother me now

There is an old man who sat on this stone stool,

 high on this mountain and laughed at me

I came to you without a gift

My heart is good

What shall I do?

Forgive me

Tell me

Then a spirit of a relative appears before Grandfather.

Ah...go home, go home

I'm simply singing here

Go away

Go home

Go away by yourself or together we will go to the red earth

We'll fly across the yellow seas

I bow before you to this very earth three times

That's all

Let's finish here

Take pity on me, Great Spirit

Great Spirit, I continue my journey

I will try to fulfill all of the rituals, all of the ceremonies

I beg of you take pity on me

Forgive me

Great Blue Star

I stop here at this altar with its ritual items

Yellow cloud together with my father

Father, Mother, help me, assist me

Two spirits have just arrived, an adult male spirit and his daughter.

It's dark all around

It's dark in my eyes

I appeal to you

Help me

Assist me here

Along the mountains

Along the seas

Along the edges of the lakes, I have traveled

Old man, don't be offended

My spine will become undone completely

My tongue and my insides

All of them will fly and be mixed together

Great star above me can see the transparent land (cosmos)

The clear land

The home of my father

Don't torture me so

Don't bother me so

If you find me here

If you want to take me

Well....what can I say?

If that's the way it shall be, then let it be that way

I fly

I turn

I fly among the golden cloud

The yellow cloud

In the great transparent land

I'm not laughing

And I will not laugh at you

Have pity on me

Assist me here!

I've become very old

Oh, with my soul

I speak to my soul

I appeal with my soul

I'm searching for myself with my soul

I ask of you, the taiga

I ask of you, the sun

I ask of you of the forest

Help me here

Help me so that I can walk upon this earth

Give me great strength
Give me my health
Give me my happiness
I ask
You've protected me
You've kept me safe all this time
Thank you
Now I give thanks
Great thanks
Now I give you thanks and ask for your help at this time
Ask for your help in the future
Hey! Growing things!
Mountains!
I ask for your help
I bow to you three times, and I touch
    my head to the ground
Until all days are foreseen, give me your protection
Give me your assistance
Help me along
Soon I will leave
Soon it will be time to sleep

Another spirit arrives.

Don't play with me!
Be calm
Be calm
Quietly here
Quietly
Go quietly away

Be quietly on your way
Forgive me
The grass and the trees are trembling
from the noise I've made

Speaking to the grass and the trees:

Forgive me
Don't take offense
I beg of you
Thank you

Personal Journey for the Shaman and Group

Grandfather Misha

Bainbridge Island, Washington
1995

So don't be offended by what I do
On the yellow earth, between the two mountains,
  is where I will begin my song
People of the moon
Listen to me
Here I sit and sing my song
Grant me that I shall sing well
Grant me that I may find a clear path, a straight road
Here I sit, and here I sing my song
People of the moon
People of the earth
Here is my song
Let me sing well
Here I begin my song
Here I have journeyed through three cities
Mother and Father
Don't be offended
Thank you for sending me here
Here I've come to visit this place, to see
  what these places are like
On the right side, a dog travels along
He will be my guide
Who will be my guide?

A black dog

As of yet I travel by a straight path

Father, Mother, Sister

Help me

Don't be offended by my noise making

In the taiga where the sun rises is where I shall go

Three years I have wandered, not knowing

 myself where I have wandered

On top of the mountain

Father, I am not a shaman

Don't let wickedness come down on my head

Grandfather Misha sees and speaks with his father, who is accompanied by another spirit.

Look

They are ahead of me

I see ahead of me sits a very old and ancient man

His head is grey, and his eyes are enormous and blue as ice

He sits

He is the guardian spirit of the earth

The guardian of this place looked at me and said

Look at these people who have come here!

Be careful and guard yourself well

You are a tiny man

I am a tiny man

Mother, Father, guard me well

Two staffs guard my way

I will pass through these staffs and see if I

 can make my way through them

Three waves at their highest point

Yesterday I made an offering to you and
  brought to you that which I gave you

Guardian of the earth

Here there are people who come to you and ask
  for their health, happiness, and safety

People live here, work here, and make their lives here

Guard these people and keep them well

Keep me from the shaking

I can feel a great shaking as I stand on the edge of the earth

In three different places, I've sung my song
  not understanding anything

It is still a long way until my birthday

My birthday is in the autumn

Keep me well, Father

Keep me well and guard me on this journey

This is not my father's path

Guard me well

Father, Mother

There are people who live in this place
  with their culture and customs

I am not a shaman

Guard me well

Show me well the path

Help me to be safe and follow the road carefully

It is already three years that I don't sleep through the night

Don't be angry with me

I have seen in my visions a great lake where the sun sets

I have seen these visions
Guard me well
Forty years I have been a shaman

The heads of many spirits appear to him.

When the earth was created, people lived
They reproduced themselves and made their living
They found food in the waters, in the oceans, in the lakes
Don't be offended by what I do
Mother, look around us
We are surrounded by great stone mountains

His mother in a surprised tone of voice says:

Why are you here?
Why have you found your way here?

He replies:

All the same, I have traveled through the mountains
The great stone mountains

He asks the people who are among him:

Is there anyone here who is a twin
  or the mother of a twin?

A woman speaks up and says she is a twin.

Daughter of the earth
Guardian of the earth
I see an old man with grey hair and a
  beard and on his body are snakes
He wants to be a shaman
Is there such a man here?

A man in the group answers yes and says he has a bag full of small snakes.

Guardian of the earth

Guardian of the heaven

Forgive me

Take pity on me

I've come to sing my song

I've seen so many snakes here

Perhaps they use them for special healings

Then the Great Spirit Ba says to him:

What are you doing here singing this song?

This is forbidden!

Grandfather Misha answers:

Ah, take pity on me

I am simply singing my song here

I thought to strengthen myself here, to save myself here

Don't throw me off my path

Help me here

I've already passed through that age

I've already passed through that age

Referring to being old:

I speak to the Red Tumba

A Red Tumba is a special type of saven, cut from paper, sitting upon a stick.

Take pity on me

Assist me here

I see the faces of my ancestors

There are many people here, people of all
    cultures, and people of all nations
Don't be offended by what I do
I've only come here to tell them my legends, and I've
    only come here to take a legend home with me
They speak different languages, and I
    don't understand what they say
Take pity on me
I'm not a shaman
My father said to me before his death
Watch out
Be careful
The path of a shaman is a very dangerous path
My father was a great shaman
My father had the gift of clairvoyance
My father walked among the clouds
My father played the thunder
I am but a small person
A small person
Take pity on me
Here is the road of my father
The house of my father
This is the road of the thunder shaman
It is a dangerous path, and I am not seeking this path
I know it is a dangerous path and one who
    travels down it might be struck down
I will begin now
Ah, they've made me a shaman, laughing at me

They refer to his ancestors.

Here I step through the portals
Here I step through the doorway
Here I shall break free
Can I break free?
Can I tear loose?
On top of Kadi Mountain there stands a great
stone pillar, and from that place, I will go
Take pity on me
Guard me on my journey
Father, Mother
Help me
Protect me as I sing

He sees a spirit and yells out:

Hey! Why are you bothering me?

Grandfather Misha then led everyone outside in a procession to help them to drive away any harmful spirits. Grandfather Misha said, "It helps people themselves if they participate in their own healing ritual. Through the dance and drumming, we are able to rid ourselves of negative spirits and ill health. Then each person will dance their own soul's dance, which is unique to that person's own self-expression. We Ulchi sing in the voices of the birds, ravens, and animals. When we play our drums, we would improvise our dream beats within the framework of the shaman's rhythm. When you participate in a conjuring, your soul also goes flying and traveling, therefore you must bring it back through the door (the top of the head) and close it." The procession went on for about twenty minutes. It took place under a moonless sky, and the starry heavens above were especially visible from this island location. After Grandfather and the other people in the procession had drummed, danced, sung, and moved in a snake-like promenade around the outer perimeter of the building, the music ended, and the procession went back inside to complete the final section of the conjuring, involving the shaman saving himself.

Here I begin, Guardian spirit of the Earth

I bow to you

I begin here

At the top of the mountain and the voice of the larch tree

I begin

Don't be offended by what I do

I have not defiled anything

I haven't offended anyone

I have not traveled far

At the top of the mountain

At the edge of the precipice

I sing my song

Pity me

Think good thoughts of me

Two mountains

Kadi Mountains

Don't be offended by what I do

You see I crawl here before you

Here I come crawling

Here I come stepping

Walking with my daughter (Nadia Duvan) *at my side*

We don't come to offend you

Take pity on us here, Kadi Mountain

Here Grandfather Misha sings to Kadi Mountain about all of the beautiful places he has seen and visited in Washington State—transparent (clean and clear) places and locations where the mountains and oceans meet.

See these places I've seen, Mountain Spirit!

Here I turn on my journey

Amba, Tiger Guardian of the Earth

Grandmother, Grandfather asked me why I am here

Take pity on me

I've come to save myself

Think of the good people who live here

Here I begin

Here I will begin my journey

Take pity on me

You see I am still a small, small person

I am a small person, and I know nothing

Now the ritual to the house and house spirits begins. Grandfather Misha addresses himself to the four corners and the Spirit of the House.

Here I stand and begin my journey

Take pity on me

In the voice of the star I sing and with

  lightning I shall strike!

Oh mountain, little mountain

I pity you

My mountain by the edge of Kadi, Lake Kadi

Oh mountain, I pity you

Is everything all right there?

I will go there

I will travel there

I will travel there to investigate if everything is all right

This is the location where I guard the souls

    of children and other people

This is the place that I keep them safe

Grandmother of the Mountain

Guardian Spirit of the Mountain

Hold the doors open for me

In the center of this floor, I fly

Grandmother, strong grandmother

I am afraid

Help me fly to the altar in this house

To the sacred section of this house

I give my intentions

I've only come here to sing my song

Think of the good people here

I am singing my song here for them

I've only come to show them what I know

Take pity on me

From here I shall break free

From here I shall fly

In the three voices of the cuckoo bird

In the three voices of the swan

Shall I fly three times?

I will circle around myself, and from this city, I shall fly

So give me then my great stone book

I have just traveled here

I have since traveled here and sung my legend

I am simply a guest here
I bow before you
I turn around myself and bow before you empty-handed

Now speaking to his spirit helpers:

Fly away now
Make haste
Fly away well to your places
Go away now
Fly away
Gold and silver
Breaking free
Flying from here
Go away and break free
Fly away from here
You know that it is the rule
Fly away from here, so fly away
Fly away from here
Be gone!
Let all of these children stand and you
     shall fly away with them.
We will send them off together

This insures that all of the people's harmful spirits are taken away with Grandfather Misha's spirit helpers.

Personal Journey for the Shaman and Group

Grandfather Misha

Portland, Oregon
1995

> *Blue Star*
> *I have traveled to the Blue Star*
> *Three stars within the center star where I strengthen myself*
> *Grandmother, Grandfather*
> *Help me find the tudja* (shaman's tree or pillar)
> *My mother, who was a twin, has raised me*
> *The two sacred spirits will guard me and guide me*
> *Mother, do not follow me*
> *I cannot find my place on the road of my father*
> *My size is too small*
> *I have traveled here by these two cities*
> *Sister, listen to me*
> *I have traveled these two cities, and I am singing here*
> *Don't be offended by what I do here*
> *Grandmother, don't cry*
> *I am simply singing here*
> *I am simply showing what I know, sharing*
> *   what I know with these people*
> *With my right foot, I step forward*

A spirit enters, and Grandfather Misha says:

> *Hey, what are you doing? Don't block my path here!*
> *On the edge of Lake Kadi*
> *Great star, help me to find you*

Help me here

Help me to find my way

I've grown weary here, and my tongue doesn't work

My bones are dry, and my skin has withered

My wings are limp

Help me find my path

There are three windows where I stand

The sacred places of the corners

The house altar

This sacred place

Grandfather Misha begins to address the home in which the healing ceremony is taking place.

Forgive me, take pity on me, and enable me to fly

I have said nothing offensive about you

Guardian spirit of this house

Guardian spirits who dwell in the corners

Spirits that inhabit this sacred space

I bow down on my knees to you, these

knees that have grown old

Guardian spirit, take pity on me and forgive me

Give me still some time to live

Speaking to the corner spirit in the west, Grandfather Misha sees an old humpbacked grandmother spirit in that location.

Grandmother, I bow down to you

I bow three times to you

I bow down to my knees, and my

knees are bruised and blue

With my two hands, I give you greetings

Grandfather Misha has an extensive conversation with the spirit of this corner, introducing himself to her and telling her about his family and clan history. He tells her that he comes from a great clan and of his wonderful son-in-law. He speaks to her about his shaman father and how both of them are able to fly to the other worlds. "Take pity on me because I am the last living shaman of my clan." Then he turns to the altar and says:

Old man, take pity on me

I am not a Kasa shaman

I am not a shaman

Father, help me

Great spirits, help me

Give me your aid

There are two tables on the sacred mountain

The stone mountain Tolchema

There are two great stone books, and in one of
*   those books my father has written my name*

I know, and I am afraid

Father, you have the power to call down the thunder

I am so reluctant to travel the path of my father

I wish to live a few years more

Dark clouds aid me here

I won't sing much more

I have a family

I have children

I have grandchildren

Take pity on me, grandmother of the western corner

Take care of me and allow me to return home

I have traveled here with my daughter (Nadia Duvan)
We have come here together to show and
share the rituals of our people
I know you are strong
Take pity on me
I cry to you and beg you to take pity on me
I will turn here around myself
Most likely you hear me here
Don't allow me to lose my path
I bow down to you three times touching
my head to the earth
Soon my waist will tear apart and together
with this rope I shall fly away
So that's enough! All right!!

Now addressing his spirit helpers:

Fly away, fly back to your homes and your lives
Tell everyone that we are fine
Okay, enough
I will turn around myself and fly away
Give me the power to fly well
(Crossing to the other side of the room, saying)
Guardian sun, guardian window, pity me
I see my mother's flame of fire
Don't destroy me
I bow to the guardian spirit of the window
and to the guardian spirit of the sun
Enough, enough, fly away

Commentary

Grandmother Nadia

"Grandfather had to end the ceremony here because he traveled very close to the edge of where he could travel. He had to stop because he was facing a condition or situation where only another shaman could save him and bring him back. He had fallen into yuyun (a deep shamanic ecstatic state). He had entered another world where it was difficult for him to return. Sometimes it could take three, five, seven, or eleven shamans or elders in attendance to be able to help such a shaman to come out of this world. I was very afraid."

Personal Journey for the Shaman and Group

Grandfather Misha

Bainbridge Island, Washington
1995

On the yellow earth, between the two
mountains, here I will begin
People of the moon
Listen to me
Here I sit and sing my song
Grant me that I should sing well
Grant me that I should find a clear
path and a straight road
Here I sit
I sing my song
People of the moon
People of the earth
Hear my song
Let me sing well
Here I begin my song
I have traveled
I have journeyed through three cities
Mother, Father
Don't be offended
Thank you for sending me here
Here I have come to visit this place, and here I will
examine, visit, see what these places are like

So, to my right side, a dog travels along
He will be my guide

Asking his mother and father:

Who will be my guide?
A black dog
As of yet, I travel a straight path
Father, Mother, Sister, help me
Don't be offended by my noise making
In the taiga
Where the sun rises
That is where we shall go
Three years I have wandered, not knowing
*   myself, where I have wandered*
On top of the mountain
Father, I am not a shaman
Don't let misdeeds come down upon my head

His father and a spirit appear.

Look, there ahead of me
I can see an ancient old man whose head is grey
Whose eyes are large and luminous
He is sitting
He is the guardian spirit of the earth
This guardian spirit of this place looked and me and said
Look at those people who have come here
Look well on them, but be careful and guard yourself
You are a tiny man
I am a tiny man
Mother, Father, guard and protect me well

Two shaman's pillars guard my way

I will pass through these two pillars

Three waves on the very heights

Yesterday, I made an offering to you

I brought you that which I could

Guardian of the earth

Here there are people who come to you

They bring offerings

They ask for their health, happiness, and protection

People live here

Work here

Make their lives here

Guard these people

Keep them well

Don't make any mistakes

Guardian of the earth

Guardian of the mountains

Protect me well

Keep me from the shaking

I can hear a great shaking

I stand on the edge of the earth

In three different places I have sung my song

I understand nothing

It is still a long time till my birthday

My birthday is only in the fall

Keep me well, Father

Keep me well and protect me on this journey

This is not my father's road

Protect me well, Father and Mother
There are people who live in this place
   with their cultures and customs
Guard me well
I am not a shaman
Protect me well
Show me well the path
Help me sing and follow a safe road
It has been three years that I haven't
   slept through the night
Don't be angry with me
I have seen in my visions a great lake where the sun sets
I have seen these visions
Protect me well
Forty years I have seen visions

The heads of many spirits appear.

When the earth was created, people lived
People created (reproduced) *one another*
They found food in the waters, in the lakes and oceans
Don't be offended by what I do here
Mother
Look around us
We are surrounded by great stone mountains

His mother is surprised and says:

Why are you here?
Why have you found your way here?

Answering his mother:

All the same, I have traveled through the mountains

Through the great stone mountains

Here he sees among those seated:

A woman, says the daughter of the

earth, guardian of the earth

He asks if there is a twin or someone who has given birth to twins among the people seated. A woman speaks up and says that she is a twin. Nadia says to the woman, "Grandfather is speaking to you. In our culture, twins are considered sacred people and are seen as part spirits in the Middle World." Then Grandfather sees an old man (sitting in the crowd) with grey hair. On this old man's body, Grandfather sees twisted snakes. Grandfather says, "Perhaps he wishes to become a shaman. Either that or this person has received strong visions of snakes."

Guardian of the earth

Guardian of the heavens

Forgive me

Take pity on me

I have come here to sing my song

I have seen so many snakes here

Perhaps they use them for a special purpose

He then hears the voice of Ba, master spirit of the heavens, saying:

Ah, what are you doing here singing your song?

This is a taboo

Grandfather responds:

Take pity on me

I am simply singing my song here

I thought to strengthen myself
To save myself here
Don't cast me off my road
Help me here

Grandfather speaking to Ba:

I have already passed through that age
I have passed through that time
I see the Red Tumba
Take pity on me
Assist me here

Grandfather sees the faces of his ancestors.

Hey, there are many people here
People of all cultures
People of all nations
Don't be offended by what I do
I have only come here to share my legends
I have only come here to take a legend home with me
They speak different languages
I don't understand what they say
Take pity on me
I am not a shaman
My father said before his death
You should be careful
Watch out
The path of a shaman is a very dangerous path
My father was a great shaman
My father had the gift of clairvoyance
My father walked among the clouds

My father played the thunder
I am a small person
A small person
Take pity on me
The road of my father
The house of my father is the road of the thunder shaman
It is a dangerous road, and the ones who
      travel it may be struck down
I will begin now
Ah, they have made me a shaman
They are laughing at me
Here, I step through the portals, through the doorway
Here, I shall break free
Can I break free?
Can I tear loose?
On top of Kadi Mountain stands a great stone tudja
From that place, I shall go
Take pity on me
Protect me well in my journey
Father, Mother, help me as I sing

A spirit appears before Grandfather.

Oh, why are you bothering me?
Here I begin, Guardian Spirit of the Earth
I bow to you
I begin here
On the top of the mountain with the
      voice of a larch tree, I begin
Don't be offended by what I do

I have not offended nor have I defiled anything

I have not offended anyone

I have not traveled far

On the top of the mountain

On the edge of the precipice, I sing my song

I cry

Pity me

Think good thoughts of me

Between these two mountains

Kadi Mountain

Kadi Mountain

Don't be offended by what I do

You see, I've crawled here before you

Here I've come, crawling

Here I've come stepping, walking with

my daughter at my side

We don't come to offend you

Take pity on us here, my daughter and me

I sing to you, great Kadi Mountain

I sing of the transparent lands, the beautiful places

The lands where the mountains and the oceans meet

See the places that I have seen?

Look at these places I have seen!

Have pity on me

Protect and guard my journey

Amba Tiger, Guardian of the Earth

Grandmother, Grandfather, have

asked me why I have come

Take pity on me

I have come here to save myself

Take pity on me

Think of the good people that live here

Here I begin

Here I will begin my journey

Here I turn two times around, and I break free

Take pity on me

You see, I am still a small, small person

I am a small person

Grandfather stands to sing, addressing himself to the four corners of the house.

Here I stand

Here I begin my journey

Take pity on me

Oh, mountain

Oh, shaman mountain

I pity you

Oh, mountain by the edge of Lake Kadi

Oh, mountain, I see you

Is everything all right there?

I will go there

I'll travel there to check and see if everything is all right

This mountain

This is the place where I guard the souls
    of children and other people

Grandmother

Grandmother of the mountain

Grandmother of the mountain
Guardian spirit
Hold the door open for me
Hold the door open
I fly through the center of the door
Grandmother
Strong grandmother
I am afraid
Help me here
Help me to fly
To the altar of this house
The sacred area of this house
I turn my attention
I have only come here to sing my song
Think of the good people here
I am singing my song for those here
I have only come to show them what I know
Take pity on me
From here I shall break free
From here I shall fly
In the three voices of the cuckoo
In the three voices of the swan, I shall cry out
Three times shall I turn around myself
    and from this city I shall fly
So, give me my great stone book
I have just traveled here
I have just traveled here and sung
    my legend for these people

I am simply a guest here
I bow before you
I have turned around myself and bowed
    before you empty-handed
Forgive me

Speaking to his helping spirits:

Fly away now, make haste
Fly away, fly away well to your places
Go away now
Fly away
Be gone
Gold and silver, breaking free, flying from here
Go away
Break free
Fly away from here
You know that it is the law, the rule
Fly away from here
So, fly away, fly away, fly away from here
Be gone
Let all these children stand, and you shall fly away instead

Village/Group Healing

Grandfather Misha

Sonoma County, California
1996

Who's bothering me?

Spirits are bothering him.

Spirits say:

> *What are you bothering us for?*
> *I came here not to bother you*
> *I came here to show you my knowledge and ability*

Grandfather begins speaking in a secret spirit language about the full moon being turned around. Referring to the Ulchi legend that the migration along the land bridge started in North America and ended in Siberia:

> *My source of my ancestors is in this place*
> *Don't frighten me*
> *Don't be angry with me*
> *I beg you*
> *My three stars go on my path*
> *On the path of my father, I'm leaving*
> *I depend on your help*

Speaking to his father:

> *As of this present time I have traveled*
> *over seven mountains*

I came here to see your country
I came through the three stars where the
  sun falls into the middle clouds
And entered the middle clouds, falling
  through the yellow cloud

Another spirit shows up and bothers him. Speaking to this spirit:

Don't worry
I didn't come here to find out whether
  or not I was a shaman
I came with my daughter (Nadia Duvan)
  here to see and look and speak
I beg you, Mother and Father
I do not know anything
I am not a shaman
I have arrived here on foreign ground

Grandfather plays intricate rhythms on the drum for a few minutes and journeys to the corners of the room to speak to the guardian spirits. Each spirit master of the corners has Grandfather perform different drum rhythms. Grandfather is moving around the room addressing each corner spirit with a different rhythm, and once finished, returns in front of the main house altar:

I'm not looking for a shaman
I've come here to save myself

He continues to move about the room, playing various drum rhythms and then, turning, begins to address the main house spirit:

Completely closing my eyes, I came here to discover

To look and the land

To look at the rivers and lakes

To look at the mountains

My bones are ancient

My hands already shake

I came crawling

A long, long time ago my parents lived here

My relatives lived here (referring to his ancestors)

We traveled over the mountains and the sea

    to the land in which we live now

I sit outside on the road

Oh, serpent spirit

Please feel sorry for me

Please show me mercy

I have been suffering for a long time

My body has become dark blue

I am looking for something

And I turn here and there

You can see me well

My place

A new spirit appears.

What could you ask?

I cannot give you anything

I cannot give you anything

I stopped at the nine stars along the path

I stopped in the white fog

Grandfather moves around in a circle, moving through the fog, changing the drum rhythms.

Speaking to a spirit:

What do you want?

Answering the spirit:

I don't know
Thank you very much
Please help me

Addressing his father and mother:

I am going to rest a little
The sun has fallen into the red sea
In the far regions of my father, I am wandering
Please help me
Take me carefully home
I and my daughter (Nadia Duvan)
I am flying
I am closing my eyes
I am resting on the North Star
My waist hurts
Did I do something wrong?
Please help me
I am singing here
Here there are different taboos
There are different traditions
Don't be offended by my song
Help me
I beg you
Please accept all of my offerings
I don't need anything

Everything has come together
Master spirit of the Heavens
Master spirit of the Earth
Help me
My spirits, help me
I close my eyes working with the clouds and stars
I fly to the Upper World with my daughter

Grandfather begins going around the room and begins healing and speaking to the individual participants who are gathered in the ceremony.

Woman, you have great headaches

Moves to next participant.

Man, do not suffer, don't worry so much
Go and straighten out your path
Flying in the red and yellow clouds, I see that
   sometimes your soul is very dark
Sometimes it is fine, but always keep ahold of yourself
Be able to heal yourself
Renew yourself
Ask the Master spirit of the Earth
Bring an offering
I will ask the clouds to help you
Nature!
Do not be offended by what I do here

Moves to next participant.

Woman
I am resting on the three stars and on
   the six stars I am resting

I have asked Nature, and nothing is serious with you

Moves to next participant.

Woman
Don't pay attention to bad news
If you hear something which is unpleasant to
you, then you take it very much to heart
I have asked my spirit helpers to help you
Make an offering and pray
Ask for forgiveness and help from Nature

Moves to next participant.

Man
I ask my Yako ancestors for help
You have illness in your hands and feet

Moves to next participant.

Woman
I fly over the nine seas
When you find good news keep it to yourself
Don't keep the unhappy news in your heart
You have a wooden spirit idol at home that you work with
Make offerings to this spirit

Moves to next participant.

Woman
If I sit and work with you for a while, I will
find your path, but I am just looking now
I think you will find your own path on your own
So travel on the path of the father
Travel to the tops of the mountains and ask for happiness.

Grandfather finishes with this participant and continues his own journey.

On the edge of the sea, I begin my flight

On the roads of the ancient ones

On the road of the father I go

I tear myself away from the clouds and fog

I am going to check now

I am going to examine this room

I have traveled through three cities

I have flown through three cities

I am a small person

I am just in my body

What are you doing? (speaking to a spirit)

Why are you bothering me?

I don't want to do this!

I don't want anything

I beg you

I am just saving myself

Please speak to the guardian spirit of the heavens

Speak to me

What can I do?

I am beginning

I am just starting out

My father, my brother, my ancestors were great shamans

They asked me to follow their path

I am just a small person

Please do not bother me

Please forgive me

Don't be offended by me, spirit
I am looking for my happiness
Please let me walk a little longer on this
    earth as long as I have the strength

Another spirit appears, and he speaks:

Please don't touch me
I feel spirits crawling on my skin

A star spirit arrives and asks him what he wants here.

If the guardian spirit of the father and the guardian
    spirit of the heavens and sun arrive
I beg you, star spirit, do not touch me
Please address my father and my mother
Don't be offended that I have walked this path
Let me go through the road
I am just asking
I am just asking a little
Probably many have gone before me
    on this road into the taiga
There were many of us before, but now I am left alone
I am turning nine times
I'll stop on the three stars at night

Now addressing the Guardian spirit of the Earth:

I beg you
I am sitting on the clouds; I am resting

Grandfather proceeds to the altar and makes an offering, asking for forgiveness from the spirit of the house and asking that this spirit not be offended.

I ask you, House Spirit, permission
   to go straight on the road
To go out
I am flying
Mother
What are you doing with me?
Don't bother me!
Do not laugh at me!
Do not tease me!
I am just sitting here singing

Grandfather's ancestors arrive and start to bother him. He stands up in the center of the room, making offerings to the guardian spirits of the corners.

I am not doing anything
I am just asking you
Do not pay attention to me

Grandfather walks over to the first corner of the room and says:

Please, I beg you
I am not doing any harm to anyone
I know nothing
I can't do anything
Please spirit of this corner, give me your good help
I ask you to let me travel on this path
   without any ill consequences

Grandfather travels to the second corner.

I bow to you
I bow to you on my blue knee

Please save me somehow

I beg you

Grandfather travels to the third corner, addressing his mother:

Please forgive me that I am dancing here

That I am making noise here

I know that my ancestors, my father, my mother

> *lived here a long, long, long time ago*

I know that my people were on this water

I beg you

I beg you, guardian spirit of this corner

I beg you, Pole Star

Red Star, give me air

Red Star, let me breathe

Let me breathe these things

I am falling through the yellow clouds

I am moving

I have spoken to all of the corner spirits

Do not be offended by me

I have put out three chairs

Do not hurt me, I beg you

I don't need what you are saying

Three suns

Three stars

Three moons

Addressing the three suns and three moons, he asks:

May I travel though this passage?

I beg you

Allow me to proceed without any hindrances

I don't know where to go

I have found my path

I have traveled through the seven clouds

Ancestors, sky, and clouds

Please help me

I want to sit here in my father's place

Please help me

Mother, Father

Next month I am going to sing

You are letting me go through this terrible path

I beg you

Please let me through

I am turning seldom now

Grandfather's drum rhythm changes and he travels over to speak with the door spirit.

Don't move anything

Don't turn

I came here with my daughter

Do not be offended by me

Oh, my spirits

Fly away with the Heavenly Dragon

Grandfather begins the ritual of "saving himself" and reclaiming his own strength.

I came here

Don't say anything harmful about me

Don't think unpleasant things about me

Please permit me to go straight on my path

I am being torn away
Please, guardian spirit of this place
Don't be offended by me
I beg your forgiveness
I am saving myself

The spirit of an ancient old man appears.

Don't bother me
I am bowing my head to you, guardian spirit of this place
I travel to the altar
The guardian spirit of this place is raising up my heart
I have three larch trees in the taiga
Please hold me up
Do not let me fall, my shaman's pillar
Help me travel though straight along my path
The guardian spirit of this place will probably
*   find out himself what it is he needs to do*
The guardian spirit of this place is a very great spirit
I am not bothering you
I am not touching you
I am only here to look
My spirits
Do not hurry me along
Don't hurry, I beg you
Please wait
There is nothing there
I am singing with the voice of a bird
I am flying here and there
My father cried

I will probably go on the path of my father

It is a terrible road

It is a path of lightning and of threats

I beg you, guardian spirit of this house

Please protect these people who have gathered around me

Give them good health

Master spirit of this room

Take care of the people here

Grandfather begins the dance of his yampa shaman bells and casts out all of the harmful spirits of the place, saving the souls of the participants gathered in the home.

I am closing my eyes

Grandfather continues around the room, working with different participants.

Woman

Don't laugh at me!

She does not actually laugh, but Grandfather feels that she is insincere. He moves away from this participant.

Mother and Father

I am working with the sacred streamers (gemsacha)

Do not be angry

I am tearing myself away from my father

Do not do anything harmful to my path

Forgive me

Protect me

I see three birds flying

I see their eyes

What are you doing here?

What have you been searching for?

His spirits, in the forms of birds, answers:

We are just singing
Don't be offended by us

Grandfather chases them away with his hat and continues.

Do not make noise out of good news!
Go away!
I am flying away to the three stars
I am stopping at the head of a cloud
I am resting
Fly away, my spirits
This is good
Very good
You have helped me

Grandfather moves toward a different participant.

Woman
You love everyone
Your heart is large
You do good for everyone
You need many helping spirits to protect you
I don't know your customs
I can't give you my helping spirits
But I'll ask my spirits to protect you sometimes
You sing happily
Your head is always singing

The participant revealed later that she was a professional singer.

Fly away
Fly away from the legs
This is an unusual woman
I think she has unusual dreams
She does not want these dreams
She tries to pull herself away from them

Grandfather leaves and moves on to the next participant.

Woman
I am tearing myself away from the three clouds
All of the people have one blood (referring to humankind)
I am asking for your happiness
You know everything in your dreams
Present and future

Grandfather is finished and moves on to the next participant.

Woman
You are a very wise woman
You know what to do
Don't be offended by me
Sometimes things are dark for you

Speaking to the spirits:

Help her
She is not a simple woman
She has a very large spirit
A very intelligent woman
I will not touch her

Speaking to his spirits:

Please don't bother me

Stop that!

Let me look at her

Grandfather moves on to the next participant

Woman

You are on your path

My spirits are sitting on your shoulders

Do not be offended

You must absolutely ask for happiness

Moving on to the next participant.

Woman

Your soul glows from within

You are not a simple woman

Sometimes there is fog in your head

I am just asking

Do not be offended

I am just looking

Especially at the time when the moon grows full

You need to make offerings

I think you probably already do this

Three of Grandfather's helping spirits take the form of snakes and Grandfather says to them:

Go away!

Leave her alone!

Go away!

Crawl away!

Moving on to the next participant.

Woman

You are looking for your path

It's important that you make offerings for

   your entire family and for yourself

Make offerings to Nature and in the taiga

This is not a simple woman

I am just looking at the surface of her

If I were able to work with you, one on one,

   I would be able to see your path

To see everything

Grandfather moves on to the last participant.

Woman

I see the soul of a crow

You should work with the spirit images

   of snakes and lizards

If you had a snakeskin that you could use to

   make an image that would be satisfying

You could also make an image out of paper

Then sleep with it under your pillow

Make offerings every month

Don't let anyone touch the snake or lizard spirit

The participant relates a story of recently walking down a road and finding a dead crow in the center of her path. Grandfather replies:

I am a little worried

Your soul may be in danger

If you are in contact with something recently dead, it

   can drag your soul along the path of the underworld

You should make the images of a crow and snake

There is a connection
You must make offerings one, two, or
three times a month saying
"Do not take my soul, do not affect my body"
You must travel through the taiga and
travel up the mountains
Make the ritual of happiness in both environments
Afterwards, take the images of the crow
and snake and save them
Place them in a box for safe keeping

JOURNEY TO RELAY INFORMATION FROM THE MOUNTAIN SPIRIT TO THE PEOPLE

GRANDFATHER MISHA
Bulava village, Ulchi territory

The Rock Master and the Earth Master
    together made the mountains
Altogether these master spirits know all of the people
They taught the people how to live well
It is forbidden to live at the top of the mountain
Do not make a house here!
The mountain spirit will not like this
Never cut a tree, said the Master Spirit

Journey to Kadali

Variation of Autobiography

Grandfather Misha

Bulava village, Ulchi territory

This is the story of how I traveled to the
*   dangerous country of my mother*
It took me one month to travel to this place
I was eight years old when I traveled
*   there with my relatives*
It was 1911, and we were living in
*   Kadi village at that time*
From the bank of the Amur, we stopped
*   during evening time*
We set up camp in a beautiful mountain meadow
It was a very quiet place.
The red river is a large river with many fish
The sun travels toward the red river
*   when she is going down*
Where does the sun set?
She sets in the red sea
My father could see my road in life
He showed me these places in nature and
*   told me I must remember them*
We walked through the land of the animal people (taiga)
He taught me where the rivers would run and the places
*   to catch fish, and the places that fish would not be found*

The red and blue meadows were so large and expansive
You could not touch or spoil this place
My father taught me that what you eat, you give
back to nature by making offerings of tobacco
We traveled until we came to a rock house (cave)
In this rock house was a rock table and
chair, so we all went inside
We then made a fire inside the house and
made our offerings to this place
I was young, but my father insisted that I learn to
give the chicturi (offering of water or alcohol)
This was the thunder road of my father.
I slept all night and had so many different types of dreams
When I woke up, the next day, I saw
that my uncle was gone
He had gotten up earlier and had met the
Haja Kalta (the Ulchi name for peoples
who live in the northern territories)
He saw the Yako (Yakut) *people*
These lands were the places of the Yako, Kela
(Negidal), *and Sela* (Even) *people*
The people who had arrived had come
from three different villages
In my dream, I saw that we were
walking and saw a rock house
My uncle said, do you see?
I said, yes, yes I do!
My uncle said, here your father plays with the thunder

This territory is the place that you want to make

*   offerings, and if you want to live for a very long*

*   time, you make your offerings inside the rock house*

The red, blue, and yellow mountain meadows

*   of the earth are such a wondrous place!*

*   You can really breathe here, I said*

My uncle said, remember this well!

No one ever comes here except your father

I looked and saw my father and older

*   sister's faces on this rock table*

The Thunder Master placed those faces into the rock table

My uncle said, your father plays with the thunder

The Thunder Master that killed your older sister

That is why your father can play with the thunder

The white clouds, white bird, red clouds and red birds fly!

We all awoke from our sleep and began

*   our journey back to our home*

We first made offerings and then began

*   to walk and walk and walk*

We arrived at another Yako home

There we stayed the night to sleep

My uncle had decided to go hunting

He was gone for about one week

When he was in the taiga, he killed a bear

When we left, we traveled in a jayji (a small birch boat)

Then I walked with my uncle to where the sun was setting

It took us one month to travel back home

When we arrived back home, a great shaman

   relative (name unknown) *came to*

   visit our home from the black sea

He was such a powerful shaman

He could point his finger at an iron cable

   and cut it into like a knife

When I started on this journey to Kadali,

   I was a very young child

When I returned, I was a young man

We stayed with our relatives for three or four years

Long Distance Healing

Grandmother Tika

Bulava village
1994

Father, Mother, please help me (referring
    to the client's parents)
I don't know this person
I am confused
Mother Ba and Father Ba
Help me to find the soul
I plead with the father
Her father
Convey me to this woman's body
The father helps
But the mother leaves
The mother is blind and does not listen well
Poor thing
I weep
The father is helping
What land is this?
She (the client) *sent me her clothes*
She asked that I quickly sing for her
I have never been to this land
What territory have I arrived at?
The father is shy
Enduri knows
I sit down

What will be her future?

Why does she have pain?

I don't know

The father's soul is good

And travels around his daughter

I'll just sit here

I beg her father to help her

Is this enough for her?

I don't know

How can I help

I don't know

Is it her head?

Does her body feel pain?

She worries too much what will be in the future

She worries and worries and worries

She walks and walks and walks and worries

Is this true?

I ask the father

Yes, this is what creates her strong illness

Maybe she worries too much

The father is good

And the mother helps

The father helps from above and below

The mother gives protection

How is she now?

The father wants me to give more

Father Mountain

I now fly above you, turning round and round

I turn above the earth

Three times I turn round

And as I turn I completely search for her soul

I fly with my tiger children

I have no strength, so I fly with them

Her soul is sometimes very calm and relaxed

I now mark her with my song, and I give offerings

Different foods

Manchu foods

There is a light by her bed

I recognize everything which is completely clean and clear

Father, Mother, please assist me with your good traditions

I know this well

Her heart and soul are good

Give me completely your heart and soul

They make such a thing

I am not a shaman

Her father combs her hair one hundred times

Is her head full of pain?

I am surprised

The father sees everything well

He sees this cap

Is this cap for her head?

She comes from a clan of powerful shamans

They want her to take the road

The ancient shaman grandfather sits beside her

I ask my old clan to help me

At the three altars, I plead to him

Three times I turn round and round
In the fog and mist, I turn
I am enveloped in this mist
I turn into a mosquito
And I turn and fly in this house
I travel up to the rafters turning round and round
Which road shall I take outside?
I will sit here in her home
The good father opens the door for me
I come inside of this place
The father has opened the door for me
I come inside and search for the altar
I bow three times touching my head to the floor
I come inside and see everything well
I see everything as I search for her bed
I ask the father
The father helps
Pay-pay-pay

Tika drives away the offending spirits.

Here the father stands in the darkness
The mother is deaf and blind
How will I find help?
Here outside I beg you
Is it okay that I do this?
I am suffering
I must go back
I turn round three times
I stand up

I ask her if everything is fine
Her heart and soul suffer
The father sees well
So I will return
I ask the father

Asking the father:

Were there great shamans in your clan?
Is it your daughter's dream to take the shaman's road?
What do you think will happen?
Is this true?
Her ancient clan wants her to become a shaman
Father, Mother
She comes inside as the sun is setting
She sees well all that is inside
The good father searches within the home
Please do not make a mistake
Inside her home are many spirits
In her house is an ancient man
He has long silver hair and is sitting outside in the garden
The father and mother see well
Watch well I say!
I will never overstep my position within her home
Excuse me, Father and Mother
Please don't be offended by what I do here.
I offer the nine types of Manchu food
I take these offerings to the altar
Here the ancient shaman grandfather offers protection
There are many powerful shamans here

I ask the father, is this true?
Here I am like an orphan
But I cannot say anything more
Mother, Father, give your good help
I think she will find this good help
Sometime she will be at peace and rest
Here I have made my mark!

Glossary of Ulchi Terms

• A •

Adawu poktoni • Road of the Twins

Ajaha • powerful spirit who serves and protects shamans

Agdipanyani • Rainbow, soul manifestation of the Thunder spirit

Agdi • the Thunder spirit

Amba • name usually given to the Siberian Tiger but can also refer to any powerful spirit

Apu • shaman headdress or cap, also *Dayligda*

Araki • alcoholic beverage

• B •

Ba Enduri • Dragon form of the Great Spirit

Ba, Ba Adja, Ba Ama, Ba Unya • various titles for the Great Spirit of Creation

Bakini • sky people

Bay • the Moon spirit

Bibe • a novice shaman, also *Nuchka sama*

Buchu • main spirit mediator between shaman and Upper world

Buni • lower world

Burikta • the Red Star or Venus

Busawu • vampiric sky spirits, also *Ebaha*

Buyu • Bear

• C •

Chanko • ventilation hole in Ulchi home

Chicturi • giving liquid offerings

Chuvachi • solid offerings of food, etc.

• D •

Daro • sacred tree associated with families and shamans, also *Taro, Tudja*

Darpu • glue made from sturgeon bladder

Dayligda • shaman headdress or cap, also *Apu*

Doe, Doe meva • heart/mind soul

Domki • tobacco

Dorkin • lower world located in the water realms/invisible world of the shaman

Dorkini • people who reside in Dorkin

Doro • natural laws or organic patterning in Nature

Duentey • Taiga or Forest

Duenteyni • People of the forest or the wild animals

Dusey • Tiger

• E •

Ebaha • vampiric sky spirits, also *Busawu*

Ewu • the ritual act of calling a spirit into a container or amulet

• G •

Galbu Khosta • the Pole Star or Blue Star

Gemsacha • wooden streamers uses in conjuring, healing, and protection, also *Sisakun*

Gespu • shaman's drumstick

• H •

Harkume, Harkowu yiyee • song of a Kasa shaman on tree platform

Hogduwa Tuambuwu • a conical house made from straw for Kasa ritual

Humahu • ritual for the deceased

Huraka • frogs

• I •

Isachula • shamans who work only as intuitives/psychics, also *Nairigda*

• J •

Jakpa, jakpachi sama • shaman who possesses dangerous or powerful spirits

Juli • wind soul or wandering soul

• K •

Kamchu • birch bark container for navel cords of newborns

Karpa • trance dances

Kasa • most powerful
type of shaman able to
perform death rituals

Kenapu • magical walking staff

Keselemi • shamanic illness

Kesi Guliyi • offering of thanks

Khadai • first ancestral
shaman associated with
the constellation Orion

Khargi • shaman's soul

Khasisi • initiation for
novice shamans

Khondari • trance dance by
twins or mother of twins

Kolinga • lizards

Kombo • the Big Dipper
or Ursa Major

Kori • container that holds
the navel strings and
afterbirth of twins

Koori • iron eagle spirit

Kulamukachi • shamans who
sing in glossolalia (tongues)

Kuljamu • race of Bigfoots who
inhabit Eastern Siberia

• L •

Lavji • shaman assistant

• M •

Mali • main altar in the
Ulchi household

Mapa • honorary name for Bear
meaning Ancient One

Masi • House spirit

Meu • spirit house or material
with characters or designs

Mui • snakes

Murgen • hero

• N •

Na Adja • Earth spirit

Nairigda • shamans who
work only as intuitives/
psychics, also *Isachula*

Nani • people of the earth,
Ulchi's self-name

Nuchka sama • a novice
shaman, also *Bibe*

• O •

Odi • shaman's payment
for conjuring

Ome • a person's first
Celestial soul at birth

Oto • ritual dish or container

• P •

Panya • shadow or soul of the physical body

Ponga Saven • wooden spirit idol used for divination

Pujen • Fire Spirit, or female heroine

Puta • pouch used by shamans to carry errant souls

• R •

Red Tumba • spirit helper of shaman usually made of paper

• S •

Sisakun • wooden streamers uses in conjuring, healing, and protection, also *Gemsacha*

Salcha saven • grass effigy used to imprison harmful spirits

Sama • shaman

Sankura • main smudging plant used in ceremonies, also known as Labrador tea (Ledum Palustre)

Sava/Savens • spirits

Saycha • a special mark

Seu • the Sun spirit

Siljuni • somatic tingling experience throughout the body

Sisajaha/Sisayagi • ritual act when using the wooden streamers in conjuring

Sukpungi • act of shaman biting top of client's head

• T •

Taro • sacred tree associated with families and shamans, also *Daro, Tudja*

Temu • Water spirit

Toli • bronze mirror used by shamans

Tudja • sacred tree associated with families and shamans, also *Daro, Taro*

Tuandame • name of Kasa ritual on tree platform

• U •

Uchey Bukini • threshold spirit

Udjadyu • log drum

Umtahu • drum

Ungi • shaman procession

Urgan • adult or full grown soul

• V •

Vaysi Nyalau • name of
the Water ritual

Vaysi • dried wild onions
used in outdoor rituals

• Y •

Yampa • shamans sprit
belt with iron cones

Yiyee • shaman's song

Yuyun • shaman's ecstasy

Map

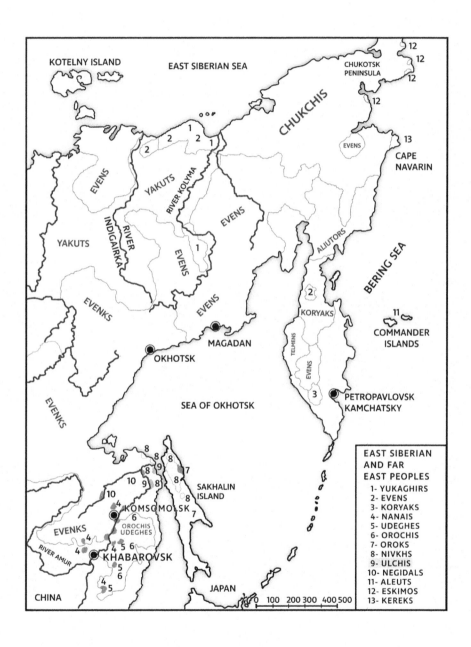

KOTELNY ISLAND

EAST SIBERIAN SEA

CHUKOTSK PENINSULA

12
12
12
12

CHUKCHIS

EVENS

13

CAPE NAVARIN

EVENS

YAKUTS

RIVER KOLYMA

EVENS

1
2
2
2
1
1

YAKUTS

RIVER INDIGAIRKA

EVENS

1

ALIUTORS

BERING SEA

EVENKS

EVENS

EVENS

KORYAKS

2

11
COMMANDER ISLANDS

MAGADAN

OKHOTSK

TELMENS

EVENS

3

PETROPAVLOVSK KAMCHATSKY

EVENKS

SEA OF OKHOTSK

8
8
8
9
8
7
8
10
9
8
8
10
4
SAKHALIN ISLAND
8
KOMSOMOLSK
7
6
OROCHIS UDEGHES
4
5
6
EVENKS
4
RIVER AMUR
4
5
6
KHABAROVSK
5
6
4
5
JAPAN
CHINA

EAST SIBERIAN AND FAR EAST PEOPLES
1- YUKAGHIRS
2- EVENS
3- KORYAKS
4- NANAIS
5- UDEGHES
6- OROCHIS
7- OROKS
8- NIVKHS
9- ULCHIS
10- NEGIDALS
11- ALEUTS
12- ESKIMOS
13- KEREKS

0 100 200 300 400 500

Made in the USA
Coppell, TX
29 June 2020